CIRCLE
OF FIRE

*Dickens' Vision &
Style & The
Popular Victorian
Theater*

*WILLIAM F.
AXTON*

UNIVERSITY OF KENTUCKY PRESS

725348

Circle
of Fire

"Mr. Carker in his Hour of Triumph." Illustration by
Phiz (Hablôt Knight Browne) for *Dombey and Son*

To Joanne Lewis Axton
IN MEMORIAM

PREFACE

THE SUBSTANCE of this study began in a suggestion for a doctoral dissertation made to me ten years ago by Professor E. D. H. Johnson, when I was a graduate student at Princeton. At that time we thought it would be interesting and profitable to examine Dickens' style in the hope of discovering what if any principles might be said to govern it. A little reading and reflection led me to conclude that, whatever else it might be, at least one important facet of Dickens' style was derived from theatrical idioms—and, presumably, from the theater actually known to him during his life.

With this in mind, I embarked on a program of reading that alternated between volumes of and about the early Victorian theater and drama and volumes of and about Dickens. The present study has grown out of these researches. In the meantime, it struck me that a certain amount of preliminary work needed to be done on the unity, coherence, and structural integrity of Dickens' novels, particularly as the novelist's appropriation of dramatic literature bore on that question, and the intervening years have been devoted for the most part to investigations along these lines. I have regarded these studies as premises upon which to base this volume, and I am indebted to the editors of *PMLA, ELH, Modern Language Quarterly,* and *Studies in English Literature, 1500- 1900* for allowing me to refer to some of the material contained in those essays. The main thrust of the present study, however, takes up where they leave off.

To achieve economy and coherence I have thought it wise to confine my discussion to a relatively small number of Dickens' works—*Sketches by Boz, Pickwick Papers, Oliver Twist, Dombey and Son, Bleak House,* and *Great Expectations*—which I believe to be more or less representative of the novelist's early and mature manner. By and large I have employed the early works to establish the theatrical premises of Dickens' vision but have included so late a novel as *Great Expectations* to indicate the continuity of that vision throughout the novelist's career. The mature works I have reserved for stylistic analysis of their theatrical underpinnings, because in them I believe can be found the full development of Dickens' borrowings from the playhouse. At the same time I have tried to indicate in passing where and how both early and late works share certain theatrical preoccupations without at the same time attempting any study of Dickens' artistic development. Within this general framework I have also chosen to deal at length and in detail with a relatively small number of passages which seemed to me to be representative of Dickens' stylistic "voices." Many of these passages are employed elsewhere in this study in quite different contexts of discussion. I have followed this practice intentionally, realizing the dangers of repetitiousness and obscurity it might entail, in the hope of offering a more nearly holative approach to Dickens' work.

I use the phrase "borrowings from the playhouse" advisedly, for this is not a study of Dickens' appropriation of specific technical devices from the early Victorian drama so much as it is an attempt to indicate where and how the general spirit, idiom, or "style" of that theater underwent a transmutation into the very different vernacular of prose fiction. My concern has been more with demonstrating shared artistic attitudes, modes of vision, and general procedures than with isolating a particular technical indebtedness to some one genre, play, or theater, although in certain instances that seemed to warrant it I have indicated where such a borrowing might have occurred.

Similarly, I have allowed myself a good deal of latitude, once having established the theatrical counters I am using, in carrying my approach as far as I am able. Difficult as it may be to follow the thread that leads from Grimaldi, say, to *Dombey and Son,* my hope is that I have done no violence to my initial premises and that I have obtained results which someone will find interesting.

I owe a debt of gratitude to a host of people and institutions for their help and encouragement in bringing this study to completion: to Professor E. D. H. Johnson, for the sympathetic rigor of his direction of the early phases of this volume; to the staff of the Firestone Library at Princeton University, and particularly to the librarians in charge of its Theatre Collection, for their great assistance in running down chap-books, play texts, and the like; to the Kentucky Research Foundation for its help in preparing this manuscript for the press. To acknowledge specific indebtednesses beyond this point would be to extend this list indefinitely. Suffice it to say that many who cannot be named here have had a hand, or at any rate a thumb, in this study. To them all, my thanks.

CONTENTS

BOOK ONE
Dickens
and the
Theater

Chapter One
THE WRITER
AS ACTOR

FROM THE TIME when John Ruskin deplored Charles Dickens' habit of speaking as it were "in a circle of stage fire,"[1] until today, when Edmund Wilson can claim that Dickens was "the greatest dramatic writer the English had since Shakespeare,"[2] the manifest theatricality of Dickens' genius has been a critical cliché, and a sizable literature dealing with the relations between the novelist and the theater has grown up over the years.[3] But no one, as far as I know, has attempted any extended study of the influence of the theater actually known to Dickens—particularly the popular Victorian theater —on his techniques as a novelist.[4] This is the task proposed by the present study.

The biographical facts of Dickens' lifelong love affair with the stage are well known. Many of his most vivid memories of childhood centered on the Theatre Royal at Rochester, visits to Chatham of Richardson's traveling pantomime and melodrama troupe, and the backstage world of his uncle's amateur theatricals.[5] Dickens' first juvenile literary work was a tragedy, *Misnar, the Sultan of India;* and as a student at Wellington House Academy he was the leading spirit in toy theater productions of such plays as *The Dog of Montargis, Cherry and Fair Star,* and Pocock's famous melodrama, *The Miller and his Men.*[6] Later, as a young man in London, Dickens seriously contemplated an acting career, and only an illness postponed an audition with Charles Mathews the Elder, one of the first English comedians to attempt realistic domestic character parts.[7] Not long after, one of Dickens' sketches appeared in print, and the stage-struck young shorthand writer was fairly launched on a career in journalism and literature.

Yet Dickens never deserted the stage. In addition to his duties as a novelist and editor, he found time to write six plays (for the most part farces) and to turn out a great quantity of journalism on theatrical subjects.[8] His amateur theatrical tours on behalf of various charitable causes earned him a reputation as a talented actor.[9] Many of his most intimate friends were closely connected with the Victorian theatrical world.[10] Dickens' love for popular and classical drama continued undiminished throughout his lifetime, as evidenced by his heavy patronage of almost every kind of theatrical production and by his special fondness for the unlicensed theaters "on the Surrey side" of London.[11] He was a staunch supporter of the Royal Theatrical Fund and was often called upon to serve as toastmaster at its fund-raising dinners.[12]

Dickens' character reveals a deep histrionic strain, quite aside from his interest in amateur theatricals and the like, which suggests that it was a fundamental aspect of his psychological makeup. His favorite games, for example, were those which demand some kind of impersonation, like charades; and he was given to playing practical jokes on his family and friends in which he disguised himself in costume and makeup.[13] His penchant for dramatic readings of newly completed works to a circle of friends was so remarkable that he sometimes went to very considerable trouble to arrange such sessions. In the winter of 1844, for example, he rushed all the way back from Genoa in order to read his Christmas book for that year, *The Chimes,* to a group that included Thomas Carlyle, Douglas Jerrold, John Forster, and Clarkson Stanfield.[14] The psychological forces behind Dickens' histrionic bent finally pushed him to embark, on April 29, 1858, on the first of those public dramatic readings from his own works which he vigorously pursued, against the mounting pleas of his family, friends, and doctors, until his death twelve years later—a death at least in part caused by the physical and emotional strain of the readings themselves.[15]

Since his theatrical and histrionic interests were inseparable from the very nature of the man, it is not surprising that they play an important role in the theory and practice of the artist. On the simplest level, theatrical personages crowd the pages of Dickens' works. As we shall later see in some detail, Dickens' earliest fiction, *Sketches by Boz,* is deeply imbued with a vision of life derived from the playhouse and populated with actors of all sorts. *Pickwick Papers* has for its principal rogue that superb charlatan, the strolling actor Jingle. Codlin and Short figure prominently in *The Old Curiosity Shop,* as do the immortal Crummles family in *Nicholas Nickleby;* and F. R. Leavis has defined the important thematic uses to which Dickens put Sleary's Circus troupe in

Hard Times.[16] Even so late a novel as *Great Expectations* (1860-1861) gives a large place to that wretched thespian, Wopsle, whose career on the London boards is a comic paradigm of Pip's disappointed expectations.

Dickens' concept of the novel had as its cornerstone the dramatic presentation of story, and his theoretical statements are uniformly couched in terms taken from the playhouse. Premised on his belief that "every writer of fiction . . . writes, in effect, for the stage,"[17] Dickens' practical criticism everywhere insists on dramatic impersonality. To Mrs. Brookfield he wrote, "You constantly hurry your narrative (and yet without getting on) *by telling it, in a sort of impetuous breathless way, in your own person, when the people should tell it and act it for themselves.* My notion always is, that when I have made the people to play out the play, it is, as it were, their business to do it, and not mine."[18] To another would-be novelist he offered the following advice: "The people do not sufficiently work out their own purposes in dialogue and dramatic action. . . . What you do for them, they ought to do for themselves."[19] To a third, "There is too much of the narrator in it —the narrator not being an actor. The result is, that I can *not* see the people, or the place, or believe in the fiction."[20] As one recent critic has remarked, "Dickens' canon of dramatic presentation of his story did not stop with action and dialogue but extended to the revelation of the inner life of his characters. Formal psychological analyses of the states of mind of his people were out of the question in a novel that was meant to be dramatic, to have the same impact on a reader as a swiftly moving play."[21] And to this end Dickens had recourse to the formal dramatic soliloquy, to the inserted autobiographical narrative, and to the direct rendering of his characters' thoughts —almost to the point of using the stream-of-consciousness technique.[22]

Indeed, since for Dickens, as for his influential friend Carlyle, all life was a great drama gradually unfolding itself, it behooved the novelist, as he once wrote Wilkie Collins, "only to *suggest,* until the fulfilment comes. These are the ways of Providence, of which ways all art is but a little imitation."[23] That life, behind its superficial appearance of being an anarchy of unrelated phenomena, was in reality controlled by some intelligible and purposive order constitutes the central premise of Dickens' world-view; and typically, he spoke of this conception in essentially dramatic terminology. Acutely summarizing the novelist's temperament, his friend and biographer John Forster once remarked, "On the coincidences, resemblances, and surprises of life, Dickens liked especially to dwell, and few things moved his fancy so pleasantly. The world, he would say, was so much smaller than we thought it; we were all so connected by fate without knowing it; people supposed to be far apart were so constantly elbowing each other; and tomorrow bore so close a resemblance to nothing half so much as to yesterday."[24] And Dickens himself, in a transitional passage in *Oliver Twist,* made the same point in specifically dramatic terms:

It is the custom on the stage, in all good murderous melodramas, to present the tragic and the comic scenes, in as regular alternation, as the layers of red and white in a side of streaky bacon. The hero sinks upon his straw bed, weighed down by fetters and misfortunes; in the next scene, his faithful but unconscious squire regales the audience with a comic song. . . .

Such changes appear absurd; but they are not so unnatural as they would seem at first sight. The transitions
in real life from well-spread boards to death-beds, and
from mourning-weeds to holiday garments, are not a whit
less startling; only, there, we are busy actors, instead of
passive lookers-on, which makes a vast difference. The
actors in the mimic life of the theatre, are blind to violent
transitions and abrupt impulses of passion or feeling,
which, presented before the eyes of mere spectators, are
at once condemned as outrageous and preposterous.
(V, 153-154)

And in another place the novelist makes a similar
claim in even more forceful language: "A pantomime
is to us, a mirror of life; nay more, we maintain that
it is so to audiences generally, although they are not
aware of it, and that this very circumstance is the
secret cause of their amusement and delight." (II, 427)

Dickens argued in these passages that the conventions of the popular theater contain an inherent truth
to life which was obscured from the man in the street
by his own dullness of vision, and that it was the
function of the creative artist to revivify this vision
by depicting the commonplace—as it really seemed to
Dickens—in all the glowing color, light, movement,
and surprise of the playhouse. It was on these grounds
that the novelist defended the cheap, popular theaters
of London against puritanical attack: they offered the
workingman an opportunity for imaginative enrich-
ment and for an escape from the ugliness of his life.[25]
The same ideas governed the editorial policy of
Dickens' popular magazines, *Household Words* and
All the Year Round, which was to stress "the romantic
side of familiar things."[26] Indeed, similar views stood
behind his sense of the novelist's high calling in a
utilitarian age. Defending himself once against a

charge of imaginative excess, he wrote: "In these times, when the tendency is to be frightfully literal and catalogue-like—to make the thing, in short, a sort of sum in reduction that any miserable creature can do in that way—I have an idea (really founded on the love of what I profess), that the very holding of popular literature through a kind of popular dark age, may depend on such fanciful treatment."[27] This "fanciful treatment" of life, it need hardly be stressed, took the form of dramatic or theatrical treatment.

In defending his own works from the charge of exaggeration leveled against them, Dickens elaborated this position when he wrote,

What is exaggeration to one class of minds . . . is plain truth to another. That which is commonly called a long-sight, perceives in a prospect innumerable features and bearings non-existent to a short-sighted person. I sometimes ask myself whether there may occasionally be a difference of this kind between some writers and some readers; whether it is *always* the writer who colours highly, or whether it is now and then the reader whose eye for colour is a little dull?
On this head of exaggeration I have a positive experience. . . . I have never touched a character precisely from the life, but some counterpart of that character has incredulously asked me: "Now really, did I ever really, see one like it?" (XIV, xvii)

As Dickens saw it, the "common observer's" lack of dramatic imagination leads him to accuse the "writer of genius" of "intentional exaggeration, substitution, addition;" he has "never been able in society to see the startling phenomena which he condemns as melodramatic and unnatural. The reason is, that such an individual has never developed the sense required for seeing such things; and, because he is partially blind, he accuses his informant of wilful invention."[28] The artist's imaginative vision is peculiarly able to see into the heart of things and perceive the dramatic order of reality in all its brilliance and unity. Compelled to communicate this vision of the truth behind the surfaces of things in appropriately dramatic terms, the artist's aim is to make the "common observer's" view of the multiplicity of his experience meaningful and ordered: "Facts . . . from their very abundance, have to be refunded into the unity of the principle of which they are examples; and this, once declared, has a tendency to impersonation."[29] The novelist was, then, a man dedicated in a fact-minded era to re-organizing his readers' modes of perception of the real world around them along imaginative lines—and by imaginative Dickens meant dramatic or theatrical.

Far deeper matters of Dickens' personality and the peculiar operation of his creative imagination demonstrate equally well how profoundly theatrical were the conditions under which he wrote. Leaving aside the tendency Dickens shared with Thackeray to conceive of and express himself as an author in the role of a stage manager or actor,[30] which suggests the degree of intimacy he wished to share with his reading public as a result of his serial mode of publication and of his personal predilections, much evidence testifies to the specifically theatrical character of his creative process. From the testimony of his daughter Mamie, who was once accidentally left on a couch in her father's study, we know that in the act of writing Dickens often laughed, grimaced, and otherwise acted out his stories as they rose in his imagination, often with the additional aid of mirrors placed in view from his desk.[31] What G. H. Lewes described as an "hallucinative" process of creation—that Dickens was a "seer of visions" which had the "coercive power of realities"—was confirmed by the novelist himself: "When . . . I sit down to my book, some beneficent power shows it all to me, and tempts me to be interested, and I don't invent it—really do not—*but see it,* and write it down."[32] It would seem, then, that for Dickens the very act of creation took on many aspects of the witnessing of a dramatic spectacle, in which Dickens' role was alternately that of spectator or performer, depending upon whether he was imagining or writing.

It is in the light of these peculiar conditions under which Dickens' imagination seems to have operated that we may understand the nature of the intimacy which subsisted between the novelist and what he quite literally regarded as his audience. Because he apparently thought of himself in some sense as a witness to and reporter of events transpiring almost independently, the creatures of his imagination had about them an unusual order of reality which made his novels take on the character of an imaginative experience which he was actively sharing with his readers. Dickens was stating the simple truth when he once wrote—what he was never tired of repeating—that if any of his readers "have felt a sorrow in one of the principal incidents on which this fiction turns, I hope it may be a sorrow of that sort which endears the sharers in it, one to another. This is not unselfish in me. I may claim to have felt it, at least as much as anybody else; and I would fain be remembered kindly for my part in the experience" (XVIII, xiii). Here the pathos engendered by the untimely death of young Paul Dombey (where elsewhere it might equally have been humor or melodrama) is the means of drawing author and reader more closely together on the ground of a deeply felt communal sympathy. That the original emotion was a powerful one we know from Dickens' own testimony: "My remembrance wanders for a whole winter night about the streets of Paris—as I restlessly did with a heavy heart, on the night when I had written the chapter in which my little friend and I parted company" (XVIII, xiv) .[33] This sense of personal intimacy between himself, the created personages of his novels, and his readers was greatly increased by Dickens' serial mode of publication, as he well knew. At another place he likened the "freedom of intimacy and cordiality of friendship" between himself and his public as a result of monthly serialization to the relationship between writer and reader of an informal essayist like Henry Mackenzie (VI, xv-xvi) , and in his abortive *Master Humphrey's Clock* project he attempted to combine in one person and form the functions of both periodical essayist and serial novelist. What he succeeded in doing, however, by the publication of *The Old Curiosity Shop* out of that experiment, was "to make the bond between himself and his readers," as John Forster correctly saw, "one of personal attachment."[34]

Similar motives prompted Dickens' ventures into journalism. Outlining the idea of *Household Words,* his first magazine, to Forster, he wrote, "I could approach them [the reading public] in a different mode under this name, and in a more winning and immediate way, than under any other. I would at once sit down upon their very hobs; and take a personal and confidential position with them which would separate me, instantly, from all other periodicals periodically published."[35] And at the beginning of its publication, in outlining his editorial policy to the public, he concluded, "We have considered what an ambition it is to be admitted into many homes with affection and confidence; to be regarded as a friend . . . and to be associated with the harmless laughter and gentle tears of many hearths. We know the great responsibility of such a privilege; its vast reward; the picture it conjures up . . . of a multitude moved by one sympathy" (XXXV, 107-108). Dickens' unifying intention, to be achieved through what George Eliot was later to call the "sympathetic imagination," extended to include a kind of social communion among all classes of his readers as they joined in the common imaginative experience of his fiction and journalism. As he wrote in the same place, "to bring the greater and the lesser in degree, together, on that wide field [the field of the romance in familiar things], and mutually dispose them to a better acquaintance and a kinder understanding—is one main object of our *Household Words*."

Dickens' hunger to experience more immediately that sense of "a multitude moved by one sympathy" drove him to undertake a series of dramatic readings from his own works during the last twelve years of his life. In retrospect this decision, however bizarre it seems, was no more than the final step in Dickens' lifelong effort to establish an ever more intimate contact with his audience. Given the dramatic basis of his vision and inspiration, his serial mode of publication, and his desire to stand on terms of personal attachment with his readers, such a step now appears inevitable. It was in partial recognition of all these mixed motives operating on his genius that Dickens described his public readings as "like writing a book in company,"[36] for in them the novelist was reenacting his original creative experience in the actual presence of an audience responding with tears and laughter. Indeed, to bring this intimacy into actual physical being before his very eyes had been from the first a major attraction of a reading tour. "Think of this reading project (as I do)," he wrote a dubious Forster, "solely with a view to its effect on that particular relation (personally affectionate and like no other man's) which subsists between me and the public."[37] And later, when his public readings were a resounding success, he revealed that from the beginning he had counted on "that peculiar personal relation between my audience and myself" to guarantee their popularity.[38]

Quite aside from his delight at the money he made from the reading tours, Dickens was perhaps most moved by the strong sense of personal attachment he encountered in the audience at a critical point in his personal life. Beyond these feelings, however, one other emotion dominated his enthusiastic accounts of the readings in his letters, and that was of a man overwhelmed by the emotional power of his own genius over an audience whose reactions swept him along with them into a thrilling sense of sympathetic unity. He found himself "knocked off my legs" and "simply bowled over" by the emotions he engendered and was caught up by. At one of his most successful readings, at the British Embassy in Paris early in 1863, the sense of emotional participation, and even the new insights into his own works he discovered in consequence, strike the major note:

I suppose that such an audience for a piece of Art is not to be found in the world. . . . I got things out of the old Carol—effects I mean—so entirely new and so very strong, that I quite amazed myself and wondered where I was going next. I really listened to Mr. Peggotty's narrative in Copperfield, with admiration. When Little Emily's letter was read, a low murmur of irrepressible emotion went about like a sort of sea. . . . As to the Trial, their perception of the Witnesses, and particularly of Winkle, was quite extraordinary. And whenever they saw the old Judge coming in, they tapped one another and laughed with that amazing relish that I could hardly help laughing as much myself.[39]

So complete was Dickens' identification with the subjects of his readings and with his audience's responses that, when he read Sikes' murder of Nancy from *Oliver Twist,* his pulse rate rose to dangerous heights, often in mere anticipation of the reading.[40] In short, the readings had become the last phase in Dickens' practice of his art.

Chapter Two
MODES OF THE
POPULAR VICTORIAN
THEATER

I F IT IS DIFFICULT for us now to realize the extraordinary hold the theater and the actor had on
the Victorian literary imagination, it is no less
difficult to reconstruct the forms, styles, and conditions of the stage known to Dickens and his age. By
and large scholars and critics have ignored or condemned the hundred years of British theatrical history that lay between David Garrick and Tom
Robertson; and only recently has a revival of serious
interest in the nineteenth-century theater brought
with it some effort to discover just what it was really
like.[1] The task is complicated, first, by the fact that
during Dickens' lifetime the English theater underwent a series of profound transitions—in acting style,
production, dramatic forms, even playhouse construction—so that it is next to impossible to speak about
a definitive Victorian drama; and second, by the fact
that much of what was most characteristic of that
theater has either disappeared or has been so changed

by the passage of time as to be unrecognizable. No one now living has ever seen a Planché extravaganza, a burletta or burlesque, a *feerié,* or one of Charles Mathews' "At Homes." Even modern English pantomime or motion-picture melodrama is radically different from its Victorian counterpart.

Undoubtedly the most important force for change in the Victorian drama was the enactment of the Theatre Regulation Act of 1843, which terminated the century-long monopoly enjoyed by Covent Garden, Drury Lane, and (latterly) the Haymarket theaters of "legitimate" drama—that is, five-act comedy and tragedy. This act also ended the restriction of the "minor" or unlicensed theaters to the production of what had come to be called burletta—properly speaking, a one-act comedy or farce with music and a minimum of five or six songs—and other forms of musical drama.[2] During the period when the patent-theater monopoly was in effect, however, the nature of what was called burletta, under pressure from managers and audiences, was broadened to include almost any kind of dramatic production which involved a great deal of music, song, dance, verse, or recitative. Indeed, so popular had the form become in the minor theaters that the patent houses were forced to meet competition by producing their own musicals of various sorts.[3] Nor was the triumph of musical drama by Dickens' time the only consequence of the patent-theater monopoly. As a result of the loose definition of burletta, the stage in the 1820's, 1830's, and 1840's was marked by a wholesale proliferation and confusion of genres and forms. Burlesque, extravaganzas, true burlettas, melodramas, revues, pantomimes, burlesque-pantomimes, operettas, comic operas, opera—all were more or less characterized by the introduction of musical or poetic devices.[4]

The seminal form which spawned this welter of musical drama was most likely the harlequinade tradition inherited from *commedia dell' arte* and domesticated in the eighteenth and early nineteenth centuries by John Rich and Joseph Grimaldi as English pantomime—the form that Dickens once thought to be "a mirror of life."[5] As the novelist knew it, a typical Christmas or Easter pantomime opened with a half-serious story of a conflict between two lovers, a heavy father, an unwanted suitor, and a comic servant or old dame, all dressed in spangled imitations of street clothes and huge *papier-mâché* masks designed to caricature contemporary types. When the struggle between the lovers and the father reached an impasse, a fairy interceded and with a magic wand instantly transformed the scene. The actors, who had previously underdressed (that is, had put on a second costume under their outer dress), meanwhile doffed their masks and street clothes to stand revealed as the personages of harlequinade. The two lovers became Harlequin and Columbine, the heavy father Pantaloon, and the rest clowns, mischievous followers of the lecherous, scheming, and gluttonous Pantaloon. Strung on the thread of the disreputable characters' pursuit of Harlequin and Columbine, the ensuing pantomime constituted the main portion of the piece and was for the most part either mimed or spoken in recitative but with comic songs, music, and dancing often inserted. Within this framework structure was episodic, usually consisting of a series of frauds, impostures, or tricks perpetrated by Pantaloon and his accomplices the clowns while masked in a variety of transparently obvious disguises; the climax ordinarily resulted in a slapstick unmasking or other contretemps. Transitions between episodes were frequent and surprising, signaled by the fairy's wand which had been given to Harlequin in order to keep the lovers' mischievous pursuers at bay. Toward the end Harlequin and Columbine were threatened with capture when the wand came into the hands of one of the clowns; but at this point the good fairy once again interceded to resolve the quarrel, mete out punishment and reward, state the moral of the piece, and bring everything to a happy conclusion in one final spectacular scenic transformation.

In addition to the burlesque framework provided by the incongruous use of a story based on some folk or nursery tale—Grimaldi's *Harlequin and Mother Goose* of 1806 set the pattern for the age[6]—pantomimes usually mixed fantasy with topicality and topical satire. Patterns of action were repeated in episodes with comic variations and inversions, and sets tended to become more careful reproductions of real places recently in the news. Conventional spangles gave way increasingly to accurate costumes, but the motley and grotesquerie of traditional pantomime remained alongside them. Scenic transformations were both ingenious and sumptuous. Properties and sets collapsed or opened out into radically different things or places which yet bore striking resemblances to their originals: palaces and temples reappeared as huts and cottages, trees turned into houses, colonnades became beds of tulips, and mechanic shops were translated into serpents and ostriches. Properties commonly played upon grotesque incongruities in scale or context, and comic animism was a favorite device. Thus clowns went disguised as kitchen imple-

ments, animals, outsized vegetables, even plants and
trees; and it was customary to see "Harlequin trim-
ming himself with an axe, hewing down a tree with
a razor, making his tea in a cauldron, and brewing
ale in a teapot."[7] Clowns turned into, or appeared
out of wheelbarrows and joint-stools, and Grimaldi
variously impersonated a chicken, sang with an oyster,
and played games with a frog.[8] Costume and disguise
often burlesqued some fad, fashion, or public figure
and were governed by the comic or satiric use of
disproportionate or incongruous materials. Grimaldi,
for example, was celebrated for his impersonation of
a hussar: he dressed in coal-scuttle boots, a shako
made out of a woman's fur muff with a watch-pocket
pinned to one side and a table-brush stuck in the
crown, tassels and cords of bell-rope, and a poker for
a sword.[9] In short, pantomime as Dickens knew it
was a curious amalgam of fantasy, realism, topicality,
anachronism, grotesquerie, burlesque, spectacle, music, verse, dance, and a serious story. Moreover, it
bequeathed most of its mixed elements to the dramatic forms that grew out of it.

Pantomime played a central role in the growth of
the burlesque, extravaganza, and revue, where confusion about the distinguishing features of the genres
was most general. It was a common practice to
describe a spectacle based on an old story, for example, as a "burlesque extravaganza," and James
Robinson Planché's early extravaganzas were billed
as "rum-antic burlettas."[10] Clinton-Baddeley defines
extravaganza as "farce written in rhymed couplets"
with spectacle added; and the same critic quotes *The
Illustrated London News* (Dec. 28, 1844) to the effect
that "at present, the burlesque, and the introductory
portion of a pantomime, are closely assimilated. . . .

A great hit might be made by producing a pantomime all opening." He goes on to add, "That is precisely what did happen. The burlesque squarely super-imposed itself on the old beginning. It came to be the habit to play a long fairy extravaganza with a superb transformation scene at the end of it—and then to tack on to that a harlequinade which had no reference to the particular story and which got shorter and shorter with the passing of the years."[11] But even here hard and fast definitions are next to impossible. Burlesque gradually lost its satiric meaning as it became identified with the jocosities and absurdities of debased extravaganza, in contrast to the wit and charm of its chief practitioner, Planché; and panto-mime, in its frequent appropriation of some old chil-dren's story for a framework, involved a considerable amount of burlesque.[12]

A typical burlesque like Albert Smith's and J. Taylor's *Dick Whittington and his Cat* (Lyceum, 1845),[13] for example, was similar to both pantomime and extravaganza in that it retold, with many incon-gruous topical touches, a traditional story in an ex-travagant or absurd manner; but it did not so much make fun of the original story as extract laughter from a wide discrepancy between subject and style. To this end the cat was played by a girl in a breeches part; and a pantomime-like good fairy with a wand arranges Dick's vision of future happiness and pros-perity if he returns to his employer, Mr. Fitzwarren. Cast upon the shores of Araby with his master, Dick's cat aids the local Sultan by driving the rats out of his realm—but the "rats" are French troops engaged in reducing Algeria to colonial status during the 1840's. And Mr. Fitzwarren arrives in North Africa (having been bankrupted by unwise investments in railway shares) aboard a "flying machine." From this play with anachronism and topicality, scenic transformation by magic, incongruity, and the like, it can be seen that much of the machinery and spirit of pantomime was alive in burlesque.

Burlesque was also often confused with burletta and farce, partly, Rowell believes,[14] because of the music and song common to all three; but a more likely reason is that their comedy was similar. While burlesque, narrowly defined, ridicules either some literary or dramatic work or some event or person made absurd by an inappropriate context, the form has always been careless of its comedy and willing to elicit what Hughes calls the "non-reflective guffaw" of farce from the clever handling of incongruous materials and the ridiculous, antic difficulties of stock types.[15] Pantomime, the progenitor of burlesque, was itself an outgrowth of harlequinade much influenced by farce; burletta was musical farce; and extravaganza merely added poetry and spectacular scenic effects to the mixture. And farce, pantomime, and burlesque shared a fondness for improbability, extravagence, and comic anachronism, together with a preference for action and business to dialogue. Structurally these forms were episodic, exploiting all the possibilities of machinery, sudden changes of scene, incongruous transformations, and surprise reversals; what unity they achieved lay in their common delight with stock patterns of action: intrigue, disguise, the chase, accidental unmasking, and comic repetition with variation in motif, episode, gesture, and action.[16]

Burlesque was equally confused with two other popular Victorian theatrical forms, the revue and extravaganza, partly as a result of Francis Talfourd's extension of burlesque into fantasy, which brought the genre close to the extravaganzas of Planché, and into topical satire, which was the province of the revue.[17] In addition to sharing the features of the forms discussed above, all three genres strove to achieve an air of gaiety and sprightly satire, chiefly through the use of fantastic plots based on legendary stories and loose iambic pantameter couplets, all mixed together in a medley that included spectacular transformations, music, song, and dance.[18] Furthermore, while they developed the stage use of fantasy as far as possible, these genres participated in the general tendency in the nineteenth-century theater toward realism and accuracy in costume, setting, and properties.[19] If there is one feature of the drama known to Dickens, then, it is this grotesque mixture of the real and the fantastic.

The moving spirit behind these two forms was James Robinson Planché, whose revue, *Success* (1825), and extravaganza, *High, Low, Jack and the Game* (1833), defined their respective genres for twenty years.[20] The revue was a light-hearted, gently satiric survey of recent dramatic or public events linked together (if at all) by the loosest of plot lines. Extravaganza was much more pretentious. It was a blank-verse or rhymed-couplet fantasy based on some ancient and usually mythological story, often premised on a fantastic allegorical theme.[21] Like burlesque, extravaganza had its probable origin in pantomime: its immediate source seems to have been the *feerié,* a French form whose predecessor is thought to have been *Arlequin dans un Oeuf* (1798).[22] According to Planché, extravaganza stressed a "whimsical treatment of a poetical subject" as distinct from "the broad caricature of a tragedy or serious opera which was correctly described as burlesque."[23] Like burlesque in its use of traditional stories, extravaganza rather played on the charm of the tale itself than on gross travesty or grotesque incongruity as in burlesque. While both used some distortion of a received story for contemporary application, burlesque sought to ridicule where extravaganza sought only a lightly humorous or satirical tone, a whimsical interplay between the original legend and its topical subject.[24]

The most characteristic form of the nineteenth-century theater, melodrama, was no less closely related to pantomime. Whatever encouragement may have been given to its development by the tale of terror, the romantic novel, nautical song, and eighteenth-century sentimental comedy, Victorian melodrama had its most likely parent in pantomime. Out of eighteenth-century *pantomime dialoguée* Guilbert de Pixérécourt evolved the essential melodrama form, and his *Coeline* (1800) became, in Thomas Holcroft's *A Tale of Terror* (1802), its pirated English version, probably the first true melodrama in England.[25] The Dibdins developed the genre, Edward Fitzball domesticated its characters and setting in his nautical *The Pilot* (1825), and melodrama was given crude social overtones by John Buckstone's *Luke the Laborer* (1826). By the 1830's, following Douglas Jerrold's immensely popular *Black-Eyed Susan* (1829), *The Press Gang* (1830), *The Rent Day* (1832), and *The Factory Girl* (1832), melodrama had taken English theaters by storm.[26]

The characteristic traits of melodrama reveal its descent from pantomime. The earliest melodramas were hardly more than mimed action plays with musical accompaniment, and throughout its career the form has leaned more toward visual action than the spoken word.[27] Like many other nineteenth-century theatrical forms, melodrama tended to appropriate historical, legendary, and folklore materials: Jerrold's *Black-Eyed Susan,* for example, is based on John Gay's popular nautical ballad, "Sweet William's Farewell to Black-Ey'd Susan" (1720).[28] The principal dramatic effect of melodrama, as of many genres contemporary with it, depends upon a sharp contrast and mingling of exaggerated moods; but where pantomime, say, relied on the mixture of realism and fantasy which creates the grotesque, melodrama rather contrasts or fuses pathos, sentiment, and suspense with farce. Yet all these dramatic forms exploited striking alternations of scene and mood, a pronounced burlesque approach to comedy, parallel plotting, and the same preoccupation with masking and unmasking, especially, in the case of melodrama, with the hidden relationships between disguised characters and with the transparent mask.[29]

Any further discussion of popular Victorian theatrical forms would extend this study to unmanageable dimensions and force us to consider such subspecies as vaudeville, burletta, comic opera, operetta, comedietta, farcetta, opera, and a half-dozen other offshoots and combinations of these and other minor types. But at least the overall spirit of the theater Dickens knew has been indicated, and it remains only to glance at some of the other forces bearing on the stage of that time to complete this sketch. Of these influences, the most important were the replacement of the apron stage with the proscenium, the gradual expansion in size of the major playhouses, and the unruly behavior of early Victorian audiences, all of which discouraged subtlety in acting and staging and made it necessary to communicate by coarse visual devices—sweeping gestures, flamboyant costume, mass blocking, spectacular effect, machinery, business, miming—and by music, song, and dance. Add to this the encouragement given to the visual aspect of drama offered by new developments in stage lighting, scenic design, and realistic costume, and it is little wonder that the nineteenth century produced so little great drama and so much delightful theater.[30]

The gradual evolution of the star system, type-casting, stereotyping, and traditional "parts" which specified members of these repertory companies were expected to perform, all combined to produce a unique extra-histrionic familiarity between actor and audience at the very time when the intimacy of the older theater had been lost and that of the "fourth wall" theater was not yet in being. The playgoer came to see his favorite actor do the tricks, play the parts, and make the "points" with which he was identified as much as to be absorbed by the drama; and lesser actors played directly to the audience, grimacing, doing their familiar business, and whispering asides in violation of credibility. Yet the spectators were willing to hiss the villain, cheer the hero, and weep with the beleaguered heroine with equal sincerity.[31] Victorian audiences thus were to a peculiar degree involved in that willing suspension of disbelief—as well as of belief—which constitutes theatrical illusion. Indeed, they were simultaneously called upon to lose themselves in imaginative identification with the personages and events on stage as if they were real, and yet to remark the artifices of actor and designer as well—to be equally engaged by the actor and by his impersonation. Victorian audiences seem to have been able to sustain this ambiguous state throughout the four to six hours of an average theater's evening bill and, what is more extraordinary, to take pleasure in it.

The outstanding feature of the nineteenth-century theater is perhaps this very mélange, this "balance or reconciliation of the opposite or discordant qualities," of realism and fantasy. Anachronism and topicality, grotesque incongruity and scenic verisimilitude, and that extra-histrionic intimacy between actor and spectator which so complicated dramatic illusion combined to create a fascinatingly ambiguous theater. All the devices of actor, machinist, and scenic designer kept an antic surface constantly in view, while transformations, pantomime, and burlesque comedy stressed the discrepant likenesses between discordant but familiar realms and the interplay between appearance and reality. In general the categories of comedy, satire, and humor were blurred because their treatment by actors, playwrights, and designers emphasized absurdity rather than ridicule: they played for the "non-reflective guffaw," not the sneer. Similarly, dramatic ambiance linked fantastic patterns of action and archetypes with their counterparts in commonplace life, and in so doing sought to give the audience the pleasure that goes with unexpected recognition and reoriented perspective. Structure was dominated by equally impure motives, as startling contrasts vied with unlooked-for analogies, and variety with proliferation and repetition. Indeed, the line between character and setting was as hard to draw as that between comedy and satire, chiefly in consequence of pantomime's conventional confusion between animate and inanimate realms.[32]

If this welter of forms may be said to have had any governing spirit, however, it was that of grotesquerie, considered not merely in the figurative sense associated with "bizarre"—that is, extravagant, fantastic, caricatural, or capricious—but as a mode or structure with its own distinguishing elements. It is not an easy task to describe the grotesque, nor have I yet seen a fully satisfying definition of its traits.[33] But we know that this style is associated with such practitioners of "dark" grotesque as Breughel, Grünewald, Bosch, and Kafka, on one hand, and with *commedia dell' arte,* harlequinade, and the drawings of Callot on its lighter, gayer side. In any event, it seems clear that the development of grotesque style is firmly linked to important precursors of English pantomime, burlesque, and melodrama, and that these later forms retain many of its leading features.

The most prominent trait of grotesque style, perhaps, as of that of Dickens and of the popular nineteenth-century theater, is its tendency to estrange reality without dispensing with it. The grotesque aims to subvert the familiar world (as distinct from fairy tale, which creates its own special world) by means of sudden, surprising transformations of its elements, so that the processes normally associated with the working of everyday life are undone, or the conventional relations between things are dislocated. Similarly, grotesque style is marked by a host of techniques identical with those of the nineteenth-century theater and of Charles Dickens' works. In pursuit of the discrepant, all three play with disorganization and incoherence between functions, disproportion or incongruity between scales and contexts, or unexpected transposition of realms. For

whatever ends, the grotesque spirit seeks the subversion of tradition, convention, and customary usage,
often carrying this work to that point at which it
reveals the disruptive elements concealed in language.
The final effect of grotesque style is to create the
impression of a world turned upside-down, as in K's
roach, for ends not easily defined and in a tone that
remains ambiguous. It asks us, as Dickens asked his
readers to do in his "realist fairy tales," to perform
an unlooked-for reorientation of our perspective
toward the commonplace.

In the popular theater loved by Dickens—whose
"infirmity" it was "to fancy or perceive relations in
things . . . not apparent generally"—he would have
found innumerable kinds of the unapparent relationships that define grotesque style. There were inventions of unlikely beings and objects tumbling about
amid incompatible juxtapositions of everyday things.
There, too, eccentric figures gamboled in the caricatural, gestic modes of pantomime and burlesque or
pursued their humors and crotchets with the mad
consistency of *farceurs*. There, finally, Dickens must
have been pleased to see the sprightly transposition of
animate and inanimate worlds, where pantomime
clowns became animals, vegetables, and objects, and
where machinery, inanimate things, and vegetable life
turned into people or took on some extraordinary
activity of their own.

From these considerations follows as corollary and
consequence the second major trait of the grotesque
popular theater known to Dickens and reflected in
his work, its special kind of comic effect here rather
lamely called burlesquerie, for want of a better term.
This curious mode of grotesque style when applied

to comic ends is so named because it evades classification according to the traditional categories of comedy,
satire, burlesque, farce, humor, or irony. Rather,
burlesquerie emphasizes the absurd, the ridiculous,
the ludicrously pointless; although it may make use
of any or all of the devices normally associated with
the categories indicated above, they fail adequately
to define the ultimate intention of that grotesque
comedy we have named burlesquerie. In its lighter
mode with which we are mainly concerned here,
grotesque comedy subsumes commonplace character
and action under the rubric of a *theatrum mundi,*
much as Dickens did when speaking of the "Pantomime of Life." From this perspective, all the men
and women are indeed, in Jacques' phrase, "merely
players" in an immense puppet show or pantomime
in mufti, a grand compound of actors furiously and
all unconsciously running through the parts assigned
them by their humor, place in life, environment, or
any one of a thousand other causes. Its intention,
then, is to achieve that helpless laughter at the human
condition in all its manifold antic life; but in its
darker vein, it may seek a recognition of the sinister
or macabre elements which lie concealed just beneath
the commonplace surface of things.

In the hands of Buchner, Hoffmann, or Kafka, this
grotesque play may issue in horror, unreasoning fear,
or terrified helplessness before the spectacle of a
world wholly estranged and alienated, in which one
glimpses ominous or demonic forces arising out of the
reassuring, familiar surface of commonplace life. But
this "dark" grotesque, which Mark Spilka among
others has found to be an important strain in Dickens'
vision, was largely absent from the nineteenth-century

popular theater, aside from an occasional pantomime "dark scene." Rather, the drama best known to Dickens—and, as we shall see, Dickens' own work—located its interest principally in that aspect of grotesque comedy to which we have given the name of burlesquerie. As it was then rather loosely construed, burlesquerie embodied a comedy of discontinuity and incongruity which had no clear and final satiric intention, although it made use of any or all of the usual comic and satiric devices. Broad humor, mixed fantasy and realism, bustling and inconsequential action, ludicrous caricature, extraordinary costume, setting, and property—these are the materials of nineteenth-century burlesquerie.

True grotesque comedy thus finds its peculiar effects precisely in the balance or juxtaposition, rather than the reconciliation, of discordant rather than opposite elements. Its play is with the laughable possibilities of discordance, incongruity, disproportion, and incoherence. More especially, burlesquerie capitalizes on the disruptive potentialities of subverted typicality, convention, and—in language—cliché. It is particularly fond of exploiting conventional norms of language: it plays fast and loose with the discontinuous aspects of cliché and the confusions between literal and figurative dimensions of meaning. It is this latter aspect of burlesquerie that makes it elude the classical categories: it employs typicality and parody for unsatiric ends.

Such free-wheeling comedy may at times incline more toward fantasy, and at other times toward satire, depending upon how character is depicted. Yet its permanently caricatural bias always suggests that in the *theatrum mundi* character operates as it does in

pantomime and burlesque, by the manic persistence
of a few eccentric traits. Caricature of this kind,
whether in the masked and motleyed figures of harlequinade or the humorous stereotypes of farce, may
make use of comedy, but it is finally a different form.
For comedy innocuously annihilates dignity and great-
ness, especially if they are falsely assumed, on some
secure basis of real values; but burlesquerie in effect
aims to do away with familiar footholds of tradition
and convention—even with dramatic credibility. In
comedy and humor, again, though both may exploit
incompatible elements, a certain detachment is maintained which is not proper to true grotesque. With
the latter, on the other hand, we find ourselves becoming more involved than we had anticipated as, for
example, one moment's cheater turns out to be the
gull of the next, and as no unequivocal moral response is indicated. This insecurity of moral view-
point results largely from the fact that the grotesque
seeks neither to teach, warn, nor arouse compassion,
as other modes do, but simply to portray its vision
of the ludicrous or incomprehensible in the commonplace. Its aim and method is to unsettle perspectives
derived from tradition or convention.

   In the case of nineteenth-century popular dramatic
practice, the exploitation of grotesque style was perhaps occasioned as much as anything else by the
cynicism and triviality that ruled company and audience alike; and it would be dangerous indeed to infer
any profoundly alienated world-view from such evidence. But in the hands of a great artist like Dickens,
whose "highly coloured" imaginative vision was shot
through with theatrical perspectives, a grotesque style
like that found in the theater was readily adaptable

to the modes of prose fiction. In the hands of an artist who was committed to the "fanciful treatment of reality," who boasted of the "fantastic fidelity" of his characters to their originals, and whose works have been defined as "realist fairy tales," the techniques of theatrical grotesquerie could be used to achieve his announced intention of undermining conventional ways of looking at the familiar world and commonplace experience. It does not require any traumatic alienation of vision in Warren's Blacking Factory to account for Dickens' desire to subvert his readers' safe, conventional sense of the relations between things; on the contrary, this reorientation and revivification of perspective was his conscious aim as an artist. "Impersonation," he once said, is the act of refunding facts "into the unity of the principle of which they are examples." In a world seen from the point of view of theatrical grotesquerie and burlesquerie, things and people do become suddenly discrete, wanton, eccentric; and one discovers the curiosity of all around him that had gone flat from familiarity and "dullness of vision." The commonplace is viably estranged, and the alien suddenly seems near and disturbingly relevant. The total effect is, as it were, to open one's eyes to the vital interest of his immediate world.

This mode is close to what Schiller once defined as "pure comedy," the comedy of passion as distinct from that of intrigue or character, in that the effort to mediate a sense of the "totality of a world forms the substance . . . and events and characters subserve the creation of a compact poetic universe, not one of the ingredients of which attracts attention by itself, but the overall animation of which engenders an extreme feeling of freedom, gaiety, and ease."[34] Perhaps this "overall animation," this "extreme feeling of freedom, gaiety, and ease," most nearly summarizes the popular Victorian theatrical atmosphere. Certain it is at any event that a similar spirit transfigures the vision and style of Charles Dickens.

BOOK TWO

Dickens'
Theatrical
Vision

Chapter Three
SKETCHES BY BOZ
AND THE
THEATRUM MUNDI

DURING THE transitional years 1834-1838, when Dickens grew from a journalist-cum-actor into a novelist, the grotesqueries of the theater he had frequented as a would-be thespian and a spectator apparently came to hold great relevance for him as means of depicting an emergent bourgeois England in terms of a *theatrum mundi*. His first published works, at any rate—the short journalistic pieces later collected in the two volumes of *Sketches by Boz* and the brilliant but ambivalent first novel, *Pickwick Papers*—are controlled by this vision of society and take their inspiration from the techniques of the early Victorian popular theater.[1]

As we have already seen, Dickens' effort when writing about the theater or about his own work was to demonstrate its congruence to the real world—when seen in all its rich coloration and high contrast through the eyes of an imaginative artist. In order

to mediate this view it was first necessary to under-
mine the conventional assumption that, because the
antic, gestic modes of pantomime, burlesque, and
other dramatic forms were apart from familiar life,
they were in consequence false to it. To this end
Dickens went to some pains to show that the rapid
alternations of comedy and tragedy in melodrama,
for example, are no more violent than those in real
life, but that the man in the street is blinded to this
fact by his participation in those events, much as an
actor is blind to the artifices of the stage because he
participates in them. Viewed imaginatively, however,
the commonplace world appears to be a no less melodramatic mixture of bright and dark.

A similar point of view stands behind Dickens'
defense of his caricatural mode of drawing his characters. To the common reader, such characterization
seems exaggerated because conventional dullness of
vision in a fact-minded age prevents one's seeing with
the eyes of creative imagination. But to Dickens, as
to Thomas Mann, grotesque distortions, eccentricities,
and manic persistence of type are "neither arbitrary,
irreal, or absurd, but excessively true to life."[2] They
are so because their apparently incongruous surface
is only a means of revealing the underlying reality of
such phenomena. Dickens' closely argued brief for
his "fanciful" treatment of reality, his stress on the
"romantic" side of familiar things, and his recognition of the "fantastic fidelity" of his characters to their
real-life counterparts, all point to the novelist's awareness of the theatrical grotesquerie of his vision. To
"fancy or perceive relations in things not apparent
generally" is simply to juxtapose incompatible realms
in such a way as to estrange—or what is more to
Dickens' purposes, to transform—the existing world.

In this Dickens merely demonstrated his participation in a movement of aesthetic ideas that carried across the whole of the nineteenth century.

In a little-known sketch entitled "The Pantomime of Life," the novelist argues that the grotesque distortions, the gestic caricature, and the antic treatment of life that define pantomime and burlesque were "a mirror of life; nay more, we maintain that it is so to audiences generally, although they are not aware of it, and that this very circumstance is the secret cause of their amusement and delight" (II, 427). Dickens' thesis here is more subtle than might appear on a casual reading. He affirms, first, the substantial congruity to reality of the grotesque stylization of pantomime; and second, that the spectators' unconscious awareness of this fact is what has given the mode its potency. There is to Dickens, apparently, a special impact to be gained by the subliminal recognition of the theater's hidden relevance to real life.

A statement such as this would not be accorded great significance were it not for the fact that "The Pantomime of Life" occupies a critical juncture in Dickens' early career: for the *Sketches,* it is the *terminus ad quem;* it was published near the midpoint of *Pickwick Papers,* and, as we shall later see, near the beginning of *Oliver Twist,* to fill out the short second number of that latter novel. In this position, it appears to offer a summary of the ideas that occupied the novelist's mind during the period of composition of these volumes.

However that may be, the vision of society as *theatrum mundi,* implicit in the opening words of the sketch quoted above, is ratified by its conclusion, which takes its text from the speech of Shakespeare's Jaques:

A gentleman, not altogether unknown as a dramatic
poet, wrote this a year or two ago—
>   "All the world's a stage,
>   And all the men and women merely players":

and we . . . venture to add, by way of new reading,
that he meant a Pantomime, and that we are all actors
in The Pantomime of Life." (II, 437)

To ingratiate this view of the world's stage with his
readers, Dickens went beyond invoking the immortal
authority of the Bard of Avon. He employed the
simple strategy throughout the essay of alternating
episodes taken from pantomime with their counterparts in real life. By witholding identification of
each realm, occasionally reversing the order of comparison, and playing down the extravagances of
pantomime while heightening the descriptions of real
life, Dickens misleads the reader into confusing the
two realms and hence into accepting the author's view
of the congruence between the grotesqueries of theatrical pantomime and the characteristic types and
events of ordinary life. The conventional way of
looking at the familiar world is clearly the target of
subversion.

Early in the essay, for example, the reader is introduced to "an elderly gentleman, with a large face and
strongly marked features," a "sunny smile, and a
perpetual dimple . . . on his broad, red cheek. . . . He
is richly, not to say gaudily dressed" (II, 427-428).
It is not until later in the paragraph, however, that
the unsuspecting reader is informed of the identity
of this personage: he is a pantomime clown, his "large,
strongly marked" face a huge papier-mâché mask, and
his "rich dress" spangles and motley. His similarity
to a real-life type is then drawn, followed by a com-

parison between the lecherous behavior of a pantaloon and that of an old man "making such comical
and ineffectual attempts to be young and dissolute,
that all beholders are like to die with laughter"
(II, 429).

This identification of life and playhouse is extended to include the clown's characteristic "swindling everybody he possibly can" (II, 431). At this
point the reader meets an "honourable Captain Fitz-
Whisker Fiercy, attended by his livery servant Do'em,"
who egregiously bilks a number of eager and fawning
merchants. Dickens comments:

> Who can fail to recognize in this, the exact counter-
> part of the best portion of a theatrical pantomime—Fitz-
> Whisker Fiercy by the Clown; Do'em by the pantaloon;
> and supernumeraries by the tradesmen?[3] The best of the
> joke, too, is, that the very coal-merchant who is loudest
> in his complaints against the person who defrauded him,
> is the identical man who sat in the centre of the very
> front row of the pit last night and laughed the most
> boisterously at this very same thing,—and not so well
> done either. Talk of Grimaldi, we say again! Did
> Grimaldi, in his best days, ever do anything in this way
> equal to Da Costa? (II, 433)

Here the novelist's rationale for the truth to life of
theatrical artifice is clearly enunciated: the gross and
antic exaggerations of pantomime clowns do not belie
reality but represent its grotesque dimensions faithfully. Only in real life, men are unable or unwilling
to perceive in its true colors the histrionism of human
actions owing to their participation in the conventions of social intercourse. In real life men are "the
busy actors, instead of passive lookers-on, which makes
a vast difference." And like actors, who are blind to
the "violent transitions and abrupt impulses of pas-

sion or feeling," men are equally incapable of seeing the essentially grotesque extravagance of their own ordinary behavior. Life in middle-class England of the 1830's was to Dickens no more nor less than a great playhouse, in which typical people mimed and strutted as egregiously as if they were actors in a pantomime, though all unaware; and the world embraced by the confines of London seemed a ludicrous burlesque of gestic eccentrics.

To Dickens the astonishing feature of this society was not its histrionism, but that the actors in it were wholly unaware of how flagrantly histrionic were their gestures. To the young writer such impercipience must have seemed all the more incredible under the impress of his recent theatrical experience, his clearing sight, and his widening imaginative horizons. The joyous power of an awakened consciousness of life's absurdity when bringing the familiar London scene into form and expression is the dominant impression one carries away from these early sketches. So it is that the remainder of the piece broadens and darkens its discussion of the likeness between the two realms of theater and life as Dickens extends his analogy to include the supernumeraries (the dull, luckless people of this world), harlequins (the fortunate few who have happened on the magic wand of success), and finally the entire parliamentary system in which party hacks become tumbling clowns prompted by the magic wand of office, who perform astonishing transformations in principle in response to the same agent.

If "The Pantomime of Life" were an isolated instance, no case could be made for the theatrical springs of Dickens' grotesque vision, but the rest of the sketches are unified by their participation in a similar perspective. Considered in respect to their subject matter, *Sketches by Boz* falls into three categories according to the kind and degree of relationship to a theatrical scene which is an incongruous paradigm of the world outside the playhouse. In the first group of sketches belong those pieces which deal directly with the theater and back-stage life: "Greenwich Fair," "Astley's," "Private Theatres," "London Recreations," and "Vauxhall Gardens by Day," among others. In these, the pattern established by "The Pantomime of Life" is more or less faithfully observed: the grotesque interplay between appearance and reality both before and behind the footlights receives studied attention, and the hollow contrivances of the stage to simulate the appearance of reality are exposed and ridiculed. But the final intention of this group of sketches seems to rest on the paradox that the incongruities which destroy dramatic illusion, or at least render it grotesque, are precisely what make the playhouse a true picture of the world outside. There too are found grotesque masks, eccentricities performed in the name of convention, absurd posturing and gestic bustle, and people miming their own stereotypes with all the single-mindedness of puppets moved by another hand.

In "Astley's," for example, the writer finds himself one of the audience at Astley's Circus, an equestrian show interlarded with melodrama and farce, which he had not visited since childhood. He notes that all the fustian traditions and conventions remain unchanged in every respect; but now, he writes, "with shame we confess, that we are far more delighted and amused with the audience, than with the pageantry we once so highly appreciated" (I, 123-124). The rest of the sketch sets side by side for comparison the invariable routine of the show—the impudent clown, the elegant and imperturbable ringmaster, the beautiful equestrienne—with a no less conventional bourgeois family of spectators—a large, proud, and condescending mother, a servile nurse, an adolescent son too anxious to appear grown-up, and a daughter already a coquette. The inference is clear: characteristic behavior constitutes an activity comparable to that of an actor in his role and thus validates the gestic, caricatural mode of the mime or *farceur*. This interplay between the boards and the great world is carried to its logical conclusion in the final scene of the sketch, where the members of the troupe, now stripped of their gorgeous costumes and clad in tattered mufti, are discovered lounging outside the stage door. The narrator's voice focuses on two responses: first, astonishment at the great discrepancy between actor and role; and second, the recognition that, even returned to the everyday world, the actors participate in the general "pantomime of life" and strut, pose, and strike attitudes as falsely and characteristically as they did on stage—and as people do, universally. Life is indeed a *theatrum mundi,* a bizarre spectacle of stereotypes in antic movement, when it is viewed from a perspective that undermines conventional relationships and juxtaposes realms normally kept separate.

In "Private Theatres," again, Dickens turned to explore that half-world where the real and the fantastic join—backstage, where amateur actors appear in costume but out of their roles, and before the footlights, where the audience are out of costume but in their several characteristic parts. Behind the scenes appearance and reality meet and mingle to create grotesque discrepancies and incongruities, thus: a plate basket becomes a witches' cauldron in a tawdry *Macbeth,* and "the three uncouth-looking figures, with broken clothes-props in their hands, who are drinking gin-and-water out of a pint pot, are the weird sisters" (I, 148). Similarly, in the audience, "That gentleman in the white hat and checked shirt . . . is Mr. Horatio St. Julien, alias Jem Larkins. His line is genteel comedy—his father's, coal and potato" (I, 147). In "Greenwich Fair" Richardson's traveling melodrama company stages an affecting scene in the following manner: "The rightful heir is discovered in prison, carefully holding a long chain in his hands, and seated despondingly in a large arm-chair" (I, 138). In the audience at the same time, one can see "young ladies, who are persuaded to indulge in a drop of the . . . right sort, display a pleasing degree of reluctance to taste it, and cough afterwards with great propriety" (I, 135). In Dickens' writings, the grotesque emerges when incompatible realms mingle: pit and boards, backstage and stage door, plate baskets and witches' cauldrons, pint pots and weird sisters, prisons and easy chairs, the histrionic subterfuges of genteel respectability, and the manic persistence of the type.

A second group of *Sketches by Boz* embraces a somewhat broader spectrum of subjects than those with explicitly theatrical topics, but they are linked together by a common theme implicit in the first group—the recognition of the grotesque histrionism at the heart of middle-class manners and morals. At one extreme are those pieces which are closely related to theatrical subjects, as, for example, "Miss Evans and the Eagle," "The Dancing Academy," "The Mistaken Milliner," and many others, in which the genteel ambitions and affectations of lower middle-class types lead them into the snares of swindling actors, dancers, and musicians. Played before a backdrop of the stage and the demimonde, these sketches bridge the realms of playhouse and street through the character of their rogues, who are imposters in private life as well as on the boards, and whose transparent frauds and impositions are concealed only from the eyes of their gullible and affected dupes. Usually, some farcical catastrophe exposes the imposture at last, or deflates the soaring ambition of the victim, who then returns to his former station in life a sadder, wiser, and less pretentious person, having been forced by humiliation to give over his hope of emulating the great and fashionable.

At the other end of the same scale are a larger group of sketches which explore in detail what "The Pantomime of Life" indicates in outline form—that is to say, they view the entire social and political life of the time through eyes on the lookout for the discrepant and incongruous modes of the playhouse. Among these may be counted such pieces as "Horatio Sparkins," "The Tuggses at Ramsgate," "Watkins Tottle," "The Parlour Orator," and a host of others, including most of the pot-boilers later published in collections such as *Sketches of Young Gentlemen* (1838), *Sketches of Young Couples* (1840) , and *The Mudfrog Papers* (1837-1839) . Peopled by middle-class pretenders to cultivation and genteel status, by hypocrites, humbugs, poseurs, newly rich social climbers, and the rogues who prey upon them, these sketches have for their central action the farcical difficulties encountered as a result of the affectation of the outward forms of genteel respectability and the mechanical adherence to conventional forms of conduct, speech, and manner. Invariably the poseurs are hoist on their own petard in some wildly funny disaster, confusion, or humiliation. The causes are manifold. Sometimes the inability of genteel forms of speech to communicate any substantial meaning results in a comic contretemps, or the maladroit use of cliché, circumlocution, or euphemism by some untutored tradesman culminates in a mildly risqué confusion. On the other hand, the skillful impostures by the rascals who play on the genteel susceptibilities of the *petit-bourgeoisie* often involve broad parody of conventional types, manners, and speech to which their victims are wholly blind.

The pattern of action and technique outlined above is taken whole from farce, pantomime, and burlesque. The people assume outrageously transparent disguises in pursuit of complicated double and triple intrigues and chicanery. The frauds are grossly obvious to everyone but the willing, gullible dupe; and imposture is exposed by some accidental plot crossing that brings about a farcical discovery or unmasking, usually with a good deal of slapstick and tame ribaldry. Much incidental business, bustling action, and word play marks the texture. The staples of comedy since Plautus and Ben Jonson, these materials nevertheless bear the stamp of the early Victorian theater. The settings are of real places, for example, uniformly described in a carefully documented, realistic manner, even though the action that takes place in front of this backdrop is as wildly fantastic as any caper of Harlequin or Pantaloon. The characters are stereotypes borrowed from the playhouse: elderly lechers and gormandizers in the mold of Pantaloon; swaggering military types like Grimaldi's hussar; slightly tarnished ladies patterned after Columbine; and palpably extravagant frauds in the broad, gestic manner of pantomime clowns. The rest are monomaniacal eccentrics and humorous characters taken from farce.

Characterization proceeds in the theater's caricatural mode. A few rigid traits reassert themselves with antic persistence, and feeling and motive are subordinated to the recitation of gesture, action, and speech. The narrator often affects perplexity in the face of wholly conventional behavior and stereotype. The total effect, in true grotesque style, is of that frenetic half-world between recognizable human types and the ageless counters of puppeteer and *commedia dell' arte*. The personages seem to be moved by some external mechanical contrivance and to be prompted by forces which lack the coherence necessary to shape a personality.

Thus it is that much of the stylistic texture of this group of sketches is infected by terms appropriate to the playhouse. In "The Boarding House" (I, 334-381), for example, Septimus Hicks, one of the boarders, is likened to Hamlet (I, 347). Another lodger, Simpson, "was one of those young men, who are in society what walking gentlemen are on the stage" (I, 338), that is to say, a fashionable clothes-horse who resembles "the distinguished unknown who condescends to play the 'swell' in the pantomime at 'Richardson's Show'" (I, 342). Mr. Calton, an elderly inmate, reminds the author of "a Punch with a cold" (I, 342); and another lodger, the ill-kempt O'Bleary, is compared to Orson. One scene opens in this manner: "'Tap, tap.' 'Come in.'—Door opens, and discovers Mr. Calton sitting in an easy-chair. Mutual shakes of the hand exchanged, and Mr. Septimus Hicks motioned to a seat. A short pause. Mr. Hicks coughed, and Mr. Calton took a pinch of snuff" (I, 347). This mode of narrative might very well have come from the stage directions in the beginning of a playbook; "Door opens, and discovers . . ." is direct paraphrase of script terminology. Another typical instance of Dickens' dramatic bias in these early sketches is the climactic scene of "The Tuggses at Ramsgate," in which the son is discovered innocently involved with the wife of "Captain" Waters; it concludes when "Mr. Cymon Tuggs and all the ladies forthwith fainted away, and formed a tableau" (II, 26)—the latter a characteristic way of ending a farce.

It is, however, not enough to indicate where and how theatrical terminology crops up in the narrative style of the sketches, for Dickens' vision of his society as a *theatrum mundi* sees into underlying middle-class attitudes and values and finds them histrionic. "Shabby-Genteel People" provides the keystone to this framework of ideas (I, 318-323). Hardly more than a vignette of a London type, "Shabby-Genteel People" carefully chronicles the increasingly futile efforts of a middle-class gentleman who has suffered reverses to keep up respectable appearances and a falsely prosperous façade. Since the author strongly implies that the man's sense of his own identity is dependent upon maintaining the outward appearance of gentility, it soon becomes apparent that in the bourgeois scheme of values, as Dickens saw it, the outer man defines the inner, appearance in this realm *is* reality, motive is displaced into manner. This point is delicately driven home in the opening words of the piece, where the shabby-genteel type is invidiously distinguished from another characteristic London type with whom he might be confused by a careless observer, the out-of-work actor, dressed in his tawdry chic. The reader is left to infer that somehow the shabby-genteel type is subtly embroiled in the same system of values as that to be found by the stage door. Moreover, the tone of this sketch is so deliberately ambiguous as to escape easy classification under any of the ordinary modes of satire, comedy, humor, pathos, or irony. Although many of these elements are present, they serve a larger intention of presenting a commonplace type in such a way that he appears slightly grotesque in his single-minded devotion to keeping up the minutiae of respectability. To this end a key element in the transformation of the familiar into the strange is the opening suggestion of the essential histrionism of conventional genteel attitudes and codes of behavior.

"Watkins Tottle" goes even farther. Tottle, a middle-class bachelor living on the income from an estate that is just too small to support him in perfect genteel respectability, agrees to try to win the hand of an ugly but well-to-do spinster, Miss Lillerton, in an effort to make himself comfortable for life. In the process he hopes to repay the money he has borrowed over the years from his friend, Mr. Gabriel Parsons, who first suggests the marriage scheme to Tottle. Unfortunately, both Tottle and Miss Lillerton are decked out in the entire armory of genteel taboos, and the course of true love must circle and recircle through an elaborately roundabout punctilio. At last Tottle proposes in a very high-flown and circum-locutionary speech, to which Miss Lillerton replies in kind. Thinking that he has been accepted by the lady, Tottle shortly learns to his chagrin that Miss Lillerton had thought him an emissary from the local curate, Timson, who is also after her fortune and to whom she has already pledged her heart. Rejected and on the eve of being arrested for debt, Tottle drowns himself. Meanwhile a subplot develops an antiphony to the main story in the narrative of the sufferings of a young couple who have been ruined and jailed for debt by their wealthy parents, who had intended that each of the children should make a morganatic marriage.

Quite aside from the grotesque intermingling of farce and melodrama in this sketch, the tone of "Watkins Tottle" is highly ambiguous, for while the main action is carried on in a high-spirited caricatural manner, with much gestic, eccentric activity and incidental word play, there is always an ominous undercurrent beneath the superficial comedy of genteel manners and mores. This fact points, if not to the theme of the piece, then to the world-view implicit in it: behind the finicky taboos and arbitrary conventions of genteel respectability lies a substratum of bald economic self-aggrandizement which exploits social norms to further these aims and to disguise its egocentricity from the *bourgeoisie* themselves. Throughout the elaborate ritual of Tottle's courtship, with all its reading of expression and gesture, pregnant remarks, genteel cliché, euphemism, circumlocution, and banal sentiment, the very artificiality and indirectness of the forms of discourse and intercourse prohibit meaningful communication, with the result that confusion and disaster follow for schemer and victim alike. The high point of the main action, the proposal scene, amply illustrates this thesis. So abstract, so artificial, so hedged about by taboo, conventional observance, and trite formularies is the

vocabulary of genteel courtship—the point is underlined throughout by Parsons' cynical view of courtship as an entirely mechanical operation divorced
from real motive—that neither Tottle nor Miss Lillerton is able to express any truth of feeling to the
other and seem rather to be engaged in a grotesque
monologue à deux. Each seems isolated, alienated,
and estranged from the other, from others, even from
the deeper springs of his own personality. Were it
not for Tottle's suicide and the scene with the young
couple in the sponging house, "Watkins Tottle"
would be almost pure farce, and the reader would
follow the antics of the ridiculous stereotypes with
complete detachment. But he is brought up short
by the somber undercurrent of debtor's prison and
feels an unpleasant sense of involvement with these
marionettes, whose actions and sentiments are disturbingly real if eccentric, and who thereby estange
the familiar world of social convention.

In part this sense of estrangement results from
Dickens' exploitation of a rootless burlesque humor
that finds its characteristic expression in a continuous
verbal play with no identifiable satiric, comic, or
ironic intention; lacking this, it has the effect of
creating grotesquerie. Thus, when we first meet
Tottle, we learn all we need to know about him in
terms which are grotesque in themselves as well as
with respect to the stereotype they describe:

Mr. Watkins Tottle had long lived in a state of single
blessedness, as bachelors say, or single cursedness, as
spinsters think; but the idea of matrimony had never
ceased to haunt him. Wrapt in profound reveries on
this never-failing theme, fancy transformed his small
parlour in Cecil Street, Strand, into a neat house in the
suburbs; the half-hundred-weight of coals under the

kitchen-stairs suddenly sprang up into three tons of the best Wallsend; his small French bedstead was converted into a regular matrimonial four-poster; and in the empty chair on the opposite side of the fireplace, imagination seated a beautiful young lady, with a very little independence or will of her own, and a very large independence under a will of her father's. (II, 124-125)

Gabriel Parson's house is described in terms no less gratuitous as "a cardboard-looking house with disguised chimneys, and a lawn like a large sheet of green letter-paper" (II, 130) ; and Miss Lillerton comes perilously close to being a puppet, for she was "a lady of very prim appearance, and remarkably inanimate." "She was one of those persons at whose age it is impossible to make any reasonable guess; her features might have been remarkably pretty when she was younger, and they might always have presented the same appearance. Her complexion—with a slight trace of powder here and there—was as clear as that of a well-made wax-doll, and her face as expressive. She was handsomely dressed, and was winding up a gold watch" (II, 132). In short, the realm of Watkins Tottle is one in which the familiar is lightly made to seem strange—even mechanical—by means of comparison to discrepant things—toy houses, dolls, and the like—and by verbal play to no special purpose.

"The Parlour Orator" and "Sentiment" carry the play of grotesquerie, like the later passages of "The Pantomime of Life," into broader social areas of middle-class English life. The former is hardly more than a portrait sketch of the articulate political humbug, a master of senseless rhetoric, who has achieved an ascendency over his fellows by the vigor of his tongue. Like the other characters of *Sketches by Boz,*

he is a hollow poseur drawn with a few vivid traits
and defined by the caricatural, gestic mode of burlesque, as in the following speech:

"What is a man?" continued the red-faced specimen
of the species, jerking his hat indignantly from its peg
on the wall. "What is an Englishman? Is he to be
trampled upon by every oppressor? Is he to be knocked
down at everybody's bidding? What's freedom? Not a
standing army. What's a standing army? Not freedom.
What's general happiness? Not universal misery. Liberty
ain't the window-tax, is it? The Lords ain't the Commons,
are they?" And the red-faced man, gradually bursting
into a radiating sentence, in which such adjectives as
"dastardly," "oppressive," "violent," and "sanguinary,"
formed the most conspicuous words, knocked his hat
indignantly over his eyes, left the room, and slammed the
door after him.

"Wonderful man!" said he of the sharp nose.
"Splendid speaker!" added the broker.
"Great power!" said everybody but the greengrocer.
(I, 288-289)

"Sentiment" is a more broadly ranging sketch than
"The Parlour Orator" and manages to embrace within a single piece hilarious ridicule of the conventions
and clichés of literature, female education, political
economy, and the party system on the tacit premise
that they are all governed by histrionism—pretence,
jargon, imposture, and empty gesture. As in "The
Parlour Orator," burlesque treatment of banal forms
of speech is the chief comic device. For example,
Cornelius Brook Dingwell, MP, a canting back-
bencher, is a ludicrous travesty of a legislator who
promotes a bill for the "better observance of Easter
Monday" instead of coming to grips with matters of
real social injustice. To circumvent an attachment
between his daughter, Brook, whose ideas are pat-

terned on the sentimental novels she reads, and a
jargon-loving young political economist, Theodosius
Butler, the author of a pamphlet entitled "Considerations on the Policy of Removing the Duty on Bees'-
wax," Dingwell enrolls the girl in the fashionable
boarding school of the Misses Crumpton. There
young ladies "acquired a smattering of everything
and a knowledge of nothing" (I, 395). There is a
front parlor filled with "highly varnished maps which
nobody ever looked at" and "books which no one
ever read, appropriated exclusively to the reception
of parents, who . . . could not fail to be struck with
the very deep appearance of the place" (I, 396).
Unfortunately, the two lovers meet at a school ball,
elope, and marry. Their life thereafter is wretched:
the girl's sentimental daydreams prove false to the
realities of marriage on a modest income; the Misses
Crumpton's genteel prudence is found wanting; and
Dingwell's stroke of diplomacy in sending his daughter to the school backfires.

This group of sketches, then, carries over into the
larger life of London the principal features of theatrical burlesque, pantomime, and farce: chiefly, the
gestic, eccentric devices of characterization, ambivalent burlesque comedy and word play, bustling mechanical action, and the exploitation of transparently
obvious disguise, pretense, and intrigue that concludes in some farcical unmasking or other catastrophe. So close is the spirit of these sketches to that of
the popular playhouse, that their language often
approaches the terminology of the theater and narrative technique approximates scenario; indeed, one
of them, "The Great Winglebury Duel," was successfully adapted by Dickens for the stage as a burletta, "The Strange Gentleman." But their tone is

not easy to identify, for much that seems satiric must compete with much that elicits only the "non-reflective guffaw" of farce, and much that is apparently farcical reveals disturbing relationships with darker strains of pathos. Above all, however, is the impression of a society in manic, rootless action and motiveless speech and gesture: cliché and convention reduce human beings to the status of puppets dancing to a crazy tune.

There remains a third group of sketches which demonstrates its origin in quite a different aspect of the popular nineteenth-century theater. This group comprises, first, those sketches which present a vivid picture of typical or out-of-the-way corners of the London scene, such as "The Streets" series, the "Our Parish" series, "Omnibuses," "Hackney Coach Stands," "Criminal Courts," "A Visit to Newgate," "The River," and many others in the same vein. But these pieces merge imperceptibly with a considerable number of other sketches in which familiar locales serve as a pretext for sentimental, pathetic, melodramatic, or macabre subjects, like "The Hospital Patient," "The Black Veil," "The Prisoners' Van," "The Drunkard's Death," "The Old Lady," "The Half-Pay Captain," "The Pawnbroker's Shop," "Brokers' and Marine-Stores Shops," "Shops and their Tenants," "Meditations in Monmouth Street," and "Our Next-Door Neighbour." The most suggestive of these pieces are those which have a foot in each camp, that is, those which begin with a description of some commonplace locale but develop an unexpectedly dramatic narrative within a humdrum setting. The thematic significance of these sketches lies in their formal analogies to the stage: the dull world of static material objects and everyday places comes to be invested with a vigorous, even melodramatic human life, with strangeness, terror, pathos, sentiment, or manic activity; and this life may be found immanent in the most obscure and commonplace things.

These are sketches designed to transform the reader's habitual vision of the world around him to a perspective comparable to that of an audience at a theatrical performance. They encourage him to look behind the prosaic façade of the daily London scene with eyes made ready to perceive human drama and passion, to glimpse the curious, strange, and discrepant from an imaginative point of view, and to subject the conventional and banal to matter-of-fact scrutiny. Ultimately, these sketches seek to invest the realm of inanimate things with a vital implicit animation and humanity. Where those sketches dealing with theater and society share a point of view derived from an equation of motley with mufti, this third group of pieces participates in a common movement from fact, object, surface, or scene to indwelling human motive, feeling, or life. This movement gives them form and meaning, just as the other sketches were organized around the idea of histrionism as a key to understand conventional middle-class attitudes and actions. Nevertheless, this last group of short pieces remains firmly tied to theatrical grotesquerie in that the physical world is depicted as being as vital as that of pantomime and burlesque, and the interpenetration of animate and inanimate realms is calculated to dislocate the ordinary person's conventional vision.

The typical pattern of these sketches may be seen in "Our Next-Door Neighbour," which begins with a humorous analysis of the way that different sorts of door-knockers summarize the character of householders. As a particular object is imbued with a life implicit in or associated with it, so the entire house next door, and a particular apartment-to-let, become the pretexts for brief narratives, each successively darker in mood than the last, of three boarders: the first anecdote humorous, the second ironic, and the third pathetic. "Meditations in Monmouth Street" similarly takes its departure from a chance arrangement of old clothes in the window of a second-hand shop to develop the conjectural life story of a man who might have worn them. "Shops and Their Tenants" demonstrates how physical changes in the façade of a block of shops, if read by a casual passerby with sympathetic imagination, can be made to tell sentimental or pathetic stories of the lives and fortunes of their occupants. A prisoners' van or a hospital bed provides the physical framework for sensational tales of obscure personal dramas, and business and professional men are unexpectedly thrown into macabre, sinister, or melodramatic events in the course of their routine duties. Even the furniture and decor of an old lady's house form a paradigm of her personality and personal history. In all of these sketches, in short, fact, thing, and physical setting give way to passion and human interest, material form yields to animate life, objects are informed with an associated human motive, and the humdrum becomes filled with curious interest.

Throughout *Sketches by Boz,* then, an analogy to the theater, and especially to theatrical burlesque, pantomime, and broad farce, defines conventional middle-class society and the commonplace London scene. In the former case, a newly enfranchised *bourgeoisie* but recently raised to prosperity and leisure finds its identity in costumery, role-taking, and genteel mannerism; and this to Dickens suggests the transparent histrionism of the popular playhouse as well as the grotesque comic premises of pantomime and burlesque. In the latter case, the interpenetrating realms of animate and inanimate to be found in pantomime and burlesque provide a suggestive key to Dickens' handling of scenic description and to the organization of sentimental, pathetic, and melodramatic sketches, in which setting and object provide the mode of entrance into the realm of human life. In both cases, however, it is the object world, the physical and material realm, the context of thing, surface, appearance, or external manifestation with which the writer deals. It is a universe simplified to its gestic essentials, heightened by repetition, and estranged by a spectatorial point of view that refuses to provide conventional links between things or that perceives likenesses between incongruous things. Indeed, the detachment lent by the author's narrative distance contributes much to the ambiguously disturbing tone of these pieces, for the reader cannot easily determine in which of the several literary modes he finds himself when reading, say, "Watkins Tottle" or "Broker's and Marine-Stores Shops."

Chapter Four
PICKWICK PAPERS
AND THE
THEATRUM MUNDI

A s ADMIRABLE as it is, *Sketches by Boz* remains a collection of occasional pieces, many of which were added later to fill out a volume, whose inspiration was found as much in editorial necessity as in the immediate experience of their young author. But the *Sketches'* successors, *Pickwick Papers* and *Oliver Twist,* use the vision of the *theatrum mundi* implicit there as a point of departure for a more fully reasoned critique of society, in which the manic incongruities of burlesque, pantomime, and farce depict the chronic histrionism of middle-class culture.

In *Pickwick Papers,* the world through which the club members wend their way is steeped in the theater. The chief rogue of the novel, Jingle, is a strolling actor-in-mufti, whose impersonations are practiced more successfully outside the playhouse than within it. His transparently obvious impostures are better received by his willing bourgeois dupes

than by an audience in a theater—thus ratifying
Dickens' thesis in "The Pantomime of Life" that the
theater is a mirror of life "to audiences generally,
although they are not aware of it, and that this very
circumstance is the secret cause of their amusement
and delight." Jingle's dupes are the Pickwickians,
Mrs. Leo Hunter, and Nupkins, the Ipswich magistrate, all of whom are variously representative of a
bourgeoisie newly arrived at wealth, leisure, and
position, ardently imitating the manners, pursuits,
and superficial traits of the upper classes, but without any informing comprehension of their forms or
traditional familiarity with their use. The members
of the Pickwick Club, for example, epitomize the
middle classes' pretension to the paraphernalia of the
aristocracy: Mr. Snodgrass is a would-be poetaster
and man of feeling who strains to summon doggerel
and who involves his friends in the farcical *fête-
champêtre* of Mrs. Hunter; Mr. Tupman, a pretended dandy and man-about-town, fails to win the
hand of a desperate old maid, Rachael Wardel;
Winkle poses as a sportsman, though he can neither
handle a gun nor sit a horse; and Mr. Pickwick, the
intellectual leader of his club, affects the posture of
a scientific amateur, though he cannot decipher Bil
Stumps' signature on a paving stone. The Pickwickians move through a society which at every level
betrays the histrionism of form without function, the
name without the thing, the pose that lacks substantial relation to character: the law, in Dodson and
Fogg, the Ipswich magistrate, and Mr. Pickwick's
trial; government, in the Eatanswill election and the
town council of Muggleton; journalism, in Pott and
Slurk; the world of letters in Mrs. Leo Hunter's
circle; and many more. In sum, the world of the

Pickwickians is one in which people mechanically perform gestic absurdities of external action, gesture, speech, and posture in impersonation of functionaries, but without coherence or relevance to underlying character or function: they approach the status of marionettes, automata, or the figures of *commedia dell' arte.*

Jingle provides the thread of imposture that ties these personages together into a grand figure of a whole society. His impostures keep the story moving through the first half of the novel, and the Pickwickians' pursuit of him and his accomplice, Job Trotter, is an important if intermittent theme until the two rogues are found in Fleet Prison. He practices his frauds—and he is a master literary parodist—on a gullible middle-class society which cannot distinguish between affectation and sincerity, role and reality, surface and substance. In a world where appearance has been substituted for reality, Jingle makes his way, an actor out of the playhouse, whose transparently obvious poses are impenetrable to his genteel dupes because they too are involved in the same activity during the normal course of their lives. Actors in the "pantomime of life," they are blinded by the conventional histrionics of genteel respectability to the empty posturing of the professional fraud.

If Jingle, the strolling actor, provides the bridge linking middle-class society to the theater, he is by no means alone in *Pickwick Papers,* where pious frauds abound. Jingle's sidekick, Job Trotter, is close kin to Dismal Jemmy, whose "part" as an actor is that of the lachrymose pietist common in pathetic and sentimental drama of the time. He is the author of the novel's first interpolated story, "The Stroller's

Tale." Job Trotter assumes an identical role in the world, and employs a tearful religious sentimentality to further his dishonest projects. In this he is like the second Mrs. Weller's protégé, Stiggins, the drunken temperance lecturer and quondam evangelist, who also exploits an affectation of piety and sentiment to pass himself off on a gullible *bourgeoisie*. And he in turn resembles Dodson and Fogg, Mrs. Bardell's solicitors in her breach-of-promise action against Mr. Pickwick, who roundly assert their rectitude to hide the fact that they are shysters.

So deeply imbued with the atmosphere of the playhouse is the middle-class world of *Pickwick Papers* that Dickens habitually turns to the theater to find terms appropriate to describe the pervasive histrionism he sees around him, just as he had done in *Sketches by Boz*. When asked if he wants something to drink while visiting Sam Weller in Fleet Prison, for example, Stiggins, "with many rollings of his eye, clenched his throat with his right hand, and mimicked the act of swallowing, to intimate that he was athirst" (IV, 297). A few pages earlier Stiggins performs a similar pantomime in order to express his mock-pious horror of Sam Weller's depravity in being jailed, when he "raised his hands, and turned up his eyes, till the whites—or rather the yellows—were alone visible" (IV, 295). In the same scene, Tony Weller "indulged in several acts of pantomime, indicative of a desire to pummel and wring the nose of the aforesaid Stiggins: the performance of which, appeared to afford him great mental relief" (IV, 299).

The world occupied by Stiggins and Mrs. Weller is but a more egregious form of that occupied by Nupkins, Mrs. Leo Hunter, Jingle and Job Trotter,

Pott and Slurk, Mr. Magnus, Mr. Dowler, and a host of other middle-class pretenders. In it, Dickens implies by his use of theatrical terminology, human beings are grotesquely reduced to the status of automata, whose gestic externals belie the coherence between act and motive which is essentially human. This discrepant world of undefined appearance is glaringly illuminated by Dickens' habit—first demonstrated in "The Pantomime of Life"—of either refraining from identifying the motive that informs an extravagant but conventional gesture, such as Stiggins' "turned-up eyes," or supplying its identification where none is needed and in terms that are inappropriately formal, as in the phrase "to intimate that he was athirst." In either case, the aim seems less ironic than incongruous, less satiric than merely discrepant, not so much to make a moral comment as to indicate the grotesque presence of mechanism in things human.

To this end, the Wellers, Tony and Sam, are essential, for it is their unremitting literalism, their absolute refusal to participate in convention—or, equally, their constant parody of convention—that reinforce Dickens' studied detachment. Thus, when Stiggins performs his pantomime of lifting his hands and eyes in horror, Sam deliberately chooses not to comprehend the meaning of the gesture and instead reduces it to some bodily function by asking, "Is this here gen'l'm'n troubled with any painful complaint?" (IV, 295). Similarly, the spectacle of pious tears, whether those of the gin-soaked Stiggins, Mrs. Weller, or Job Trotter, is ascribed to the mechanical operation of a waterworks or to a bodily process whereby "Wot they drink . . . all turns to warm water, and comes a pourin' out o' their eyes. 'Pend upon it, Sammy, it's a constitootional infirmity" (IV, 300).

Indeed, the presence of Sam Weller and his father Tony in *Pickwick Papers* is vital to the development of the novel's grotesquerie, for without their studied, ambivalent, and ceaseless burlesque of the speech, manners, and attitudes of the middle classes—assumed not only for purposes of self-defense and subversion, but for the sheer joy of the game itself—the antics of the Pickwickians and the society through which they move might otherwise have been fixed in some single category of farce, satire, comedy, or social commentary. As it is, however, *Pickwick Papers* successfully defies ready categorization and remains an inhabitant of that elusive world of grotesquerie whose geography is uncomfortably changeful. For the Wellers function in the manner of a continuous aside directed at the reader, as it were behind the author's hand, the aim of which is to keep the tone of the novel in suspension.

In the first place, the Wellers are themselves eccentric theatrical stereotypes translated into prose fiction with all the caricatural, gestic treatment of the theater still around them. They are ardent and constant pantomimists who express themselves "in dumb show" (IV, 291) and "several acts of Pantomime," as we have seen, and for whom winks, grimaces, and antic gestures reminiscent of the Victorian comedian are the mode of comment and communication, as in burlesque and harlequinade. They are, in short, the "good rogues" of clown and Harlequin. Their characteristic form of verbal expression is a kind of rootless burlesque of conventional utterance that seeks not so much to make fun of some

original style of discourse as to extract amusement
from the disproportion between what is said and the
manner of saying it and to exploit the grotesque
possibilities latent in shopworn cliché, idiom, pun,
and metaphor. To these ends, for example, when his
father bids him goodbye at Fleet Prison with breezy
"A-do, Samivel," Sam replies, choosing not to countenance a conventionality, "Wot's a-do?" " 'Well, good-
bye, then,' said the old gentleman. 'Oh, that's wot
you're a aimin' at is it?' said Sam. Good-bye' " (IV,
302). Again, when Tony Weller assumes the role of
relentless creditor in Sam's good-hearted scheme to
jail himself for debt in order to be near his master,
father and son carry on an exuberant dialogue in
the inflated clichés of melodrama and sentimental
fiction. Mr. Weller becomes a "cruel pa," an "inex-
orable" and "unnatural creditor" (IV, 269), and Sam
refers to himself as a "wictim o' avarice" (IV, 292-293).

Sam's habit of commenting on events in cliché
terms and then crediting them to some outrageously
incongruous source—"Sit down sir; ve make no extra
charge for the sittin' down, as the king remarked wen
he blowed up his ministers" (IV, 296)—reappears
when, in describing his father's action to Mr. Pickwick
in Fleet Prison, he says that the old gentleman is "a
malicious, bad-disposed, vordly-minded, spiteful, win-
dictive creetur, with a hard heart as there ain't no
soft'nin'." But he goes on to add, "as the wirtuous
clergyman remarked of the old gen'l'm'n with the
dropsy, ven he said, that upon the whole he thought
he'd rayther leave his property to his vife than build
a chapel vith it" (IV, 273). Blatantly irrelevant to
local context and without any clear ironic intention
or object, the pointlessness of such incongruous citations contributes to the grotesque tone of *Pickwick*

Papers. They serve a structural purpose as well, for repeated many times they evoke a vision of a sinister world which sees as a matter of course the gross discrepancy between conventional forms of words and the motive prompting their utterance, and the incoherence latent in the invocation of morally impeccable gentilities as sanction for cruelty, hardness of heart, violence, and hypocrisy. But such a vision is offered in the most equable tone of voice, and so further estranges these familiar, conventional expressions, and by extension the world from which they are drawn.

The Wellers' functions may be clearly seen in two famous scenes from *Pickwick Papers* in which their ruthless literalism and cheerfully jaundiced view of conventional observances serve to point out the histrionic nature of commonplace middle-class conduct. In the first of these, Sam Weller goes on his master's orders to sound out Mrs. Bardell's intentions in her breach-of-promise suit. After finishing the business, Mrs. Bardell asks Sam if he will "take a little drop of something to keep the cold out, if it's only for old acquaintance's sake":

Sam saw the advantage he should gain, and at once acquiesced; whereupon Mrs. Bardell produced, from a small closet, a black bottle and a wine-glass; and so great was her abstraction, in her deep mental affliction, that, after filling Mr. Weller's glass, she brought out three more wine-glasses, and filled them too.

"Lauk, Mrs. Bardwell," said Mrs. Cluppins, "see what you've been and done!"

"Well, that is a good one!" ejaculated Mrs. Sanders.

"Ah, my poor head!" said Mrs. Bardwell, with a faint smile.

Sam understood all this, of course, so he said at once, that he never could drink before supper, unless a lady drank with him. A great deal of laughing ensued, and Mrs. Sanders volunteered to humour him, so she took a slight sip out of her glass. Then, Sam said it must go all round, so they all took a slight sip. Then, little Mrs. Cluppins proposed a toast, 'Success to Bardell agin Pickwick'; and then the ladies emptied their glasses in honour of the sentiment, and got very talkative directly.

"I suppose you've heard what's going forward, Mr. Weller?" said Mrs. Bardell.

"I've heerd somethin' on it," replied Sam.

"It's a terrible thing to be dragged before the public, in that way, Mr. Weller," said Mrs. Bardell; "but I see now, that it's the only thing I ought to do, and my lawyers, Mr. Dodson and Fogg, tell me, that with the evidence as we shall call, we must succeed. I don't know what I should do, Mr. Weller, if I didn't."

The mere idea of Mrs. Bardell's failing in her action, affected Mrs. Sanders so deeply, that she was under the necessity of re-filling and re-emptying her glass immediately; feeling, as she said afterwards, that if she hadn't the presence of mind to do so, she must have dropped.

(III, 469-470)

Here the presence of Sam Weller is enough to indicate the elaborate charade the three ladies must go through in order to take a glass of wine without compromising their respectability. And this they perform skillfully by means of an innocently disingenuous act of role-taking designed to disguise their real motives—thirst—in sharing a glass of wine with Sam. Sam "understands all of this, of course," and takes his part in the conventional performance perfectly: the scene is the *improvisatore* of *commedia dell' arte* translated into a lower middle-class back parlor in London, *circa* 1828.

In another equally well-known scene a few pages later, Sam and Mr. Pickwick are perfectly contrasted on the score of their very different responses to the arrival at Dingley Dell of the two medical students, Bob Sawyer and Ben Allen:

> "I am glad of it," said Mr. Pickwick. . . . "They are fine fellows; very fine fellows; with . . . tastes refined by reading and study. . . ."
>
> "They're a smokin' cigars by the kitchen fire," said Sam.
>
> "Ah!" observed Mr. Pickwick, rubbing his hands, "overflowing with kindly feelings and animal spirits. Just what I like to see."
>
> "And one on 'em," said Sam, not noticing his master's interruption, "One on 'em's got his legs on the table, and is a drinkin' brandy neat, vile the t'other one—him in the barnacles—has got a barrel o' oysters atween his knees, wich he's a openin' like steam, and as fast as he eats 'em, he takes a aim vith the shells at young dropsy, who's a sittin' down fast asleep, in the chimbley corner."
>
> "Eccentricities of genius, Sam," said Mr. Pickwick.
>
> (IV, 2)

Mr. Pickwick, who has not yet seen the two young men, conceives of them in terms of stereotypes and speaks of them in orotund clichés. Sam Weller, on the other hand, preserves a relentlessly clear-sighted view of their appearance and offers a devastating catalogue of their acts, all without reference to anything except surface data. If Mr. Pickwick's view tends to formulate the world around him in inflated conventionalities and to see things more as they ought to be than as they are, Sam Weller rather refuses to look beyond externals. Neither point of view embraces the whole truth, each is false to a certain order of reality. But because these two ways of looking at the commonplace world are continuously juxtaposed throughout the novel, they dislocate the reader's manner of viewing the life depicted in these pages.

Perhaps an even more important way of mediating the grotesque perspective developed in *Pickwick Papers* is the kind of rootless burlesque which is tacit in the two quoted passages immediately above, in the Wellers' play with cliché and convention, and which rises to explicit life in the narrative and descriptive texture of the novel. Contained in extravagantly incorgruous or incoherent patterns of conventional discourse, this rootless burlesque has as its object not so much local satire, irony, or comedy as a sense of the discrepant in ordinary things, particularly the forms and attitudes taken for granted in middle-class mores and manners. It is not only the Wellers who indulge in this loose burlesque use of language. All the personages of the novel and the narrator himself variously participate in word play, jargon, linguistic eccentricity, inflated banalities, syntactical incoherence, literal deployment of figurative language, and the reverse. From the opening words of the novel, where a dispute among the club members is settled, in burlesque of Parliament, when an insult is construed as being uttered in a "Pickwickian" sense, this kind of exploration of the chaos latent in language is carried on unremittingly. Jingle's breathless phrases, for example, constitute an eccentricity of speech that subverts normal syntax, and his wholecloth, cliché-laden accounts of the revolution of 1830 and his dalliance with a Spanish beauty burlesque the style and substance of romantic prose and poetry. The Muggleton proclamation, with all its pointless pomposity, parodies legalese; and Pott and Slurk, the warring Eatanswill journalists, declaim their patriotic platitudes in the worst over-inflated terms of nineteenth-century newspapers. The election is a triumphant *tour de force* in the conventions of the hustings; Mrs. Leo Hunter's literary effusions, like those of Mr. Snodgrass and Jingle, travesty the excesses of sentimental poetry; and the footmen's "swarry" at Bath ludicrously burlesques polite society. And, of course, the Bardell-Pickwick trial is a full-blown burlesque of the Norton-Melbourne affair. The list of burlesques could be extended indefinitely without adding to the one inescapable conclusion: what would ordinarily be categorized as satire in local context combines to create a larger picture of a whole society whose norms of speech and behavior are grotesquely incoherent when seen from a detached point of view. More disturbing to a conventional perspective is the fact that even the most vicious excesses of this society are indicated in an exuberant, high-spirited tone whose very ambivalence prevents the reader's taking any firm position toward them.

The narrative texture of the novel is no less disturbing in the way in which it treats the commonplace world, for even the most familiar things are described as if they were wholly new and strange. Outside his London lodgings one bright morning, for example, Mr. Pickwick meets "a strange specimen of the human race, in a sackcloth coat, and apron of the same, who with a brass label and number round his neck, looked as if he were catalogued in some collection of rarities" (III, 3). Having thus established the grotesque appearance of this figure, Dickens then identifies him as a familiar street-type of the time: "This was the waterman." In the meantime, however, the grotesque has been mediated, the commonplace has been rendered strange. Similarly, there is much gratuitous word play with the grotesque implications of idiom. In the same place, for example, Mr. Pickwick orders a cab, and a nearby

lounger cries, " 'Here you are sir. Now, then, fust
cab!' And after the fust cab having been fetched
from the public house, where he had been smoking
his first pipe, Mr. Pickwick and his portmanteau were
thrown into the vehicle" (III, 8). Here the comic
incongruity of a "fust cab" 's having a morning
pipe depends upon a deliberate literalism—similar to
that of the Wellers—which confuses the man and the
thing, the cab and the cabbie, contained in the
metonymy of the idiom. The result, again, is grotesque.

It is not by accident that Mr. Pickwick should be
a party to these two opening cases in which the
familiar world is estranged, for as we have seen from
the comparison between Sam Weller and his master,
the Pickwickians have their own way of estranging
the commonplace—their naïveté—just as the Wellers
have a mode of alienation—their ruthless empiricism.
We may see this in the celebrated episode in which
the club members' trip to Dingley Dell ends so
disastrously when their carriage is wrecked and Mr.
Winkle's horse bolts. The high comedy of this scene
depends upon the reader's awareness of self-evident
facts to which the Pickwickians are innocently blind
—that Mr. Winkle has never been on a horse before
and that their horses are intractable. One brief
episode begins this way:

"What makes him go sideways?" said Mr. Snodgrass
in the bin, to Mr. Winkle in the saddle.
"I can't imagine," replied Mr. Winkle. His horse was
drifting up the street in the most mysterious manner—
side first, with his head towards one side of the way, and
his tail towards the other.
Mr. Pickwick had no leisure to observe either this or
any other particular, the whole of his faculties being

concentrated in the management of the animal attached
to the chaise, who displayed various peculiarities, highly
interesting to a bystander, but by no means equally
amusing to any one seated behind him. Besides constantly jerking his head up, in a very unpleasant and
uncomfortable manner, and tugging at the reins to an
extent which rendered it a matter of great difficulty for
Mr. Pickwick to hold them, he had a singular propensity
for darting suddenly every now and then to the side of
the road, then stopping short, and then rushing forward
for some minutes at a speed which it was wholly impossible to control.

"What *can* he mean by this?" said Mr. Snodgrass, when
the horse had executed this manoeuvre for the twentieth
time.

"I don't know," replied Mr. Tupman; "it *looks* very
like shying, don't it?" (III, 80)

Dickens' fine hand is at work here to augment the
comedy by refusing to supply the name for the thing
—in this case, the fact that the horse is shying—and by
his consistent detachment and limitation to cata-
loguing externals. A commonplace event is thus
made to appear mysterious and unusual.

The narrative is no less riddled with instances in
which Dickens exploits the incongruous possibilities
of metaphor. To describe Winkle's ill success at
shooting, for example, the novelist introduces the
trite axiom that "every bullet has its billet," only to
develop its implications fantastically: "If it apply in
an equal degree to shot, those of Mr. Winkle were
unfortunate foundlings, deprived of their natural
rights, cast loose upon the world, and billeted nowhere" (III, 331). Here an outworn figure of speech
is extravagantly extended to grotesque proportions
by burlesque of trite terms—"unfortunate foundlings," "deprived of natural rights," "cast upon the

world"—which serves no particular satiric purpose
save that of exaggeratedly describing Winkle's bad
shooting. Elsewhere, the Wellers are experts in the
subversion of metaphor, banality, and idiom. When
Sam offers Stiggins a drink in Fleet Prison, for example, the temperance lecturer at first offers this
pious demurrer: "All taps is vanities." Sam appropriates the figure with uncompromising rigor: "I
des-say they may be, sir; but which is your partickler
wanity? Vich wanity do you like the flavour on best,
sir?" And Dickens intervenes to indicate how Stiggins finds that "port wine, warmed with a little water,
spice, and sugar" savors "less of vanity than many
other compounds"; and later references repeat the
term "vanity" in respect to the drink (IV, 297-299).
And the same tactic is employed throughout the Bath
footmen's "swarry."

Mr. Weller is no less adept than his son in undermining trite figures of speech. When Stiggins calls
him a "benighted man," Tony translates the phrase
into coachman's terms with devastating effect: "If I
don't get no better light than that 'ere moonshine o'
you'n . . . it's wery likely as I shall continey to be a
night coach till I'm took off the road altogether" (IV,
302). In a purer vein of incongruity, Mr. Weller
expresses his outrage at Sam's being outsmarted
by Job Trotter in the following discrepant terms:
" 'Ought to ha' know'd better!' . . . 'Why, I know
a young 'un as hasn't had half nor quarter your
eddication—as hasn't slept about the markets, no, not
six months—who'd ha' scorned to be let in, in such a
vay; scorned it, Sammy.' . . . 'Here's your health,
Sammy, and may you speedily vipe off the disgrace
as you've inflicted on the family name' " (III, 409).
The grotesque discrepancy in this last passage stems

from the ordinary context in which such inflated
phrases as "family name" and "eddication" would be
found and the matter to which they refer here; for
Mr. Weller regards as an education what the respectable reader would think of as an appalling lack of
education, and what to him is a "family disgrace" is
lack of skill in cunning, double-dealing, and chicanery. Yet the satiric object is neither Mr. Weller nor
respectable society; rather, the author's aim in this
and similar passages seems to be merely a comic
estrangement of conventional language and attitude.

Much of the grotesque ambiguity of tone in *Pickwick Papers* is to be found in those interpolated tales
which have given scholars and critics so much trouble
in trying to fit them into the organizational scheme
of the rest of the novel. In part, the difficulty in
dealing with these tales arises from the simple incongruity of their presence in such a riotous narrative
as that of the club members and the Wellers, in
spite of the three somber installments on Fleet Prison
late in the story; for the interpolated tales are generally melodramatic and seem to bear little relation
to the themes of the main narrative.

Before turning to examine their relation to the
rest of the novel, however, a word or two is in season
on the subject of another disturbing aspect of the
interpolated tales—the tonal ambiguity of the tales
themselves. For in certain of them a gratuitous burlesque keeps the reader's attitude toward them in a
state of ambivalence; in certain others, the author's
attitude appears equally ambiguous. In the most
somber of them, finally, relevances to the main narrative begin to emerge that cast a sinister shadow
over the farcical social comedy of the Pickwickians'
antics and reveal the presence of infernal, nightmare,

or supernatural elements underlying the commonplace world of middle-class London.

In the first instance, such tales as that told by
Dismal Jemmy, the two anecdotes related by the one-
eyed bagman about the romantic adventures of his
uncle, the mock-historical "Legend of Prince Bladud"
on the founding of Bath, the tale of Gabriel Grubb,
and the stories related by the Old Man about Gray's
Inn, including "The Tale of a Queer Client," are
either deeply infected by parody or rendered suspect
by the suggested unreliability of the narrator. The
effect is to make the reader unsure of what his attitude toward these narratives should be. Thus "The
Stroller's Tale" is a manifest fabrication by Job
Trotter's relative, Dismal Jemmy; and its subject, the
death from delirium tremens of a drunken pantomime clown, is as much a conscious parody of such
literature as a set-piece designed to demonstrate the
novelist's versatility. "The Legend of Prince Bladud"
is pure travesty; and the melodramatic "Tale of a
Queer Client" is preceded by a spoof of the traditional ghost story and is followed by a statement that
affirms the boredom and inattention of its auditors.
The bagman's two stories about his uncle are suspect
on several levels. One is a clear parody of the "solitary
horseman" school of historical fiction, and the other
an imitation of the romantic "Was it a dream?" convention. They are related at second hand by the
nephew of a man noted for his tall stories; and their
narrator, the one-eyed bagman, is a commercial
traveler of doubtful veracity, whose face is permanently contorted into a leering wink. Even "Gabriel
Grubb" is offered as a half-serious "fireside tale" told
for the effect its supernatural apparatus will produce
and with its truth left to conjecture.

For all their ambiguity of tone, however, the interpolated tales bear disturbing relevance to the main themes of the novel, which, like the subplot of "Watkins Tottle," darken the high jinks of the central story and turn it in a macabre direction. If the story of the club members' adventures in a society whose law is that of false appearances is handled in the broad comic manner of farce and burlesque, the interpolated tales explore the darker corners of this theme, principally the way in which the mind itself plays an active role in perceiving appearance and assessing reality. They combine to suggest that what is taken for real is inextricably bound up with the state of mind of the beholder. If the main narrative seeks to indicate how false to reality appearance may be, how an entire society may be premised on empty affectation, pretension, and presumption, the inter-polated tales rather examine how reality, because it is in part a construct of the mind, is difficult if not impossible to discover.

The theme of "The Stroller's Tale," for example, illustrates this point in the story of the last hours of a drunken and brutal pantomime actor who dies convinced that the family he had abused so long are plotting to kill him when in fact they are grieving. "The Madman's Manuscript" is a supposed con-fession by a homicidal maniac of how he had suc-cessfully passed as sane while plotting to murder his wife and best friend, whom he had come to suspect were betraying him. The "Tale of a Queer Client" and the "Story of the Convict's Return" share a mutual concern with obsessive revenge masked by unprepossessing appearances. "Gabriel Grubb" re-counts the manner in which a misanthropic sexton is restored to good cheer and fellow-feeling by an

experience which may be supernatural or merely a
psychological phenomenon—a theme developed in a
lighter vein in the bagman's two tales. In the first of
these, his uncle, Tom Smart, has an experience in
his room at an old inn in which the furniture appears
to come alive and speak, warning him of the danger
to the widowed landlady posed by a self-seeking
suitor. On the basis of this ambiguous experience,
Tom Smart succeeds in winning the widow's hand,
thereby comfortably situating himself for life. In
the other, Tom Smart, after a convivial evening in
a public house, lies down to rest in an Edinburgh
coachyard and is mysteriously transported back into
the eighteenth century, where he saves a beautiful
girl from a band of highwaymen; thereafter, he carries the girl's image in his heart for the rest of his life.

The interpolated tales, in short, provide a meaningful variation in point of view from the main plot.
They approach experience from an inner, subjective,
involved angle, as against the detached, objective
mode of the rest of the novel. They are told by first-
person narrators for the most part, often by personages deeply involved in their action, and frequently in a tone of high seriousness. Where the
main narrative is devoted to exposing the discrepancy
between sight and insight, the interpolated tales, by
examining the way in which states of mind form
external reality at will, thus invert the relation
between appearance and reality developed in the
portion of the novel given over to the Pickwickians
and the Wellers. They explore the themes of the
novel from an internal, psychological rather than
from an external, social point of view.

Moreover, context plays an important role in
establishing the linkages between the two story levels,

for though the interpolated tales appear incongruous in tone to the riotous events surrounding them, they reveal curiously apt relationships to the concerns of the main narrative. "The Madman's Manuscript" is a case in point. It occurs in the midst of the "Bil Stumps" episode, a broad spoof of scientific amateurism, and seems to have little affinity to its context. But both tale and main narrative are concerned with self-delusion, the one a foolish affectation of archeological expertise by Mr. Pickwick, the other homicidal dementia; and neither the old gentleman nor the madman can recognize a plain truth before his very eyes. Furthermore, the consequence of this blindness is that both commit an injustice: Mr. Pickwick's against the "ill-conditioned Blotton" who correctly deciphers Bil Stumps' scrawl on a paving-stone, the madman's against his loyal wife and honest friend. Insanity and affectation, Dickens seems to suggest, make of the world whatever their inner state demands; and this act undermines the conventional world and makes it grotesque.

The theme of injustice alluded to in the discussion of the relationship between the main narrative and the interpolated tales bears important connections to the theme of false appearances; and this fact serves to tie the tales more closely to the Pickwickians' story. The kind of difficulty which distinguishes the Pickwickians from the more disingenuous society through which they move is one in which they become involved innocently in an apparently compromising situation, and no one will believe their protestations that what appears to be is not the real state of the case. In such episodes the injustice resulting from the difference between sight and insight, appearance and reality, fact and supposition, is drawn most sharply. Winkle's duel with Dr. Slammer, which opens the novel, is just such a case of mistaken identity, occasioned by the habit of mistaking a suit of clothes for the man in them and complicated by the inability of those who practice the code duello to distinguish between the two. After the club members' disastrous ride to Dingley Dell a few pages later, they are unable to stable one of their horses in a farmer's barn because they look to him like highwaymen, and nothing they can say or do will convince him of their true identity. "It's like a dream," ejaculated Mr. Pickwick, "a hideous dream. The idea of a man's walking about, all day, with a dreadful horse that he can't get rid of!" (III, 85)—thus indicating the disturbing grotesquerie of their situation. Elsewhere, Mr. Winkle's naïve flirtation with Mrs. Pott, his midnight discovery in the company of Mrs. Dowler at Bath, Mr. Pickwick's entrapment in Miss Witherfield's room at the White Horse Inn in Ipswich, and his exposure after dark in a girl's seminary —these are typical instances of a characteristically Pickwickian crisis, in which the club members find themselves wholly unable to make others believe that appearances do not square with reality.

One such situation, Mr. Pickwick's "proposal" to Mrs. Bardell, sets in motion the most prominent and decisive action of the novel. In this case there is a double confusion between appearance and reality, for Mrs. Bardell mistakes for a proposal of marriage Mr. Pickwick's roundabout request to keep a servant by him; and when the club members and Sam Weller come upon the scene and find the lady in their leader's arms, where she had fallen in a conventional swoon, they mistakenly assume that he has been philandering. Later Mr. Pickwick upbraids his friends for having become involved in a number of guilty-looking positions, only to be served with papers announcing Mrs. Bardell's suit. The trial scene simply repeats in broad burlesque terms the same pattern of action: in the hands of Dodson and Fogg, innocent reality takes on a spurious aspect of deep-dyed villainy, and Mr. Pickwick is unjustly found guilty. Refusing to countenance such an injustice merely for the take of appearances, Mr. Pickwick elects not to pay the fine levied against him, and thus goes to Fleet Prison. There he finds the cells filled with suffering innocents like himself or with those who prey upon them just as in the great world outside the walls.

In voluntarily imprisoning himself rather than pay damages wrongly charged to him, Mr. Pickwick effects a moral dissociation from a society corrupted by appearances, convention, and genteel respectability. Yet what sets this major action in motion is Mr. Pickwick's fondness for that society's inflated, euphemistic, genteel mode of discourse—the style that the Wellers constantly parody—characterized by indirection, circumlocution, and grandiose cliché. It is a pretentious jargon that treats of ordinary matters in a needlessly elevated manner and so betrays a disjunction between its ostensible terms and its substantial content of meaning. The effect here, as in "Watkins Tottle" of *Sketches by Boz,* is confusion and disaster, for it inhibits effective communication.

The Pickwickians' adventures in middle-class society thus posit a mode of vision that looks at rather than sees through the superficial conventions of behavior, or that refuses altogether to look at things as they are, because of its commitment to the vernacular of genteel respectability. The other half of the main narrative is devoted to the reverse of this, to the disreputable, the ungenteel, and those beyond the pale of respectability. The Wellers' campaign against the rogues who exploit the middle classes—indeed, against the attitudes and speech patterns of the middle classes themselves—supposes a point of view in which the discrepancy between reality and appearance looms large. They look through the surfaces of experience and perception and substitute a ruthless, unblinking pragmatism for rosy but bogus ideality. The interpolated tales explore the fundamental issues raised by both the Pickwickians' and the Wellers' portions of the main narrative, the necessary subjectivity of all experience and the injustice that arises in consequence of limited or perverted vision. The meaningful actions of the novel, then, become those in which innocence is thought or appears to be guilty, those which require both objective sight and sympathetic insight to interpret correctly. If there is any larger action governing the novel beyond those already isolated by critics,[1] it lies in the gradual convergence of the opposed but juxtaposed points of view of Sam Weller and his alter ego, Samuel Pickwick, Esq., into a unified sensibility that balances but refuses to reconcile looking and seeing, sight and insight.

It is in the novel's ambivalent tone, quite aside from all its incidental play with the incongruous possibilities of language and convention, that its grotesquerie consists. *Pickwick Papers* proposes a histrionic basis for character as a systematic way of looking at middle-class England, much like that offered in *Sketches by Boz*. Indeed, the novel embodies the vision of a grand *theatrum mundi* in which the actor-in-mufti is the central archetype. Yet the total intention of all the Wellers' good-humored parody, the club members' antic banalities, and the ambiguous interpolated tales seems neither solely comic, satiric, nor melodramatic but rather the creation of a "compact poetic universe . . . the overall animation of which engenders an extreme feeling of gaiety, freedom, and ease."

An essential element in the creation of this special quality is the mode of burlesquerie as practiced in the nineteenth-century popular theater. The Wellers' studied play with convention both complements and subverts the genteel pretensions of the Pickwickians and their society; and even the interpolated tales are undermined by a rich strain of burlesque. The Wellers' guerrilla warfare against idiom and cliché, the club members' bumbling efforts to ape the manners of the great, the sundry rascals' cheerful exploitation of an entire society committed to the name without the thing, the very intermixture of farce and pantomime with melodrama and pathos—all taken together defy any attempt to place the tone of the novel in any one of the ordinary categories. Rather, as in theatrical burlesque, the aim of *Pickwick Papers* is the destruction of the conventional sense of coherence and relation between things in commonplace life. Dickens' ultimate intention was not, I believe, to mediate any existential or metaphysical alienation so much as it was to revivify his readers' sensibilities, to awaken a sense of the liveliness and interest of the familiar world. However that may be, the novel remains pleasantly subversive in the way that theatrical burlesque was subversive: it indicates the presence of the discrepant, incongruous, and ambivalent —even sinister—everywhere.

Chapter Five
OLIVER TWIST
AND GROTESQUERIE

OLIVER TWIST (*Bentley's Miscellany*, February, 1837–April, 1839), which overran the last nine serial numbers of *Pickwick Papers*, may seem to bear little connection to the theatrical burlesque and grotesquerie of Dickens' first novel, aside from a shared strain of melodrama, had not its original version a far more grotesque tone than the novel with which modern readers are familiar. The explanation of this curious fact lies in Dickens' decision, when he published the novel entire, to omit certain materials which had appeared in the pages of *Bentley's Miscellany* concurrently with the serial publication of *Oliver Twist*—chiefly, the series of three burlesque sketches entitled "The Mudfog Papers." Reading the novel now, no one would suspect that "The Mudfrog Papers" were as closely integrated into its structure and texture as they originally were, nor that the overall tone of the novel was as profoundly affected by this connection as it was.

"The Mudfog Papers" have a publishing history unique in the Dickens canon, for they first appeared in the place of installments of *Oliver Twist,* whose serialization was in each case suspended for one month. The first, "Public Life of Mr. Tulrumble, Once Mayor of Mudfog," ran in the January, 1837, number of *Bentley's Miscellany,* immediately prior to the first installment of *Oliver Twist* in February, where it served in many ways as a kind of grotesque preface, introduction, or overture to the longer work. The second in the series, "Full Report of the First Meeting of the Mudfog Association for the Advancement of Everything," appeared in October, 1837, at a crucial point in the story of the parish boy that assured its importance: between the seventh and eighth installments (September and November, 1837), which recount the kidnapping of Oliver from Mr. Brownlow and the boy's return to Fagin's gang of thieves. And the third, "Full Report of the Second Meeting of the Mudfog Association," came out nearly a year later, in September, 1838, at another decisive point in the novel, between the seventeenth installment (August, 1838) and the eighteenth (October, 1838). There Bumble and Mrs. Corney sell to Monks the locket taken from Oliver's dead mother, thereby apparently extinguishing the last hope of ever discovering the boy's identity and place in life; Nancy goes to Rose Maylie to reveal Monks' plot against Oliver, thus setting in motion the machinery that will lead to the destruction of the gang and the frustration of Monks' scheme; and Oliver is reunited with Mr. Brownlow, who now resolves with Dr. Losberne's help to restore Oliver to his true name and estate.

Together with "The Pantomime of Life" (which was printed in *Bentley's Miscellany* in March, 1837, to fill out the space left vacant by the short second number of *Oliver Twist* dealing with Oliver's apprenticeship to Sowerberry, the undertaker), "The Mudfog Papers" share a broad, not to say gross gestic mode derived from theatrical farce, burlesque, and harlequinade, full of bustling, ludicrous activity, slapstick, and rather heavy-handed satire together with a great deal of rootless burlesque. Appearing as they do in suspenseful contexts in the novel, their broad burlesque tone is grotesquely incongruous; and they profoundly alter the tone of the main narrative by reinforcing the ambiguous burlesque of the chapters devoted to the workhouse people and to Bumble, the parish beadle. "The Mudfog Papers" achieve this surprising effect through one significant omission from the final published version of *Oliver Twist*: the fact that the novel was originally set in the town of Mudfog, and the social abuses of the workhouse system, the Poor Law Commissioners, and Bumble and Mrs. Corney so vigorously castigated in the main narrative are reflected in the riotous burlesque of the sketches. Indeed, Bumble, the members of the workhouse board, Justice Fang, the workhouse cook, even Mr. Grimwig, all might have stepped out of the pages of "The Mudfog Papers." *Oliver Twist,* in short, originally existed in the context of the municipal administration of the mythical town of Mudfog.

Of the three "Mudfog Papers," the latter two dealing satirically with the proceedings of the British Association for the Advancement of Science under the guise of the Mudfog Association—a theme Dickens had already been handling for nearly a year in the scientific pretensions of Mr. Pickwick and the Pickwick Club—are by far the better known, with the result that relatively little attention has been paid to the first of them, "Public Life of Mr. Tulrumble, Once Mayor of Mudfog." Yet it was conceived and written during the time when Dickens, in *Pickwick Papers,* was bringing out the chapters on Nupkins, the Ipswich magistrate, and when Mrs. Bardell's suit against Mr. Pickwick was in the making, both of which satirize the administration of justice on the municipal level. "Mr. Tulrumble," moreover, is conceived in the farcical burlesque mode of the Ipswich episode and develops the municipal setting that embraces the opening workhouse chapters of *Oliver Twist* immediately following. This background is provided by the opening words of the sketch, which describe the town of Mudfog in terms that anticipate in very primitive form the renowned introductory chapter of *Bleak House* nearly fifteen years later:

There is a good deal of water about Mudfrog. . . . Water is a perverse sort of element at the best of times, and in Mudfog it is particularly so. In winter, it comes oozing down the streets and tumbling over the fields,—nay, rushes into the very cellars and kitchens of the houses, with a lavish prodigality that might well be dispensed with; but in the hot summer weather it *will* dry up, and turn green; and, although green is a very good colour in its way, especially in grass, still it certainly is not becoming to water. . . . (II, 345)

The description of the town itself, in spite of its radical difference in tone, reminds one of Tom-all-Alone's:

The town of Mudfog is extremely picturesque. Limehouse and Ratcliff Highway are both something like it, but they give you a very faint idea of Mudfog. There are a great many public-houses in Mudfog—more than in Limehouse and Ratcliff Highway put together. The pub-

lic buildings, too, are very imposing. We consider the
town-hall one of the finest specimens of shed architecture,
extant: it is a combination of the pig-sty and tea-garden-
box orders; and the simplicity of its design is of sur-
passing beauty.... (II, 346)

Mudfog is, in short, a typical English industrial town
of the 1830's, before the establishment of modern
municipal administrative organization.

No less do the municipal authorities of Mudfog
remind one of the pretentious futility of *Pickwick
Papers'* Muggleton, Eatanswill, and Ipswich, or of
Chancery in *Bleak House*:

> In this room do the mayor and corporation of Mudfog
> assemble together in solemn council for the public weal.
> Seated on the massive wooden benches, which, with the
> table in the centre, form the only furniture of the white-
> washed apartment, the sage men of Mudfog spend hour
> after hour in grave deliberation. Here they settle at what
> hour of the night the public-houses shall be closed, at
> what hour of the morning they shall be permitted to
> open, how soon it shall be lawful for people to eat their
> dinner on church-days, and other great political ques-
> tions; and sometimes, long after silence has fallen on
> the town . . . the illumination of the two unequal-sized
> windows of the town-hall, warns the inhabitants of
> Mudfog that its little body of legislators, like a larger and
> better-known body of the same genus, a great deal more
> noisy, and not a whit more profound, are patriotically
> dozing away in company, far into the night, for their
> country's good. (II, 346-347)

A month later, in the February, 1837, number of
Bentley's Miscellany, the opening lines of *Oliver
Twist* place the workhouse in the town of Mudfog;
and in the version of the novel published entire,
with the references to Mudfog carefully excised, the
description reads as though it were a continuation

of the lines quoted above, substituting "Mudfog" for "a certain town":

> Among other public buildings in a certain town, which for many reasons it will be prudent to refrain from mentioning, and to which I will assign no fictitious name, there is one anciently common to most towns, great or small: to wit, a workhouse; and in this workhouse was born; on a day and date which I need not trouble myself to repeat, inasmuch as it can be of no possible consequence to the reader, in this stage of the business at all events; the item of mortality whose name is prefixed to the head of this chapter. (V, 1)

And the remainder of this opening chapter of the novel is conducted in the same hard, derisive mode as that of the first paragraph quoted above, a mode which corresponds exactly with the tone of "Mr. Tulrumble."

The later pages of "Public Life of Mr. Tulrumble," however, are more in keeping with the broad burlesque tone of the chapters in *Oliver Twist* devoted to Mr. Bumble and the other workhouse personages in "a town it shall be prudent to refrain from mentioning"—Mudfog. The sketch recounts the rise to wealth and landed gentility of one Mr. Tulrumble, a coal-dealer, who begins to take an unaccustomed interest in public affairs shortly after purchasing his country seat. On his absence from Mudfog to attend the Lord Mayor's show in London, he is so impressed by the panoply that he resolves, upon hearing of his election to the Mayoralty of Mudfog, to stage his own inaugural show there. He makes the mistake of employing Ned Twigger, the town drunk, to wear the ceremonial suit of armor, and the fellow appears in the procession in a highly intoxicated condition, much to the amusement of

the onlookers, and is sent packing home by his shrew-
ish wife. Following this ludicrous debacle, the new
Lord Mayor of Mudfog, Tulrumble, who has taken
to reading statistics, political economy, blue-backed
reports of Royal Commissions, and the social views of
Middlesex magistrates, decides that the fiddle and
tambourine which constitute the musical offering of
"The Jolly Boatmen," the local tavern he used to
frequent in former days, are conducive to depravity;
and he forces through the town corporation a measure
to take away its license. Thereafter, his old friends
begin to shun the mayor, now grown proud in his
wealth and his role as political philosopher; and
Tulrumble at last awakens from his folly, restores
the license, and is welcomed back into the company
of "The Jolly Boatmen" by his old cronies. There
he again drinks hot punch, smokes his accustomed
pipe, and even dances with Mrs. Twigger, resolving
never again to attempt to restrict the pleasures of
ordinary people in the name of political economy.

From this résumé it can be seen that the "Public
Life of Mr. Tulrumble" is pretty poor stuff, with the
odor of a pot-boiler hanging about it; but its context
in relation to the appearance of the overlapping serial
numbers of *Pickwick Papers* and *Oliver Twist* grants
it an importance in excess of its intrinsic merits and
indicates what was occupying Dickens' mind during
the period of their composition. In the early installments of *Pickwick Papers,* such high farce as that at
Muggleton, Eatanswill, and Ipswich is part of the
main narrative, where it functions to satirize an entire
society motivated by pretension and affectation. In
Oliver Twist, "The Mudfog Papers," although physi-
cally separated from the framework of the novel,
provide a running commentary on the melodramatic

story of the "parish boy's progress," link up with the high burlesque of the poor law administration centered on Bumble, and introduce a discrepant, grotesque note into the somber tone of the main narrative. "The Mudfog Papers," moreover, carry the concerns of *Pickwick Papers'* satire on scientific objectivity and practicality over into *Oliver Twist.* There its relevance to Dickens' attack on the new poor law of 1834 takes the form, in part, of a subversion of the philosophic principles of those responsible for the inauguration of the workhouse system—the Benthamites, Utilitarians, political economists, and "philosophical radicals," as they variously called themselves in token of their claims to having discovered the scientific principles of social and economic law. In the "Public Life of Mr. Tulrumble," the broad burlesque of philosophical radicalism is reserved for the later pages of the sketch, in which the title character's attempts to close down "The Jolly Boatmen" are buttressed with all the statistical paraphernalia associated with Royal Commissions and political economists that Dickens had earlier ridiculed in "Sentiment." But the reader is meant to understand that Mr. Tulrumble's philosophical radicalism is only a more extreme form of the affectation which motivated him to stage his Lord Mayor's show.

In *Oliver Twist,* similarly, Dickens' ridicule of the philosophical underpinnings of Utilitarianism is given to Bumble, the ludicrously insensitive parish beadle, and to the grotesque leader of the band of thieves, Fagin, while the novelist's attack on the inhumanity of the poor law administration is confined to those portions of the narrative which deal directly with Oliver's adventures. If we may trust Dickens' version of the novel's theme enunciated in the 1841 preface to the third edition, that "I wished to show, in Little Oliver, the principle of Good surviving through every adverse circumstance, and triumphing at last" (V, xii), we may begin to see the grounds of Dickens' theoretical attack on Utilitarianism. For in the person of Oliver Twist the novelist takes issue with the central assumption of the radical philosophers that man is entirely a product of environmental forces, and that he is a rational creature, motivated wholly by the selfish desire to gratify his physical and material wants. To them, only by indoctrination in the rational principles of "enlightened self-interest" can the individual rise above narrow self-interest to altruism —but an altruism based on an exchange of immediate gratification for general conditions that will insure the preservation of the individual.

In Oliver's portion of the narrative, on the contrary, the reader is continually shown that, had the boy's moral constitution not been inherently sound, the combined environmental influences of workhouse and underworld would have inevitably turned him toward brutality and a life of crime. Oliver's career, then, is meant to stand as a living refutation of Benthamistic social and moral principles. His life in the workhouse and after directly attacks the first piece of social legislation, after the Reform Bill of 1832, to bear the blessings of the radical philosophers and political economists, the New Poor Law of 1834. And his adoption by Mr. Brownlow, the Maylies, and Dr. Losberne, who intuitively recognize the boy's latent goodness and gentle birth, provides a counterargument to the rational and deterministic premises of Utilitarianism.

Nor is it any accident that Dickens should have chosen Bumble and Fagin to be the spokesmen for

philosophical radicalism. One expresses the cold-
hearted inhumanity and complacency of the system
in terms so ludicrous as to be grotesque—he is, in
short, that special Dickens figure, the comic villain.
The other presents the case for enlightened self-
interest in terms of the code of the underworld and
by so doing indicates that to Dickens the proposition
was no other than the law of the jungle. Thus when
negotiating with Sowerberry for Oliver's apprenticeship, the conversation turns to the special verdict
returned by a coroner's jury that condemned the
beadle for allowing a reduced tradesman to die of
exposure and starvation in a parish doorway. Bumble
indignantly replies that " 'Juries is ineddicated, vulgar, grovelling wretches . . . [with] no more philosophy nor political economy about 'em than that . . .'
snapping his fingers contemptuously" (V, 32).

Elsewhere, the beadle's equation of his own indifference to suffering with experimental philosophy is
calculated to provide a grotesquely outrageous type
of the attitude toward his fellowmen of the political
economist. Throughout the novel, Bumble's egregious insensitivity to human misery and his complacent dismissal of the needs of the human spirit
as depravity or rebelliousness constitute a burlesque
picture of the moral posture of Benthamism. Yet
Bumble is a grotesquely ludicrous figure of the Pantaloon of harlequinade translated into a parish workhouse: monumentally stupid and complacent, totally
lacking in sympathetic imagination, fatuously self-
important and avuncular, greedy, mean-minded, sly,
and vulgar. He is such an absurd figure indeed that,
as a personification of the Poor Law Administration,
his very real villainy is transformed from satire or
irony into the gestic mode of burlesquerie, where the

reader's moral response is as ambiguous as its tone. This is all the more incongruous in the light of the fact that Bumble's real but ridiculous meannesses lie cheek-by-jowl with Dickens' own outraged jeremaiads.

But perhaps the most telling blow that Dickens directs against the New Poor Law's Benthamistic underpinnings is reserved for Fagin, the cunning old receiver of stolen goods, who is a grotesque figure in his own right with his manic delight in crime and saccharine mode of enunciating brutalities. The occasion of Fagin's elevation to the status of an experimental philosopher arises when he inducts Noah Claypole into the underworld and articulates the criminal code in terms which burlesque the Utilitarian doctrine of enlightened self-interest:

"And so it was you that was your own friend, was it?" asked Mr. Claypole, otherwise Bolter. . . .

"Every man's his own friend, my dear," replied Fagin, with his most insinuating grin. "He hasn't as good a one as himself anywhere."

"Except sometimes," replied Morris Bolter. . . . "Some people are nobody's enemies but their own, yer know."

"Don't believe that," said Fagin. "When a man's his own enemy, it's only because he's too much his own friend; not because he's careful for everybody but himself. Pooh! pooh! There ain't such a thing in nature."

"There oughtn't to be, if there is," replied Mr. Bolter.

"That stands to reason. Some conjurers say that number three is the magic number, and some say number seven. It's neither, my friend, neither. It's number one."

"Ha! ha!" cried Mr. Bolter. "Number one for ever."

"In a little community like ours, my dear," said Fagin, who felt it necessary to qualify this position, "we have a general number one; that is, you can't consider yourself as number one, without considering me too as the same, and all the other young people."

"Oh, the devil!" exclaimed Mr. Bolter.

"You see," pursued Fagin . . . "we are so mixed up together, and identified in our interests, that it must be so. For instance, it's your object to take care of number one—meaning yourself."

"Certainly," replied Mr. Bolter. "Yer about right there."

"Well! You can't take care of yourself, number one, without taking care of me, number one."

"Number two, you mean," said Mr. Bolter, who was largely endowed with the quality of selfishness.

"No, I don't!" retorted Fagin. "I'm of the same importance to you, as you are to yourself."

"I say," interrupted Mr. Bolter, "yer a very nice man, and I'm very fond of yer; but we ain't quite so thick together, as all that comes to."

"Only think," said Fagin, shrugging his shoulders, and stretching out his hands; "only consider. You've done what's a very pretty thing, and what I love you for doing; but what at the same time would put the cravat round your throat, that's so very easily tied and so very difficult to unloose—in plain English, the halter!"

Mr. Bolter put his hand to his neckerchief, as if he felt it inconveniently tight; and murmured an assent, qualified in tone but not in substance.

"The gallows," continued Fagin, "the gallows, my dear, is an ugly finger-post, which points out a very short and sharp turning that has stopped many a bold fellow's career on the broad highway. To keep in the easy road, and keep it at a distance, is object number one with you."

"Of course it is," replied Mr. Bolter. "What do yer talk about such things for?"

"Only to show you my meaning clearly," said the Jew, raising his eyebrows. "To be able to do that, you depend upon me. To keep my little business all snug, I depend upon you. The first is your number one, the second my number one. The more you value your number one, the more careful you must be of mine; so we come at last to what I told you at first—that a regard for number one holds us all together, and must do so, unless we would all go to pieces in company."

"That's true," rejoined Mr. Bolter, thoughtfully. "Oh! yer a cunning old codger!" (V, 418-420)

Here the grounds of Dickens' burlesque are clear: Fagin's and Noah's view of human nature, like that of the Benthamites, is uniformly selfish, rational, materialistic, and pleasure-loving. In order to avoid the chaos that would result were an unrestrained and narrow self-interest the sole aim of each person, Fagin argues from the multitude of self-interested parties to an overriding self-interest inhering in society generally, without which the society itself could not exist or flourish nor any single member of that society satisfy his selfish interests. This is of course the classic argument of philosophical radicalism, although Noah Claypole, a perfect product of the poorhouse system, is not an apt pupil, being wholly given over by his training and experience to a very narrow self-interest.

And although Fagin is finally successful in convincing Noah of the necessity to sacrifice a measure of one's own self-interest to the larger interests of society, Noah is given the task of raising the obvious logical objections to such a concept that must follow from its underlying premises concerning human nature. The fault of the theory, Dickens seems to suggest, lies in the fact that when the values of the whole come into conflict with those of the individual, it is likely to be the individual's selfish interest which will triumph. This is precisely what does occur in the later pages of *Oliver Twist* when, following the murder of Nancy for her betrayal of the plot against Oliver, the gang is hunted down and brought to justice; for in the final extremity, each member consults only the preservation of his own hide, and among these last the treacherous Noah Claypole is most prominent. Indeed, at the novel's end, we find him employed reporting violations of the laws regulating public-houses, which he does by prevailing on pub-keepers to sell him drink beyond the hour of closing and then betraying them to the authorities.

It is this implicit equation of the central doctrine of philosophical radicalism with the underworld code that constitutes Dickens' attack on Utilitarianism: Bumble, Mrs. Corney, and the other workhouse personnel hold the same views of human nature and society as do Fagin, Bill Sikes, and the Artful Dodger. Hence it is a necessity of the novel's theme, however improbable it may seem, that Bumble must become implicated with Fagin in Monks' scheme to brutalize Oliver in order to retain undisputed control over his stepfather's estate; and this the beadle does when he sells the locket of Oliver's mother to the boy's stepbrother. In this equation an essential function is performed by Monks, a melodramatic type of evil incarnate, who links underworld and workhouse in the plot to discredit Oliver. Indeed, it is Monks who personifies inherent Evil to Oliver's Good in the novel's allegorical system; and Monks represents that consuming egotism and corrosive self-interestedness that in very different ways motivate the Poor Law Administration and Fagin's gang of thieves. Behind experimental philosophy there lies the theatrical figure of Monks, black cloak, slouch hat, glittering eye, manic guilt, and all, who embodies in himself the motives underlying the moral position occupied by the Workhouse Board—i.e., respectable society— and the criminal underworld: that is to say, consuming self-interest.

It is in the light of this theoretical attack on the

New Poor Law of 1834 which lies behind Dickens' overt castigation of its practical manifestation in the Mudfog Poorhouse administration that the first and second "Reports of the Mudfog Association" are to be read. Their immediate satiric target is the British Association for the Advancement of Science, founded in 1832, whose annual late summer meetings coincided with the appearance of the "Reports" in October, 1837, and September, 1838. Indeed, the "Second Report" was published in *Bentley's Miscellany* while the British Association was still in session at Newcastle, August 20-September 15, 1838. In them, Dickens broadens his attack on philosophical radicalism to include the scientific objectivity upon which political economy claimed to be based in its discovery of the natural laws governing social and economic arrangements.

The two "Reports" are like each other and different from "Tulrumble" in several important respects, the first of which being their narrative mode, for they are conducted in a broad parody of journalese that seems to have no single, clearly defined intention. In and of themselves, then, and without regard to their location in the context of the serial publication of *Oliver Twist,* the two reports are ambiguous and unsettling in tone. This is so because their parody seems only partly directed against the inflated and breathless style in which newspapers, then as now, report even the most trifling scientific discoveries and inventions. In part this burlesque throws into stronger satiric light the absurd proceedings of the Mudfog Association. The most insignificant matters, such as the choice of an inn by Doze, Wheezy, and Snore, are reported in an elaborate and sententious mode which further undermines their subjects and at the same time reveals the bias of the reporter. The narrative texture is thus another instance of that rootless burlesque already isolated in *Sketches by Boz* and *Pickwick Papers* which makes an important contribution to their grotesque tone. At the same time, the two "Reports," like "Tulrumble" and the Bumble sections of *Oliver Twist,* carry on the incidental satiric thrusts against the futility of municipal authorities, the collection of pointless or erroneous statistics, and the exaggerated importance pseudo-scientists attach to themselves and their researches, which bulk large in *Pickwick Papers.*

The two "Reports of the Mudfog Association," however, are far more single-mindedly concerned with the false claims of objectivity advanced by nineteenth-century science and by the social, political, and economic theorists, all of whom contend that they have uncovered some fundamental natural law or statistical relationship. In "Tulrumble," for example, the title character bases his attack on "The Jolly Boatmen" by sampling its patronage at the busiest hour of the week's busiest day; then, by extrapolating these figures through a simple process of multiplication, he arrives at the wildly extragavant conclusion that the offending public-house does a weekly traffic of 26,460 beer jugs (II, 366). In the "First Report," again, a statistical inquiry into the wastage of dog's-meat skewers in London concludes that some 21,900,000 are thrown away annually, "which, if collected and warehoused, would in ten years' time afford a mass of timber more than sufficient for the construction of a first-rate vessel of war . . . to be called 'The Royal Skewer' " (II, 391). Other equally ludicrous figures on the pernicious consumption by children of imaginative literature,

coupled with statistics showing their entire ignorance
of the works of Mungo Park, lead to a resolution deploring the lack of factual training for youth that is
worthy of *Hard Times'* Mr. Gradgrind. More ominous is the finding of a Mr. X. Ledbrain, showing
that among the workers in a great Yorkshire industrial town there are a larger number of human legs
than chair and stool legs. He cautiously concludes
that half of the operatives must either have nothing
at all to sit on or else use legless packing cases.

In a similar vein is an invention demonstrated before the mechanical section of the Mudfog Association that automatically picks pockets. Unfortunately,
it works so well that the underworld refuses to adopt
its use, fearing widespread technological unemployment among the tens of thousands of London thieves
—a conclusion with pointed relevance to *Oliver
Twist*. Another inventor introduces a new variety of
eye-glasses that allows the wearer to see faraway
things, such as West-Indian slavery, but not to perceive near things, such as the plight of Manchester
cottonmill operatives. No less acute in its ironic
relevance to *Oliver Twist* is a seemingly innocent
report on the advantages of the medical theory of
infinitesimal doses, which turns to social satire when
someone suggests that workhouse paupers might be
able to subsist on infinitesimal quantities of bread,
cheese, and cereal grains. The proposal, though applauded, is dismissed on the grounds that the dietary
under the New Poor Law is already based on the
theory of infinitesimal doses of food, as the reader of
Oliver Twist very well remembers from the episode
in the Mudfog Workhouse when Oliver "asks for
more."

The practical folly, misery, and indifference

amounting to cruelty that results from statistical evidence, the scientific method, and rationalism unalloyed by compassion, which are involved in this satire of the British Association, seem ultimately as much to hold up to ridicule a prevalent attitude and point of view in Dickens' time as to condemn an institution. Thus it is that many altruistic proposals are brought forward before the Mudfog Association primarily to satirize the Englishman's greater concern for animals than for his fellow men. Of these, perhaps the most amusing is a proposal laid before the Botanical and Zoological Committee for the enactment of a vast legislative program to alleviate the humiliating labor performed by the members of a London flea circus by retraining them in more socially profitable industrial pursuits, providing facilities for their moral education, creating an old-age home and a supporting fund for superannuated fleas, and passing a vagabond flea law. In another place, similarly, a report is introduced deploring the technological unemployment of dancing dogs, who have been reduced to robbing blind men's guide dogs. Even pets are not immune to the madcap investigations of Mudfog Association members, for the opening pages of the "First Report" recount the grotesque dissection of a pug-dog in all the manic, gestic style of theatrical burlesque and harlequinade—indeed, the comic dissection was one of the staples of nineteenth-century English pantomime.

"The Mudfog Papers," and particularly the first and second "Report of the Mudfog Association," which show the broad burlesque mode of *Sketches by Boz,* the proceedings of the Pickwick Club, and the chapters in *Oliver Twist* devoted to Bumble, interrupt the main narrative of "the parish boy's progress" for

the incongruous purpose of subverting the intellectual foundations of philosophical radicalism. Even
the names of the more prominent members—Wheezy,
Doze, Snore, Ledbrain, Pickle, Woodensconce, Slug,
Muff, and Nogo, to name only a few—read like the
dramatis personae of theatrical burlesque, farce, or
pantomime. And their antic, gestic absurdities of
invention, discovery, and action—like Pickle's spec-
tacles, the pocket-picking machine, and the dissection
of the pug-dog—reflect the standard business of harlequinade. "The Mudfog Papers" ' gross incongruity
of tone to that of the main narrative suggests the
grotesque transformations of English pantomime; and
the sharp alternations between comic, pathetic, and
melodramatic episodes—like the alternate layers of
red and white in a side of streaky bacon, as Dickens
put it in *Oliver Twist*—remind one of Victorian
melodrama.

If the incongruities of "The Mudfog Papers" in
relation to their contexts are grotesque, their curious
parallels and relevances to the main narrative are no
less so. The ludicrous projects of the Mudfog Association do not present the case against the scientific
pretensions of experimental philosophy in terms
more grotesquely ridiculous or broadly burleque
than those Dickens reserves in the main narrative for
the local Poorhouse Board, the poorhouse master and
cook, and Bumble, the Pantaloon-like parish beadle.
Indeed, the latter is given the grotesque assignment
of enunciating the most heartless principles of the
New Poor Law point of view in the most ludicrously
inappropriate terms, as in the conversation with Mr.
Sowerberry about the relationship between the poorhouse dietary and the size of coffins, or his genial
practice of dumping paupers near death in a wagon

and sending them to London in order to rid the parish of them without incurring the expense of their burial. Whenever Bumble appears in the novel, the reader of the original serialization in *Bentley's Miscellany* would have known immediately that he was back in the manic world of Mudfog, not only by the evidence of the beadle's name but more so by the tone of such episodes, for Bumble delivers the most outrageously callous sentiments in such ignorantly equable terms as to make their mode of expression grossly disproportionate to the real human misery they describe. What now appears out of keeping with the somber and melodramatic tone of the rest of the novel was, in its serialized version, part of a much deeper strain of burlesque grotesqueries located in Mudfog; the same incongruous mixture of modes which characterized *Pickwick Papers* reappears in *Oliver Twist,* and the tone of the whole is profoundly altered by this fact.

Other, deeper analogies and interconnections between "The Mudfog Papers" and the main narrative bind the grotesque and the melodramatic portions of the novel more closely together in incongruous relationships. For example, the first "Report of the Mudfog Association" interrupts the novel between the seventh installment (September, 1837), in which Mr. Brownlow sends Oliver to the bookstore in order to prove the boy's integrity to a skeptical Mr. Grimwig, and the eighth installment (November, 1837), in which Oliver is recaptured by Nancy and returned to Fagin's gang. At first glance, there seems to be no connection whatever between these two serial numbers, on one hand, and the awkwardly interpolated burlesque episode on the other; but further reflection reveals disturbing analogies between them. For one

thing, Oliver might never have been kidnapped had
not Mr. Brownlow been goaded by Mr. Grimwig's
doubts of the boy's honesty into sending him to the
bookstore in order to demonstrate his truthfulness.
And the contentious Mr. Grimwig—a name, inci-
dentally, as much at home in Mudfog as Bumble's—
is a man who, like the members of the Mudfog Association, has positive opinions on every subject and
constructs elaborate theories on the basis of only the
sketchiest evidence. In this instance he allows his
reason—the "head" he offers to eat in testimony of
his covictions—to overrule his heart, his habitual con-
trariness to conquer his prepossession in favor of Oliver. The result is that Mr. Brownlow determines
the boy's "prompt discharge of his commission . . .
should prove to Mr. Grimwig the injustice of his
suspicions: on this head at least: at once" (V, 131).
And Dickens concludes this chapter with the apposite
remark, "as illustrating the importance we attach to
our own judgments, and the pride with which we put
forth our most rash and hasty conclusions, that, although Mr. Grimwig was not by any means a bad-
hearted man . . . he really did most earnestly and
strongly hope at that moment, that Oliver Twist
might not come back" (V, 133).

Now, one of Dickens' implicit points of attack in
the novel against the frame of mind of experimental
philosophers lies in his belief that the unassisted reason is incapable of ascertaining human truth, since
man is not a product of environmental forces operating on an exclusively selfish nature. It is the intuitive sympathies which, as in the case of Mr. Brownlow
before his suspicions are aroused by Mr. Grimwig,
are able to grasp the underlying realities of character

behind unprepossessing appearances—a process ratified later in the novel in respect to Oliver by the
Maylies and Dr. Losberne. But at this point, when
the "First Report of the Mudfog Association" interrupts the narrative, it appears that the sympathetic
intuitionists have lost the day to the inhuman ration-
alists and that the views of human nature of the Mudfog Association, the Poorhouse Board, and Bumble
will prevail. Such a conclusion becomes inescapable
when Bumble answers Mr. Brownlow's advertisement
asking for information about Oliver, goes to Penton-
ville, and gives him an account of the boy's vicious
propensities so convincing that Mr. Grimwig's suspicions seem verified. Mr. Brownlow reluctantly concludes that, in spite of his feeling for the boy, Oliver
is beyond reformation; and only his housekeeper,
Mrs. Bedwin, who relies entirely on her intuitive
sympathies, remains unshaken in her faith in the boy.
In spite of the ridicule of the reason in the "First
Report," the broad comic treatment of Mr. Grimwig's formulation of boys into two races, the "mealy"
and the "beefy," and the high burlesque of Bumble's
interview with Mr. Brownlow, at this point in the
narrative theory and system, however, inhumane, appear to have triumphed over sympathy. The result
is that Oliver seems doomed to a life of brutality and
crime.

Similarly obscure relationships between the "Second Report" and its context in the serialization of
Oliver Twist may be seen. As in the earlier interrup-
tion, the "Second Report" intervenes in the narrative
at a decisive point between the seventeenth number
(August, 1838) and the eighteenth (October, 1838),
in which Bumble and Mrs. Corney sell to Monks

through his intermediary, Fagin, the locket taken from Oliver's mother at her death which is the last piece of evidence linking Oliver to his true name and estate. At the same time a counteraction is beginning which will lead to the downfall of Monks, Fagin, and Bumble and will restore Oliver to his rightful place in life. Nancy, having overheard Fagin and Monks plotting against the boy, betrays the scheme to Rose Maylie; and when Oliver is reunited with his first protector, Mr. Brownlow and Dr. Losberne determine to find the boy's true identity.

Most of the materials of the "Second Report" comment ironically, if incongruously, on these events in the main narrative. The invention that mechanically picks pockets has already been mentioned, and much of the remainder of this paper is concerned with the ineffectiveness and injustice of municipal government, judicial authorities, and the institutions created to relieve the widespread misery among the working classes. The foolish pretension to objective truth of the scientific projectors of the Mudfog Association is meant to stand as a grotesque indictment of the public policy which pretends to care for outcasts like Oliver and Noah Claypole. However broad the burlesquerie of the reports may be, with all their fantastic exaggeration taken from harlequinade, Dickens' attack on "scientific" political economy in them focuses clearly on its theoretical underpinnings and on its indifference to or exploitation of the helpless. At about this point in the main narrative, on the other hand, the novelist underlines the other half of his theme by showing the gradual ascendance of the primal human sympathies. By the end of the novel the total defeat of the combined forces of workhouse,

represented by Bumble and Mrs. Corney, underworld, represented by Fagin and his gang, and the
criminal self-interest which connects them in the person of Monks, makes an unequivocal statement of
Dickens' moral point.

But, under these conditions of the novel's original
publication in *Bentley's Miscellany,* what an extraordinary form to launch an all-out attack on the administration of the New Poor Law, Benthamism, and the
scientism behind them! In its original serialization,
the reader would have been in no doubt that Oliver
Twist, Bumble, Sowerberry, Mrs. Corney, and the
rest resided in a Mudfog parish, were neighbors of
Mr. Tulrumble, or that all the exploitation and oppression suffered by the boy were of the same place
and time as the meetings of the Mudfog Association
for the Advancement of Everything.

Nor, I think, could that reader have escaped feeling the modification of his attitude toward the main
narrative resulting from the presence of this gross
burlesquerie and harlequinade at three critical places
in the serialization of so melodramatic a novel as that
of the "Parish Boy's Progress." The interpolated
Mudfog episodes reach far beyond mere comic relief
or suspense by deferral. They join with a comparable
strain of grotesque and macabre burlesque in those
portions of the main narrative occupied by Bumble
and the other inmates of the parish workhouse, by
Fagin and the members of his gang, which, taken together, seriously dislocate the tone and estrange the
vision of the whole novel by virtue of their mixed
incongruities and analogies. If it include "The Mudfog Papers," *Oliver Twist* becomes a world in which
pathos and melodrama are juxtaposed with the broad-

est kind of pantomime burlesquerie, where cruelty and indifference to suffering are depicted in wildly comic terms, and where outrage jockeys for prominence with Pantaloon. The tone of the whole, it is safe to say, resists pigeonholing in the normal categories and comes to rest in that mixed mode to which we have given the name of theatrical burlesquerie.

This reading of the novel's tone is underlined by the decidedly odd choices Dickens made in disposing his materials. To the absurd figure of Bumble was allotted the task of embodying the moral attitudes of the utilitarian mentality; to Fagin, the role of enunciating the concept of enlightened self-interest; to the interpolated sketches, the job of attacking the scientific foundations of utilitarianism; to Monks, the symbolic function of linking workhouse and underworld through their shared evil; to Mrs. Bedwin, Mr. Brownlow, the Maylies, and Dr. Losberne, the personification of intuitive sympathy. Tone is not alone ambivalent on the level of the whole narrative; rather, the tone of many of its parts is internally grotesque because no unambiguous response is possible to, say, Bumble, Fagin, or the "Reports."

It is at this latter point that we perceive the method of sublimation by which Dickens appropriated the modes of theatrical pantomime and burlesque to serve the ends of a social novelist. In *Oliver Twist* all the machinery of clown, Harlequin, and Pantaloon is reproduced with fidelity. Not only is the traditional business of *commedia dell' arte* resurrected in texture, but in addition the play with fantasy, topicality, anachronism, and burlesquerie finds its counterpart as well. The antic, gestic style of the popular theater reappears in Bumble, Fagin, Noah

Claypole, and Mr. Grimwig, not to mention the Mudfog Association, side by side with the terrible realities
of workhouse and underworld, of Bill Sikes and
Jacob's Island. It is in this grotesque incongruity
that the popular theater has its deepest life in *Oliver
Twist*.

Chapter Six
GREAT EXPECTATIONS
AND BURLESQUE FORM

Iт міgнт ве expected that a talented and ambi-
tious young man deeply imbued with the cheap
theatrical life of the "Surrey side" would carry
much of that world with him when, as Dickens did,
he turned first to occasional journalism and then to
serious fiction. Nor would it be surprising to find
that many of his fundamental perspectives toward his
society and times were influenced by the idea of a
theatrum mundi, nor, indeed, that he borrowed from
the playhouse many of the grotesque techniques of
burlesque, pantomime, and farce to body forth his
vision. This much we have already seen.

Yet the question of the importance and continuity
of this strain of theatrical burlesquerie and grotesquerie in the main body of Dickens' mature work
remains unanswered. In part an answer to this question must await the later pages of this study—those
dealing with Dickens' theatrical style—where the techniques of the early Victorian theater will be found

sublimated in the essential texture and substance of the novelist's characteristic modes. In part, however, the answer has already been given in the many earlier studies of the relationship between Dickens' life and the theater of his time, and between his theatrical personages and the themes and forms of his novels. Codlin and Short of *The Old Curiosity Shop,* the immortal Crummles family of *Nicholas Nickleby,* and Sleary's Circus troupe of *Hard Times* testify to the novelist's continuing interest in incorporating the playhouse world into his mature work.

A more recent study has shown the debt owed to theatrical burlesque and nautical melodrama by the first novel of Dickens' maturity, *Dombey and Son* (October, 1846-April, 1848).[1] The novelist's manipulation of the Dick Whittington and Black-Eyed Susan motifs are there shown to have been borrowed, not from their folklore originals, but from contemporary dramatic versions. Dickens' use of such folk materials taken from the theater is also shown to be both subtle and pervasive. They are employed simultaneously to give the events and character relationships of the story an order of mythic universality and to comment ironically, through the novel's departures from the patterns of action and character of the originals, on the failure of the myth to square with the hard realities of actual life. Dickens handles his theatrical folklore materials freely and grotesquely: to arouse his readers' expectations that a realistic contemporary novel will imitate an ideal mythic action and then to frustrate or disorient these expectations by departures from, inversions of, and incongruous survivals of originally dramatic motifs. Often the transposition from myth to novel occasions a grotesque anachronism that would have warmed the heart of a burlesque

machinist, as when in *Dombey and Son* the cat of the
original Whittington story becomes the feline Carker,
the villain of the novel, who sends the Whittington-
figure, Walter Gay, to almost certain death at sea.
Thus at least in his first mature work, Dickens continued to employ the theater in multiple combinations of fantasy and realism to achieve a kind of
serious burlesque mode.

Even so late a novel as *Great Expectations* (Decem-
ber 1, 1860-August 3, 1861) reveals a similar theatrical coloration in texture, structure, character, and
technique.[2] As in *Dombey and Son, Great Expectations* goes to the theater for a folk archetype of an
apprentice and for a pattern of action and character
relationships that involve his unwilling betrayal of
his friends and benefactors. In this case, the central
allusion is to George Lillo's immensely popular sentimental drama, *The London Merchant; or, The History of George Barnwell* (1731), a play so often re-
vived and so widely imitated in the century following
its debut as to become by 1860 a basic item in the
Victorian common reader's cultural inheritance.

The London Merchant, or as it was more generally
known, *George Barnwell,* recounts the life of crime
and betrayal embarked on by a young London apprentice at the behest of an adventuress, Millwood,
with whom he has what amounts to an obsessive infatuation. Briefly stated, the plot is this: George
Barnwell, heretofore an exemplary apprentice to his
kindly master, Thorowgood, falls hopelessly in love
with the enchanting Millwood, who pretends to be
threatened by her guardian—she is a wealthy orphan
—with penury and dishonor unless Barnwell robs his
master of the money she needs to buy off her guard-

ian. Knowing the evil of such a betrayal of trust yet helpless under the spell of his infatuation, Barnwell performs the deed. Although the robbery is discovered by his faithful Maria and his fellow-apprentice, Trueman, the two friends agree to impoverish themselves by covering the loss out of their own pockets, and Barnwell's crime remains hidden from Thorowgood. Meanwhile, guilt-ridden but enslaved to Millwood, Barnwell cannot act on his friends' pleas to break off the affair. Millwood next prevails on him to murder his uncle, who had reared the orphaned boy, in order to gain his inheritance. Millwood's maid, Lucy, reveals the plot to Maria, Trueman, and Thorowgood, who attempt to prevent the crime; but they are too late, and when Barnwell presents himself, bloody-handed but without his uncle's fortune, to Millwood, the adventuress turns him over to the authorities in an effort to clear her own skirts. Both, however, are apprehended, tried, convicted, and condemned to death. Barnwell goes repentant to the gallows supported by his friends Maria, Thorowgood, and Trueman. Millwood, on the other hand, awaits her end alone, afraid but unrepentant, revealing herself to have been motivated throughout by a settled contempt and disgust for all mankind and by a desire to revenge herself upon a male sex in whom she sees nothing but evil. Thorowgood announces the *sentence:* although Millwood is evil and Barnwell frail, men judge by appearances, and only God can see into the secret hearts of men.

It will already be apparent to one familiar with *Great Expectations* that there are a number of curiously mingled parallels and differences between the novel and its original, the drama; and we may best begin to trace them by noticing the narrative context in which the invocation of *George Barnwell* occurs. It is in Chapter XV of the ninth weekly installment of the novel's serialization in *All the Year Round* for the week of January 26, 1861, that, coming out of Miss Havisham's house, Pip falls in with Wopsle, who has just purchased a six-penny edition of *The London Merchant;* the two repair to Pumblechook's parlor for an evening's dramatic reading. There is no question of the pertinence of the play to Pip's situation at this point in the novel, for it occurs precisely at the end of the first quarter of the narrative in the installment that immediately follows Pip's indenture in the forge to Joe, the bounty of £25 being provided by Miss Havisham. Indeed, Pip has just marked the first anniversary of his apprenticeship by a visit to his patroness when he encounters Wopsle. Nor is anyone in doubt about the propriety of this accidental encounter, for Wopsle "appeared to consider that a special Providence had put a 'prentice in his way to be read at; and he laid hold of me, and insisted on my accompanying him to the Pumblechookian parlour" (XXIX, 125). And Pip's account of the reading itself has the serious purpose hidden behind its comic terms of linking Pip the more firmly to George Barnwell, the errant apprentice:

What stung me, was the identification of the whole affair with my unoffending self. When Barnwell began to go wrong, I declare I felt positively apologetic, Pumblechook's indignant stare so taxed me with it. Wopsle, too, took pains to present me in the worst light. At once ferocious and maudlin, I was made to murder my uncle with no extenuating circumstances whatever; Millwood put me down in argument, on every occasion; it became sheer monomania in my master's daughter to care a button for me; and all I can say for my gasping and procrastinating conduct on the fatal morning, is, that it was worthy the general feebleness of my character. Even after I was happily hanged and Wopsle had closed the book, Pumblechook sat staring at me, and shaking his head, and saying, "Take warning, boy, take warning!" as if it were a well-known fact that I contemplated murdering a near relation, provided I could only induce one to have the weakness to become my benefactor. (XXIX, 125-126)

Immediately after, Pip finds that his sister has been felled and left for dead by some unknown assailant. The opening words of Chapter XVI (the first of the next, tenth installment, for February 2, 1861) complete Pip's psychological identification with the murderous apprentice:

With my head full of George Barnwell, I was at first disposed to believe that *I* must have had some hand in the attack upon my sister, or at all events that as her near relation, popularly known to be under obligations to her, I was a more legitimate object of suspicion than any one else. But when, in the clearer light of next morning, I began to reconsider the matter and to hear it discussed around me on all sides, I took another view of the case, which was more reasonable. (XXIX, 128)

In spite of this avowal, however, Pip soon discovers that fate has ironically implicated him in the attack on his sister without his knowing it. Finding that she had been assailed by a convict's leg-iron which had been filed asunder some time previous to its use as a weapon, Pip privately concludes to the following effect: "Knowing what I knew, I set up an inference of my own here. I believed the iron to be my convict's iron—the iron I had seen and heard him filing at, on the marshes—but my mind did not accuse him of having put it to its latest use. For, I believed one of two other persons to have become possessed of it, and to have turned it to this cruel account. Either Orlick, or the strange man who had shown me the file" (XXIX, 129).

But Pip's knowledge of his unwilling involvement in crime and violence, dating from his initial confrontation of "my convict" Magwitch in the opening scene of the novel, cannot be so easily disposed of as a fact of his consciousness. Not only must he confront Orlick daily at the forge and elsewhere, but the "strange man with the file" is an emissary from Magwitch—although at this point unknown to Pip—who had mysteriously appeared at the "Three Jolly Bargemen" three weeks earlier in the novel's serialization (Chapter X, installment six for January 5, 1861), shown the file as an identification sign, and surreptitiously given the boy a shilling wrapped up in two one-pound notes. And now the boy's continuing sense of guilt is given fresh matter to feed on:

It was horrible to think that I had provided the weapon, however undesignedly, but I could hardly think otherwise. I suffered unspeakable trouble while I considered and reconsidered whether I should at last dissolve that spell of my childhood and tell Joe all the story. For months afterwards, I every day settled the question finally in the negative, and reopened and reargued it next morning. The contention came, after all, to this;—the secret was such an old one now, and so grown into me and become a part of myself, that I could not tear it away. In addition to the dread that, having led up to so much mischief, it would be now more likely than ever to alienate Joe from me if he believed it, I had a further restraining dread that he would not believe it, but would assert it with the fabulous dogs and veal-cutlets as a monstrous invention. However, I temporised with myself, of course—for, was I not wavering between right and wrong, when the thing is always done?—and resolved to make a full disclosure if I should see any such new occasion as a new chance of helping in the discovery of the assailant. (XXIX, 130)

The engagement of George Barnwell in the rags-to-riches-to-rags career of the apprentice Pip at this decisive point in the narrative thus gives the allusion to the drama an importance in the novel belied by its single, if extended treatment. For here Pip finds himself, incongruously, another George Barnwell, an unwilling murderer, or at least an unwilling and unknowing partner in a violent assault.

More subtle and profound similarities and differences between the two stories of apprentices begin to emerge, as *Great Expectations* starts to play a series of grotesque and ironic variations on the themes and actions of its dramatic prototype. If it is Barnwell's fate to sink into betrayal, crime, and evil because of his captivation by the fascinating, heartless, and utterly ruthless Millwood, it is no less Pip's destiny, in much less violent and melodramatic terms, to betray the love, care, and loyalty of his old friends at the forge, Joe and Biddy, in pursuit of the "great expectations" personified by the coldly beautiful, heartless, and unattainable Estella. And Estella bears an affinity to Millwood through Miss Havisham, who uses the girl to further her own Millwood-like scheme to revenge herself on the male sex for Compeyson's abandonment of her. Furthermore, Pip's love for Estella is as senseless and consuming as Barnwell's for Millwood, for as Pip says later in the novel, he was captivated by Estella "simply because I found her irresistible. Once for all, I knew to my sorrow, often and often, if not always, that I loved her against reason, against promise, against peace, against hope, against happiness, against all discouragement that could be. Once for all; I loved her none the less because I knew it, and it had no more influence in restraining me, than if I had devoutly believed her to be human perfection" (XXIX, 248-249).

"Human perfection"—with these words Dickens points to the far more subtle and complex value attached to Pip's infatuation with Estella than that of Barnwell's passion for Millwood. By the time of the appearance of the *Barnwell* episode in *Great Expectations,* the symbolic value of Estella as an embodiment of Pip's unfulfilled longings for a life of human perfection free from the meannesses, vulgarities, and guiltinesses of his days at Joe's forge, has already been established. Two themes have been developed during the first quarter of the narrative: first, the moral oppression to which Pip has been subjected by his sister, Mrs. Joe, Pumblechook, Wopsle, and the Hubbles that, triggered by his unwilling complicity in Magwitch's escape, has resulted in the boy's morbid obsession with his own guilt. Second, there is the theme of Pip's feelings of shame at the commonness, ignorance, poverty, and vulgarity of himself and those at the forge—as well as the shame at being ashamed—that have been engendered by his association with Miss Havisham and Estella, coupled with his boyish infatuation with the girl, who systematically persecutes him with her contempt. This latter theme is especially pertinent to the *Barnwell* episode in Chapter XV, for Pip's shame at his humble station and the start of his yearnings for a fuller life follow hard upon his indenture as a blacksmith's apprentice in Chapter XIII (the last of the eighth number) and occupy the whole of Chapter XIV (the first of the ninth number). Furthermore, both the theme of vulgarity and the theme of guilt are woven together in the boy's aspirations for a richer, broader place in the world that are focused on the celestial Estella; for Pip's "expectations" are for a way of life free from all the limitations of the primal human condition.

Accused by his elders at every turn—such as in the Barnwell episode—of an evil nature that he knows is not his, self-accused by his own morbid conscience —made so by the imputations of his elders—for his complicity in the convict's escape, though it was unwilling and under duress, and sensitized by Miss Havisham and Estella to the meanness of his condition, Pip comes into the "great expectations" of which he had so long dreamed. It is only then that he begins, ironically, to commit real evil, like Barnwell, to those who have loved and cared for him so long. In his shabby treatment of Joe and Biddy, again like Barnwell, Pip does wrong knowing he does so and yet unable to do otherwise, just as he loves Estella hopelessly and helplessly. Moreover, the evil he does to those who love him is justified by the imputation of evil in others, as he does when, after patronizing Joe and Biddy, he accuses the girl of displaying a "bad side of human nature" because her silence pricks his conscience (XXIX, 158-160, 303-306).

It is perhaps no accident, then, that the "evil" in human nature which Pip wishes to escape by his pursuit of an impossible ideal of human perfection should be introduced into the novel in the same chapter as that which contains the *Barnwell* episode, in the person of Joe's assistant at the forge, the sullen and brutal journeyman, Dolge Orlick. If Estella represents the cold and finally unobtainable ideal of perfection to which Pip aspires, Orlick stands for all those vicious and primordial aspects of human nature from which the boy vainly flees. And the scene that introduces Orlick to the reader is one of the most powerful in the novel. In it, Orlick's resentment of Pip's half-holiday leads to a quarrel with Joe that, goaded on by Mrs. Joe's hysteria, ends in a savage fight between the gentle smith and his assistant in which Orlick is badly beaten. Nursing his bruises and his hatred of Mrs. Joe, Orlick returns that night (while Pip is being "read at" by Wopsle) and viciously attacks his tormentor with the convict's leg-iron he had found on the marshes. Moreover, Orlick represents the persistence of the "bad side of human nature" which Pip would leave behind him but cannot, for Orlick turns up repeatedly in the boy's life to remind him, as do Jaggers, Wemmick, and Newgate prison, the "man with the file," Molly, and finally "my convict" himself, of the crime and evil inherent in the human condition. Orlick reappears on the marshes in the next installment (Chapter XVII) slouching after Biddy; and he turns up in Chapter XXIX as Miss Havisham's gatekeeper when Pip comes down from London to welcome Estella back after her sojourn in a European finishing school. He is the spy on Pip's stairway the night of Magwitch's return (Chapter XL), who later betrays the secret to Compeyson and so brings about the frustration of the boy's expectations; and it is Orlick who lures Pip to the lime kiln on the marshes and there nearly succeeds in taking Pip's life (Chapter LIII).

A brief examination of this climactic episode reveals the nature of that evil in *Great Expectations* as it is personified by Orlick. Having surprised and captured Pip, he then begins to acuse him of having been his enemy throughout his life—at the forge, with Biddy, at Miss Havisham's—an accusation that is partially true but fails to take account of the fact that Orlick's own faults of character have created Pip's dislike and opposition. As Pip says, "You gave it to yourself; you gained it for yourself. I could have done you no harm, if you had done yourself none" (XXIX, 456). But the final accusation is the most telling one, reinvoking as it does all the events of Chapter XV, for Orlick tells Pip that although it was he, Orlick, who used the leg-iron to assault Mrs. Joe, "I tell you it was your doing—I tell you it was done through you. . . . I come upon her from behind, as I come upon you to-night. I giv' it her! I left her for dead. . . . But it warn't old Orlick as did it; it was you. You was favoured, and he was bullied and beat. Old Orlick bullied and beat, eh? Now you pays for it. You done it; now you pays for it" (XXIX, 458).

This famous passage has been construed to demonstrate Pip's actual complicity in evil and crime through the agency of Magwitch's escape, the leg-iron, and the persecution of Orlick.[3] But I think Dickens had a more subtle moral point to make for the themes of *Great Expectations* through the lips of the malevolent Orlick, providing that one reads the scene at face value; that is, if one accepts Orlick as representative of primordial evil inherent in human nature, and if, further, one exonerates Pip from Orlick's accusation. Granting these premises, then, one must conclude that if Orlick personifies evil, the nature of that evil is, first, a frustrated and unrealistic ambition which leads to envy and jealousy and a false sense of having been wronged. Orlick has a totally unreasonable feeling of the injustice that Pip, the master's ward, had been put ahead of him at the forge and in Biddy's affections. This kind of evil leads to acts of crime and violence in revenge. And

second, he has an outraged and wrong-headed conviction, based on the envy born of his false estimate of
what is due him, that his own wrong-doing is really
the work of others. Looked at from this point of view,
the evil so vividly personified by Orlick's extreme
case can be seen to be precisely that which riddles the
other characters in the novel. It is that which motivates Miss Havisham's revenge on the male sex
through the agency of Estella, in consequence of her
own sense of having been wronged by Compeyson's
betrayal of her. It is that which prompts Mrs. Joe's
persecution of the gentle Joe and the innocent Pip.
Sensing the unfairness of having been left at her parents' death with the task of raising Pip and with a
much-reduced social status in marriage to a blacksmith, Mrs. Joe's life is spent in suffering what she
wrongly regards as a martyrdom but which in fact
takes the form of the oppression of others. It is that,
finally, which motivates all the real evil—as opposed
to that evil falsely imputed to him by others when a
child—that Pip commits during the period of his "expectations": his shame at Joe's commonness and ignorance, his condescension to Biddy, his habit of
accusing them when he is at fault. Like Orlick at
the lime kiln, Pip imputes his own evil to others who
are innocent; and he is prompted to do this by his
pursuit of an ambition for human perfection that is
patently unreasonable and impossible of achieve-
ment. In the last analysis, it is this theme which
necessitates the protagonist's confrontation with Orlick at the lime kiln. He and the reader are required
to stand face to face with Orlick, the personification
of the particular and complex kind of evil which informs the novel, and to see it for what it is—the

hypocritical imputation of wrong-doing to others as a screen for one's own viciousness.

All this may seem a far cry from *The London Merchant* and its relatively simple moral fable of an apprentice-boy's career of betrayal and crime that grows out of his senseless infatuation with an adventuress. But Dickens invested the novel's Millwood-figure, Estella, with rich symbolic value as a personification of the unattainable state of being for which the protagonist longed and in the name of which he was willing to perform an emotional betrayal of those who loved him best. The bourgeois archetype of the traitorous apprentice, Barnwell, is transformed under Dickens' genius into Phillip Pirrip, a type of the moral fallacy of the *bourgeoisie* itself; and the pattern of action of the folk tragedy provides a mold to shape the very different materials of a novel that condemns the values of a society by turning against it its own most cherished art forms.

The grotesque mosaic of parallel and variation between *Great Expectations* and *George Barnwell* extends beyond the Barnwell-Millwood and Pip-Estella axes in a complicated skein. For if Barnwell has his loyal master, Thorowgood, Pip has his Joe; where Lillo's apprentice has Thorowgood's daughter, Maria, blindly loving and loyal to the end, Pip has the much more realistic Biddy, whose silence before Pip's condescension accuses him most, and yet whose loyalty is never threatened by his inadvertent cruelties. There is no Trueman in the novel, unless it be Pocket, but in Pip's extremity following the death of Magwitch there is the presence of his master, Joe, to care for him and to pronounce the charitable *sentence* of the novel over the protagonist. And if

Barnwell robs his master, so does Pip, though under vastly different circumstances of age, motivation, and duress; and there is no one to cover for him but his own agonized conscience.

It is perhaps in the matter of the guardian that *Great Expectations* plays its most ironic variations on the pattern of its original. *The London Merchant,* it will be remembered, has for its apprentice both a loving master, Thorowgood, as Pip has Joe, although the two are vastly different in education and social status, as well as a benefactor, Barnwell's uncle, who raises the orphan, provides for his apprenticeship, and leaves him a handsome bequest in his will. It is for the latter that Barnwell ungratefully murders his guardian. In the novel, on the other hand, Pip's ingratitude is directed toward Joe, who had reared, protected, and loved the boy throughout the years leading to his apprenticeship and who willingly gives him up when Pip comes into his "expectations." At the same time, the boy's true "benefactor" turns out to be the transported felon Magwitch, the founder of the boy's fortune. Furthermore, the protégé in the novel does not murder his patron as Barnwell does in the play, though his benefactor does die as a result of Pip's unsuccessful efforts to get the old gentleman out of England. And in the novel, the boy's guardian is a criminal, thus ironically linking Pip's rise to gentle status to the violence and criminality he seeks to escape in that position in life. In addition, Magwitch is the natural father of Estella, the girl who represents to Pip all the perfections to which he aspires. As if this last were not a sufficiently ironic discovery, Pip learns that he as much as Estella has been exploited by his patron as an instrument of revenge against the world. In the case of Magwitch, his vengeance like Miss Havisham's was prompted by the "gentleman," Compeyson, who had also betrayed him. But in a larger sense his revenge is directed against the entire polite structure of genteel society to which Pip has committed all his expectations. By manufacturing his own gentleman in Pip, the outcast Magwitch utters a huge joke at the expense of the society he feels has wronged him; and it is his monomaniacal desire to savor his sardonic jest that brings him back to England and death. In this fate he shares a common pattern of action with Miss Havisham, who is in a sense also destroyed by her obsession with past wrongs and present revenge.

Thus both Pip and Estella, like their exploiters, are as much victims as transgressors, and both must and do come to learn that in accepting this knowledge of the mixed conditions life imposes lies happiness and tranquillity. Unlike the original play, then, *Great Expectations* has as its theme the betrayal of the betrayers by society and circumstance. Whereas *George Barnwell* is a tract in support of a social and economic status quo, Dickens' novel seriously burlesques the patterns of action and character relationships of its prototype to attack the status quo by means of a complex web of parallels and variations.

This burlesque appropriation of *The London Merchant* to serve the serious purposes of a social novel does not, however, end Dickens' exploitation of the methods and materials of the popular theater in *Great Expectations*. In the character of the would-be tragedian, Wopsle, the novelist creates a counterpart and parallel to Pip and his expectations that burlesques the protagonist's career and offers a grotesquely ridiculous alter ego to the apprentice boy. It is well to remind ourselves how deeply involved in Pip's story is that of the parish-clerk-turned-thespian, for Wopsle is on hand at nearly every decisive point in the narrative, busily recasting commonplace events into the absurd, banal formularies of Victorian melodrama and declamation. It is he who, at the Christmas dinner near the opening of the novel, delivers the ludicrous sermon on pork over the head of a helpless Pip; and he is with Jo and Pip when the convict is captured and returned to the hulks. Wopsle conducts the quarterly examinations at his great-aunt's "school" by reciting Antony's speech over the dead Caesar and Collins' *Ode on the Passions*. He later guides Pip's "higher education" by making the hapless boy into that "dramatic lay-figure" to be pummeled and wept over which so irritates him. He is one of the company at the "Three Jolly Bargemen" when the "man with the file" reappears to remind Pip of his connection to the underworld. And it is Wopsle of course who performs the reading of *George Barnwell* with such pointed relevance to the young apprentice. Wopsle is also present, grandiloquently reading a London newspaper account of a murder trial, when Jaggers appears and, after demolishing the clerk under his cross-examination, takes Pip aside and tells him of his expectations. Wopsle, in short, is one of the chief instruments of Pip's education by oppression which makes the boy long for the wider zones of a gentleman's life. And this intimidation and imputation are carried on in the burlesque terms of Wopsle's declamatory melodrama.

Wopsle's major role in the novel, however, is reserved for the period after Pip has gone up to London in pursuit of gentility. Then the parish clerk, with a no less unrealistic and pretentious ambition of reforming the English stage and single-handedly ushering in a new Golden Age, follows the quondam apprentice to the great metropolis in the guise of a tragedian and there comes as great a cropper as Pip. But with this difference: where Pip's rags-to-riches-to-rags career is fraught with solemn moral overtones, the exactly parallel course of Wopsle on the London boards is handled in the broad manner of burlesque. For all its pointed relevance to Pip's story, the Wopsle subplot is as grotesquely incongruous in tone to the main narrative as "The Mudfog Papers" are to *Oliver Twist,* as much of an interpolation as "the layers of red and white in a side of streaky bacon." It thereby serves to dislocate the reader's attitude to the events of the foreground by offering a comically discrepant parallel to them.

News of Wopsle's assault on the London playhouses and his disastrous debut—presumably in one of those private theaters Dickens had handled so roughly in the *Sketches*—is brought by Joe Gargary on his first visit to Pip, when the new-made young gentleman allows his consciousness of his social position to come between himself and his oldest and dearest friend. Here, then, the reader encounters the first solid evidence that Pip's rise in circumstances has brought with it a corresponding fall in his moral stature, as demonstrated by the shabby condescension and awkward embarrassment he shows toward Joe. Precisely the same point is made in the same place about Wopsle's decision to abandon the church in favor of a theatrical career, although this intelligence is offered in Joe's grotesquely incongruous comic terms. In recounting news of home to Pip, Joe remarks that everyone is very much the same as before Pip left,

and that "All friends is no backerder, if not no
forarder. 'Ceptin' Wopsle: he's had a drop."

"Had a drop, Joe?"
"Why yes," said Joe, lowering his voice, "he's left the
Church and went into the playacting. Which the playacting have likewise brought him to London along with
me. And his wish were . . . if no offense, I would 'and
you that."
   I took what Joe gave me, and found it to be the
crumpled playbill of a small metropolitan theatre, announcing the first appearance, in that very week, of "the
celebrated Provincial Amateur of Roscian renown, whose
unique performance in the highest tragic walk of our
National Bard has lately occasioned so great a sensation
in local dramatic circles."
   "Was there a great sensation?"
   "Why," said Joe, "yes, there certainly were a peck of
orange peel. Partickler when he see the ghost."
                                        (XXIX, 235-236)

   The implication that Wopsle's theatrical debut was
as unmitigated a disaster as Pip's life as a gentleman
is beginning to seem is confirmed by several pieces of
parallel evidence contained in the chapters immediately following that of Joe's visit (Chapter XXVII).
In that chapter, Joe also brings word of Estella's return and Miss Havisham's desire to have Pip visit
them. Acting upon this invitation in the next chapter (XXVIII, the second of the seventeenth installment, for March 23, 1861), Pip travels by stagecoach
down to his former home; but during the journey the
young man is discomfited by the presence immediately behind him of the "man with the file," who
reminds him again of that involvement in crime and
meanness which he seeks to escape in genteel life. In
the next installment, the eighteenth, comprising
Chapter XXIX (March 30), Orlick reappears after

a long absence from the narrative in the role of Miss Havisham's gatekeeper—to Pip another reminder of man's animal nature. Moreover, Jaggers is also there, with the breath of Newgate around him. There too is Estella, more beautiful and accomplished than ever, who makes Pip feel again the sense of her distance and disparity from him. At the same time, her symbolic value to Pip and to the novel is defined unequivocally: "Truly it was impossible to dissociate her presence from all those wretched hankerings after money and gentility that had disturbed my boyhood —from all those ill-regulated aspirations that had first made me ashamed of home and Joe—from all those visions that had raised her face in the glowing fire, struck it out of the iron on the anvil. . . . In a word, it was impossible for me to separate her, in the past or in the present, from the innermost life of my life" (XXIX, 252-253). In the same place, however, Pip discovers the divine Estella's resemblance to someone whom he cannot at present identify. Later in the novel, following Magwitch's return, he at last determines that the proud and lofty young woman is none other than the natural child of the convict and Mr. Jaggers' murderous housekeeper, Molly, thus establishing her participation with Pip and many other characters in crime and evil. At this point in the narrative, however, only the first hint is given of this complex web of relationships which will turn Pip's dreams to dust and ashes.

The following serial number, the nineteenth (Chapters XXX and XXXI, for April 6, 1861), occupies an important position at the novel's exact narrative and chronological mid-point; and the events it describes deserve the importance given to them by this central position. The first chapter opens on an

appropriately incongruous note following the pas-
sionate meeting between Pip and Estella that confirms him in his hopeless love for her. In it the novel
lodges its most comic short episode, the elaborate
public burlesque of the proud new-made gentleman
performed by the irrepressible iconoclast, Trabb's
boy. He follows Pip through the streets of his old
home town, alternately engaging in gross pantomime
indicative of his being wholly overwhelmed by Pip's
mighty presence, or he struts along with his coat col-
lar turned up, side-hair twined, arms akimbo, smirk-
ing extravagantly, wriggling his elbows and body, and
drawling, "Don't know yah, don't know yah, pon my
soul don't know yah!" (XXIX, 263-264). So devastating is Trabb's boy's burlesque of Pip's affectations
that the would-be gentleman quits the field in utter
rout, having been made a ridiculous spectacle by the
brilliant pantomime-in-mufti of another apprentice.
This clear-eyed satirical gaze has shown Pip how
ludicrous he looks to his former townsmen. Immediately following this hilarious episode, the novel's tone
makes another abrupt and incongruous shift to the
conversation between Pip and Pocket in Barnard's
Inn concerning Pip's hopeless and tormenting love
for Estella, Pocket's sensible advice to break off the
affair on the grounds of his own parents' unsuitable
partnership and miserable life together, and, finally,
Pocket's revelation of his quiet and reasonable love
for the persecuted Clara.

The central chapter of the novel, Chapter XXXI,
takes Pip and Pocket to see Wopsle (now Walden-
garver) in the role of Hamlet; and the account of this
performance in a cheap theater, together with the
ridicule visited upon it by the audience, embraces
the whole of this chapter. Dickens' version of the

production, as it is seen through Pip's eyes, is a superbly fashioned exercise in the mode of burlesque-by-grotesquerie that characterizes *Sketches by Boz* and *Pickwick Papers*. The opening words of the episode—really a set-piece like a "Boz" sketch introduced into the main narrative with a kind of independent existence of its own—set the grotesquely comic tone of the whole:

> On our arrival in Denmark, we found the king and queen of that country elevated in two arm-chairs on a kitchen-table, holding a Court. The whole of the Danish nobility were in attendance; consisting of a noble boy in wash-leather boots of a gigantic ancestor, a venerable Peer with a dirty face, who seemed to have risen from the people late in life, and the Danish chivalry with a comb in its hair and a pair of white silk legs, and presenting on the whole a feminine appearance. My gifted townsman stood gloomily apart, with folded arms, and I could have wished that his curls and forehead had been more probable. (XXIX, 271-272)

Thereafter, the grotesque tawdriness of the production is interlarded with a faithful rendition of the derision with which the gallery receives it; it is, in short, a hugely comic disaster for Wopsle, whose reading of the melancholy Dane's role is all too reminiscent of a parish clerk. Yet backstage after the performance, Pip and Pocket discover that Wopsle is totally unimpressed by the rain of boos, catcalls, and nuts which greeted his acting at every turn, preferring to credit them to the enmity of a fellow actor who had planted agents in the gallery to embarrass him. To all this, Pip responds in the following manner:

> Without distinctly knowing whether I should have been more sorry for Mr. Wopsle if he had been in

despair, I was so sorry for him as it was, that I took the opportunity . . . of asking him home to supper . . . and he sat until two o'clock in the morning, reviewing his success, and developing his plans. I forget in detail what they were, but I have a general recollection that he was to begin with reviving the Drama, and to end with crushing it; inasmuch as his decease would leave it utterly bereft and without a chance or hope.

Miserably I went to bed after all, and miserably thought of Estella, and miserably dreamed that my expectations were all cancelled, and that I had to give my hand in marriage to Herbert's Clara, or play Hamlet to Miss Havisham's Ghost, before twenty thousand people, without knowing twenty words of it. (XXIX, 277)

The parallel between Pip's material and social expectations and Wopsle's equally foolish confidence in his ability single-handedly to reform the English stage is clearly drawn in the last paragraph quoted above. Furthermore, two essential points have been made: first, Pip's expectations of achieving all the dreams focused on Estella are as fantastic as Wopsle's of remaking the theater; and second, Pip, like Wopsle, is wholly unable or unwilling to recognize the folly of these ambitions and to rest content in a more limited and humble place in the world commensurate with his real worth. Ultimately, Wopsle's grotesquely ludicrous debacle in Hamlet comments as pointedly on Pip's present unhappy situation, and in similar burlesque terms, as Trabb's boy's pantomime satirizes Pip's affected airs.

Succeeding installments confirm and underline the tonally discrepant ironies of the central episode. The next, twentieth installment (Chapters XXXII and XXXIII, for April 13, 1861) finds Pip welcoming Estella to London for her introduction into society; but his meeting is poisoned, first, by a tour with

Wemmick through Newgate Prison which renews the boy's sense of implication in crime; second, by Estella's continued coldness toward him; and, third, by a recurrence of the feeling that Estella resembles someone whom he cannot identify. The following installment permits the reader to catch a glimpse of the disenchantment with the life of a gentleman that Pip now begins to experience, quite aside from the corrosive presence in his heart of the image of Estella. There he finds that his affluence has led him into dissipation, debt, procrastination, folly, and the emotionally sterile relationships of "The Finches of the Grove." His despairing stock-taking is interrupted by word of Mrs. Joe's death; but following her funeral he has another unsatisfactory interview with Joe and Biddy, in which his condescension and sensitivity to his new social position lead him once again to deal unjustly with his old friends and to come away again troubled in conscience.

All that now remains for Dickens to do in developing the parallel between Wopsle's theatrical career and Pip's course as a would-be gentleman is to show the actual frustration of their several expectations. This is done for Pip in the return of the boy's real benefactor, the transported felon Magwitch, the defeat of their plan of escape, together with the death of the old convict and the forfeiture of his estate to the Crown, which culminates in Pip's close brush with death. To these somber events Wopsle's later career on the boards offers a comic counterpart. The parallel is drawn—in that mixture of melodrama and burlesque with which we are by now familiar—in the twenty-ninth installment, comprising Chapters XLVII and XLVIII, for June 15, 1861. Context underlines the analogy Dickens draws between Pip and

Wopsle. In the number immediately before, Pip learns that the old convict's presence in his quarters in Barnard's Inn has been discovered. Pip spends a miserable night in Hummum's while Pocket and Wemmick smuggle Magwitch out of Barnard's Inn and hide him in the same house with Pocket's beloved, Clara. Meanwhile, Pip finds himself in straitened circumstances, pressed for debt, reduced to pawning his possessions, and developing his plans for spiriting his patron out of England. And as the young man's expectations crumble into dust in this quarter, word comes of Estella's marriage to the brutal Bentley Drummle, thus shattering the last and dearest of Pip's aspirations. Now, returning from a nightly visit to Magwitch, Pip attends a cheap theater, where he discovers his former townsman has been reduced to taking a number of minor and ignoble roles in a tawdry nautical melodrama and a wretched Christmas pantomime. The parallel is now complete: Pip and Wopsle share the bitter aftermath of their different but equally foolish expectations, and the melodrama and pantomime stand as the incongruous symbols of their sad fall in state. One further touch remains: it is from the lips of Wopsle that Pip learns, after the performance, that he is being shadowed by the man whom Magwitch had attacked on the marshes so many years before—as it turns out, Compeyson, the betrayer of Miss Havisham and the novel's presiding personification of the gentleman-criminal. With this intelligence, as later pages of the novel demonstrate, the last chance of preserving Pip's expectations of a life of gentility and luxury has gone aglimmering.

It only remains at this point to notice briefly the tacit assumptions which lie behind Dickens' linkage of his protagonist first with George Barnwell and then with Wopsle. Each is in its own way a parallel variation, discrepant analogy, or incongruous likeness; each is in part ironic, in part burlesque, in part grotesque;[4] yet each helps to carry the weight of serious commentary on the futility and consequent evil of misplaced paradisiacal expectations and their accompanying self-deceptions. Moreover, in a different way each employs the theater and drama to hold up a mirror image to real life that, like any mirror, faithfully reflects what is pictured in it and yet distorts, reverses, or inverts.

Dickens' use of theatrical materials in his maturity, then, is subtilized far beyond the vision of a *theatrum mundi* that characterizes his early works. Though the playhouse is sublimated in later novels, it no less informs his vision of the life around him as a glass does through which one sees, not darkly but too well, the antic modes of men's most sacrosanct affairs. To the last the forms of the popular theater provide the fundamental medium through which the real world may be seen and, seen so, rendered with fantastic fidelity. Trabb's boy, who finally rescues Pip from certain death at the hands of Orlick, epitomizes the theatrical presence in *Great Expectations* with his elaborate pantomime-burlesque in the streets—a crude performance in mufti that nevertheless shows Pip and the reader how absurd the new-made gentleman really appears. Similarly, Wopsle's theatrical aspirations and debacle provide a burlesque counterpart to Pip's expectations and disillusionment. And *The London Merchant* offers a pattern to hold up for comparison with the apprentice boy's progress that is both a serious burlesque and a grotesquely relevant prototype and that invests the novel with that universality that accrues to folk myth. At the same time, the novel offers a far more profound investigation into the themes of obsession, guilt, and disenchantment than Lillo's play; and in this way *Great Expectations* constitutes an indictment of the comfortable cultural attitudes of which the play is an epitome. In the most serious sense of the term, then, this novel is as profound a burlesque of *George Barnwell* as Wopsle's plot is a frivolous burlesque of Pip's career. In either case, what gives form to this novel is the play a parallel and variation between incongruous realms; and this was the mode of early Victorian theatrical burlesque.

BOOK THREE
Dickens'
Theatrical
Style

Chapter Seven

INTRODUCTORY

A BRIEF STOCK-TAKING may be in order at this point, if only because the argument advanced in these pages has at times taken us far afield from the playhouse, and a moment is called for in which to check bearings and fix location. Confident of the substantial truth to life of the mingled fantasy and realism of the popular theater of his time, Dickens sought to translate the frivolous idioms of the playhouse into imaginative prose fiction with a serious social purpose. His ultimate artistic intention lay in altering his readers' vision of commonplace life from conventional literalism to imaginative vitality, and to this end he had recourse to many of the techniques of pantomime and burlesque with which his readers were already familiar.

Dickens' belief in the theater's relevance to life is based on his conception of the *theatrum mundi,* which *Sketches by Boz* and *Pickwick Papers* adumbrate. Overt theatrical materials in these two early works provided the novelist with an avenue of approach to the histrionism he found at the heart of middle-class attitudes and norms of conduct, and many theatrical echoes crop up in their texture. *Pickwick Papers* and *Oliver Twist* are characterized by the mingling of incompatible modes and by the tonal ambiguity that results from the introduction of rootless burlesque in unlikely contexts and from the serious uses to which the coarse, gestic style of pantomime and farce are put. *Great Expectations* follows the pattern of the earlier *Dombey and Son* in employing as pattern both for parallel and anachronism an earlier dramatic original belonging to folk culture, and, in the case of the Wopsle subplot, continues to exploit antic materials for serious thematic and structural purposes. In this, Dickens seems to have been imitating practices that in cruder form are to be found in the burlesque theater of his time.

Because Dickens appears really to have followed what Lewes calls an "hallucinative" method of composition in which "created images have the coercive force of realities," he stood as an artist in a singlar relationship both to his creations and to his readers. He and his audiences were, in a sense, fellow spectators of images conjured up before them by a coercive imagination. This accounts for the delighted surprise he registered at the effects attained by public readings from his own work; and the same cause stands behind his revealing comment that his readings were "like writing a book in public." His unique ability to "fancy or perceive relations in things not apparent generally" gave him the perspective of an innocent toward the familiar world, who sees commonplace people and things with the vivid coloration and grotesque clarity of a stranger in a playhouse. By this means he was able to estrange and so revivify his readers' conventional sense of the relations between things. Furthermore, the novelist seems to have been as much an onlooker of these autonomous imaginings as his readers. This fact, as we shall see, profoundly influenced the nature of his art.

At the same time, the novelist was not timid in appropriating from the playhouse many of its stock comic types, as *Pickwick Papers* and *Sketches by Boz* so amply demonstrate; and Dickens' habitual use of sudden and dramatic transitions between comic and pathetic scenes betrays a similarly theatrical place of origination. Many of his "humourous" characters suggest Dickens' fondness for Ben Jonson, and his tendency to indulge in incidental stylistic "business" —word play, punning, comic literalism, and metaphorical gymnastics—are equally characteristic of much nineteenth-century dramatic practice in, for example, farce, burlesque, and extravaganza. Dickens' fondness for the comedy of jargon, cant, technical terminology, occupational and professional diction, and inconsequential allusions, as in Captain Cuttle's nautical vocabulary and his confusions between the Anglican prayer book and popular songs, for example, is a no less common feature of the cheap Victorian drama, although it might be found anywhere in Smollett, Sterne, or Walter Scott.

His general prose style is everywhere studded with superlatives and hyperbole. No doubt this tendency toward a loosely theatrical heightening and stylization has its source in Dickens' exuberant vision of the world around him, but its counterpart in the playhouse ought to be noted in passing. The novelist's narrative techniques in many cases bear an odor of the boards about them, notably his penchant for scene-setting in the opening installments, as in the brilliant first chapter of *Bleak House,* for truncating dialogue until it approaches scenario, and for ending episodes upon a tableau. His exploitation of leitmotif to define and maintain characterization, a common theatrical device, is so well known that it hardly bears repetition, although it should be mentioned that this technique is equally to be found in many eighteenth-century novels. Dickens' habit of lapsing into blank verse at moments of great emotional intensity is a stylistic feature that the novelist himself noticed and deplored: "I *cannot* help it, when I am very much in earnest" (XXXIX, 459). And he was equally addicted to other melodramatic devices, chiefly those violations of narrative credibility by apostrophe, invocation, direct address, soliloquy, and incidental aside for which critics have so roundly condemned him, as well as for those frequent passages of sheer melodramatic writing in which language, gesture, and sentiment seem to have been transplanted directly from the stage of a cheap theater.

Although Dickens' habit of intervening in the narrative in his own voice has been the subject of much adverse critical comment, it has not received sufficiently careful attention to discriminate between different forms of these violations of credibility. To make some discriminations in this matter in the light of Lewes' theory of the hallucinative character of Dickens' imagination may tell us something about the peculiar nature of the novelist's relationship to his narrative, on one hand, and to his readers on the other.

The most frequently cited kind of intervention by Dickens is that direct address of the reader—or rather, of the reading public generally—which usually occurs at the conclusion of some turn of plot which particularly arouses the novelist's emotional involvement, as in that famous passage in *Bleak House* that concludes the death scene of Little Jo, the crossing sweeper: "The light is come upon the dark benighted way. Dead! Dead, your Majesty. Dead, my lords and gentlemen. Dead, Right Reverends and Wrong Reverends of every order. Dead, men and women, born with Heavenly compassion in your hearts. And dying thus around us every day" (XXIII, 236). This is stylistically typical of such addresses: vaguely Biblical or at least "pulpit" diction, parallel syntactical construction, truncated sentence structure, sarcastic word play—"Right Reverends and Wrong Reverends"—a decorously solemn mood, and an accusatory tone. The passage is tightly if implicitly organized around its order of address, which in this case follows the political hierarchy of queen, parliament, church, and citizenry.

Addresses such as this do indeed violate the narrative surface of Dickens' novels and break the tacit understanding between author and reader inherent in fiction. Still, there are reasons to suppose that the novelist consciously and deliberately chose to abrogate his contract with his public at places like this. The claims of a higher reality outside the framework of this fiction may have prompted the author so to break in upon his narrative in order to indicate how events of his plot correspond to an external situation in the real world. What Dickens may be doing in such passages is purposefully altering his reader's relationship to the narrative by blurring the line between reality and its representation in fiction. If Jo's death scene appeared to Dickens in the guise of an hallucination with all the "coercive force of reality," he may have wished to use this means of projecting that extra-fictional reality to his audience. He may have wanted, in short, to make this point of tangency between two orders of reality impinge on his reader with the same intensity it had for him. Moreover, a technique like this profoundly alters the relationship between reader and writer. Now both stand together on terms quite different from those normally found between an anonymous author and his equally faceless audience, for a personal contact has been created quite outside the framework of the narrative.

Other kinds of authorial interruptions have the same general effect of altering the reader's relationship to the narrative and to the novelist. The apostrophe directed to one of the characters—or to the air, as it were—seems to owe its existence equally to Dickens' hallucinative method of creation, in which, for lack of a better term, the novelist appears to be as much a witness to events as the reader. When Jo the crossing sweeper appears at the gate of the wretched cemetery where his only friend, Nemo (né Captain Hawdon), lies buried, this passage occurs: "Jo, is it thou? Well, well! Though a rejected witness, who 'can't exactly say' what will be done to him in greater hands than man's, thou are not quite in outer darkness. There is something like a distant ray of light in thy muttered reason for this: 'He wos wery good to me, he wos'" (XXII, 172). Here again the characteristic features of Dickens' style in such passages are evident: the religious solemnity arising out of quasi-Biblical diction, rhetorical self-consciousness, and an informing structural principle in the word play on the legal and theological senses of "witness." But there is much more as well. In this case, Dickens stands forward himself as a witness of this brief episode and directs a *sotto-voce* apostrophe to the character, as if the novelist were a participant in the narrative by virtue of his position within this scene—presumably standing in the shadows near the cemetery gate, where he is surprised to see the urchin and to overhear his muttered words. The note of astonishment contained in the opening rhetorical question, together with its musing answer— "Jo, is it thou? Well, well!"—urge the reader to alter his perspective toward the narrative and to step within its framework, there to share a spectatorial position with the narrator that is peculiarly intimate and extra-fictional. Or to put the matter another way, author and reader come to occupy an audience-like standpoint from which to view together an affecting tableau arranged at one side of the stage, as it were, while a big scene is being struck in the darkness. A profound alteration in point of view —considered here in both the technical and general senses of that term—has been accomplished in this brief episode.

Dickens employs two other highly wrought rhetorical devices either borrowed from the playhouse or calculated to simulate theatrical or dramatic effects, the invocation and the oracular annunciation, both of which violate narrative credibility for the purpose of altering the reader's perspective toward the fictional surface, either by investing events with a quasi-religious grandeur or by engaging a dimension of mythic or supernatural order. The following invocation to night occurs near the end of the

episode in *Bleak House* which recounts the death and
burial of Nemo. I have taken the liberty of casting
the passage in loose blank verse lines:

Come night, come darkness, for you cannot come too soon,
Or stay too long, by such a place as this!
Come, straggling lights into the windows of the ugly houses;
And you who do iniquity therein,
Do it at least with this dread scene shut out!
Come, flame of gas, burning so sullenly above the iron gate,
On which the poisoned air deposits its witch ointment
Slimy to the touch! It is well that you
Should call to every passer-by, "Look here!"   (XXII, 172)

Such a blank-verse rhythm, together with the mannered rhetorical trappings of parallelism, repeated
imperatives, and elevated diction, give to this and
similar passages in Dickens' works a formal, incanta-
tory flavor reminiscent of Elizabethan drama. It
communicates a heavy solemnity of tone which is
clearly an instance of scene-setting designed to create
awe and horror of the place so depicted. The novelist
quite deliberately draws back the curtain to reveal
a scene of degradation and decay about which he
feels strongly; and within this invocation of the
elements are found both an apostrophe to the inhabitants of the nearby houses and a direct address
of the reader by the scene itself. The compact
between writer and reader that defines the reader's
attitude toward the truth-status of the narrative and
the kind and degree of relationship between himself
and the novelist is here broken in three different
ways; but all three are premised on the commanding
reality of the scene as it presents itself to the author's

imagination and on his sense of sharing with the reader the situation of a witness.

The oracular annunciation, on the other hand, although it generally shares with the invocation a tonal dignity and solemnity that is religious in feeling, differs from it by virtue of the fact that the prophetic utterance suggests the presence in the narrative of some divine, supernal, or at any rate superhuman power ordering events according to the "ways of Providence, of which all art is but a little imitation." In Dickens' hands the oracular announcement does not serve to evoke any suspense. Indeed, its aim is exactly opposite, for prophecy in these novels acts rather to assure the reader of the fulfillment of some anticipated eventuality and to urge him to read the intervening pages with the special point of view of one assured of a foregone conclusion. Nor was such a device a frivolous or merely novelistic matter for Dickens, to whom the "coincidences, resemblances, and surprises of life" were a simple fact of observation and gave evidence of this world's ultimate government by a darkly obscure providential hand working behind everyday events.

Dickens' conception of the relationship between external event and indwelling order is ordinarily illustrated by the example of *Bleak House,* in which two alternating narrative points of view share the burden of telling the story. In the first of these, that detached, omniscient, third-person point of view which opens the novel with its celebrated description of London's November mud and fog, the dominant present and progressive present tenses stress the undifferentiated and disorderly surfaces of things and events. Esther Summerson's first-person, deeply involved point of view in her portion of the narrative, written in the past tense from a position in time long after the events have transpired and their consequences known, rather implies a perspective which sees the order and justice immanent in human affairs, as evidenced by the novel's final revelation of the complex scheme of interrelationships which tie its characters together and by the rough sort of poetic justice that is dealt out to each of them. In short, the manipulation in point of view which marks *Bleak House's* narrative also embodies and expresses Dickens' own conclusions concerning the relationship between phenomena and meaning in real life.

Within this curious mode of conducting a narrative, moreover, Dickens was at some pains from time to time to introduce prophecy into his portion of the story. In a passage that provides a transition from the Dedlock family, moribund at their country seat, to the chief representative of the Dedlock's neglect, Jo, the crossing sweeper, there appears the following oracular announcement: "What connexion can there be, between the place in Lincolnshire, the house in town, the Mercury in powder, and the whereabout of Jo the outlaw with the broom, who had that distant ray of light upon him when he swept the churchyard-step? What connexion can there have been between many people in the innumerable histories of this world, who, from opposite sides of great gulfs, have, nevertheless, been very curiously brought together!" (XXII, 249). Making this connection between the two worlds of rich and poor, mansion and slum, the ruling classes and those abandoned by the ruling classes, is of course the main theme of the novel; and this transitional paragraph is thus a prefiguration of the whole. Indeed, the pages immediately following recount the visit to the place of

Nemo's burial of a mysterious woman, who, as it turns out, is Lady Dedlock. Her involvement with Nemo, or Captain Hawdon, is the cornerstone of all the subsequent events of the main plot of *Bleak House,* culminating in her death upon those same churchyard-steps and the extinction of the Dedlock family many chapters later. The passage in question occurs in Chapter XVI (the last chapter of the fifth monthly installment, for July, 1852), which marks the exact end of the first quarter of the narrative, during which Lady Dedlock's inexplicable interest in Nemo and dark connection to Esther Summerson have been strongly hinted at. This prophetic utterance, then, should not so much arouse suspense and mystery as confirm earlier implications and suggestions and by that token urge the reader to adjust his attitude toward forthcoming events accordingly. It asks the reader, in short, to unravel the web of interrelationships among the novel's personages knowing that their foreordained connections will be revealed and that all, high and low alike, will be found at last deeply involved in the fortunes of the others. Dickens' prophetic intervention in his part of the narrative is meant to make the events of the novel participate in a stream of tendency which the writer finds operative in the real world outside. It urges the reader to take up an attitude toward the novel which corresponds to that of the novelist himself toward life. In any case, it asks that the reader alter his perspective toward the fiction in a profound and fundamental way, so that he comes to look at events with a share of that omniscience enjoyed by the novelist.

The perhaps more usual form of prophecy in Dickens' works—that which anticipates the immediate death of a pathetic or villainous figure—confirms the conclusions drawn above. The death scene of Little Nell in *The Old Curiosity Shop,* of Paul Dombey and Carker in *Dombey and Son,* of Jo and Gridley in *Bleak House,* and a host of others, all contain some annunciation of this sort, designed not so much to create suspense or to milk the last drop of pathos as to confirm in an almost ritual manner an already existing belief of the reader, and by so doing to grant the episode a measure of religious solemnity. Ultimately, these announcements constitute a means of invoking superhuman inevitability within the narrative similar to that occasioned by the oracular passage from *Bleak House* quoted above. A certain supernal mechanism of fatality invests the episode with a power that seems independent of the author's control, with the result that he and the reader stand apart together as fellow witnesses of a meaningful consummation. At the same time their ties to theatrical practice are obvious, for they act much like the chord sounded at some pathetic or melodramatic moment by the orchestra in the pit of an early Victorian playhouse to signal, say, the last moments of the heroine as she sinks upon her death bed.

A particularly striking instance of this sort occurs near the end of *Dombey and Son,* when Carker flies from Dijon only to expire under the wheels of an onrushing locomotive. An entire chapter, the fifty-fifth, is given over to this episode, making of it a kind of set-piece; and the whole is devoted to chronicling the inevitability of his death, in spite of all Carker's efforts to evade that fate. The chapter is everywhere invested with mannered language and rhetoric designed to create an aura of awful religious dignity surrounding its horrific events. When the annunciation comes—"Death was on him. He was marked off from the living world, and going down into his grave" (XIX, 390)—it appears immediately before the terrible event of his death. It functions only to confirm ritually the presence of a sublime fatality directing Carker's last moments which the entire chapter has been at great pains to establish and define. But these earlier tokens existed only in the form of hallucinations, the result of Carker's disturbed psychological state; now, in Dickens' utterance, the reader is asked to understand that the manager's imminent demise has been ordered by the nature of things or by the "ways of Providence," and novelist and reader as it were stand aside to witness the fulfillment of some larger scheme.[1]

Quite aside from these narrative interventions, there remains in Dickens' work a large, undifferentiated body of materials which are theatrical or melodramatic in the very loosest sense of the term. A case in point is the confrontation scene between Carker and Edith Granger Dombey at a Dijon inn, where they had flown apparently to consummate their betrayal of Dombey in physical union. Edith Dombey has other plans, however, and she contemptuously brushes aside Carker's advances. The scene is described and the episode narrated as though they were staged in a playhouse. It opens with a patent tableau: "She was standing with her hand upon the velvet back of a great chair; her figure drawn up to its full height, and her face immoveable" (XIX, 366). When Carker moves toward her, "She caught up the knife from the table, and started one pace back. 'Stand still!' she said, 'or I shall murder you.' The sudden change in her, the towering fury and intense abhorrence sparkling in her eyes and lighting up her

brow, made him stop as if a fire had stopped him"
(XIX, 368). Frustrated in his immediate design,
Carker lapses into a pose of his own, and the two
figures form a tableau that Dickens appears to have
wanted them to hold throughout the ensuing tête-à-
tête, to judge at least by Hablôt Browne's illustration
(see frontispiece) :

Disdaining to reply, she stretched her arm out, pointing to the chair. He bit his lip, frowned, laughed, sat
down in it, with a baffled, irresolute, impatient air, he
was unable to conceal; and biting his nail nervously,
and looking at her sideways, with bitter discomfiture,
even while he feigned to be amused by her caprice.
She put the knife down upon the table, and touching
her bosom with her hand, said—
"I have something lying here that is no love trinket;
and sooner than endure your touch once more, I would
use it on you—and you know it, while I speak—with less
reluctance than I would on any other creeping thing
that lives."
He affected to laugh jestingly, and entreated her to act
her play out quickly, for the supper was growing cold.
But the secret look with which he regarded her, was
more sullen and lowering, and he struck his foot once
upon the floor with a muttered oath.
"How many times," said Edith, bending her darkest
glance upon him, "has your bold knavery assailed me
with outrage and insult? How many times in your
smooth manner, and mocking words and looks, have I
been twitted with my courtship and my marriage? How
many times have you laid bare my wound of love for
that sweet, injured girl. . . ." (XIX, 368-369)

And so on. Edith's speech, with its elaborate parallelism, rhetorical questions, elevated diction, and
heroic metaphors, carries as strong an odor of gas-
light and painted canvas as her stylized gestures and
the stagey blocking of the two figures. Any reader of

Dickens' works can name offhand a dozen comparable scenes, such as that melodramatic encounter in *Bleak House* between Esther Summerson and Lady Dedlock, or that in *Hard Times* between Mr. Gradgrind and his disgraced daughter, all with the same formal theatrical staging and the same highly wrought rhetoric.[2]

More to our purpose here, now that these generally dramatic, theatrical, and melodramatic aspects of Dickens' style and technique have been examined, is the isolation and analysis of those major stylistic strains which the novelist appropriated from the playhouse of his time and turned to the uses of serious prose fiction. In this connection it is well to remember two fundamental premises that underlie Dickens' deployment of theatrical style in the very different medium of prose: first, that his overriding intention was the profound readjustment of his readers' perspective toward the familiar, commonplace world around them, whether by serious or comic means, by melodrama, burlesque, or grotesquerie. We have already seen how variously the novelist asks his readers to realize the ways in which commonplace characters, scenes, and events participate in theatrical modes and forms, often in grotesquely incongruous ways. Latterly, I have sought to demonstrate the manner in which an adjustment in point of view—in the technical sense of that term—suggests a corresponding alteration in point of view—in the general sense of the term: that is, how Dickens' narrative interventions consciously rearrange the reader's relationship and attitude toward both the fiction and its author. Elsewhere, the novelist employed theatrical materials to suggest the discrepant, incoherent, and incongruous elements in the ordinary conventions and familiar objects, places, people, and events of life. But this desire to alter and estrange our vision of life does not have as its object any twentieth-century existential sense of the absurd. Rather, Dickens exploits the possibilities of absurdity—in the traditional sense of the word—in order to awaken and heighten his readers' view of the things and people around them, their liveliness, their comic and pathetic intensity, their hints of deeper ordering principles, and the like. And second, we must always remember that Dickens' prose style is an *accommodation* of the modes of the theater of his time to their novelistic projection in a manner equally in keeping with his essentially theatrical vision and the necessary conditions of prose fiction. The stylistic devices of farce, extravaganza, burlesque, pantomime, and melodrama undergo as great a sea-change when they are taken out of the playhouse and put down between the boards of a novel as do those folk archetypes which Dickens borrowed from the popular drama in *Dombey and Son* and *Great Expectations*. The latter technique was employed by the hack writers of theatrical burlesques; and a similar practice defines the genius of Dickens, though in a serious if not solemn way. Nevertheless, the inherent features of the originating theatrical style remain, even if they have been transmuted into the figurative and rhetorical organization of the novelist's prose style.

Keeping these premises in mind, then, one may discriminate between three principal theatrical modes or voices in the characteristic Dickensian manner, each of which corresponds to a strain of early Victorian dramatic practice, and each of which, in addition, has its typical area of employment in the larger scheme of the novelist's fiction. The first of these is the grotesque voice, ordinarily a descriptive mode, which is marked by a discrepant use of figurative language to render strange the familiar object-world by discordance and incongruity. The second is the burlesque voice, primarily a mode of characterization, which is defined by the ambivalence of its tone through the use of rootless burlesque for ends that elude the traditional comic and satiric categories. And the third is the melodramatic voice, a narrative mode, which seeks to adapt to prose fiction the musical, rhythmic, and "poetic" resources of the nineteenth-century theater.

Even thus early in our discussion of these voices, however, a word of caution is in order concerning the absoluteness of these categories; for each of them has a point at which it touches on or overlaps one or both of the other two. They are, after all, no more than aspects of a unified artistic sensibility; they do not comprise the whole of that sensibility nor did they, surely, exist as separate entities in Dickens' mind. I have said that the grotesque voice, for example, is mainly deployed in scenic description, where it may be identified by the presence of incongruous imagery to depict commonplace objects. In particular, grotesquerie takes the form of figurative transposition or juxtaposition of incompatible or discrepant realms, much in the manner of theatrical pantomime: the inanimate and animate, the bestial and the human, the familiar and the exotic. Or it may equally involve the intermixture of commonplace items drawn from two or more widely separated contexts, the fantastic proliferation of concrete realistic details far in excess of any descriptive necessity, together with a no less extravagant proliferation of fanciful imagery drawn from nursery rhymes, fairy tales, children's literature, legend, and folk mythology. All of these materials were, as we have seen, the stuff and tactic of early Victorian harlequinade, burlesque, and extravaganza.

On the other hand, Dickens' burlesque voice is a mode of characterization, and its features include the creation of an ambiguous comic tone that defies the categories of comedy, satire, irony, humor, parody, and the rest. Instead, it employs all of these categories indiscriminately in achieving a rootless burlesque effect all its own. This rootless burlesquerie depicts conventional, stereotypical, or eccentric human action in terms of discontinuity, incoherence, and capriciousness, plays upon indications of gross disproportion between manner and motive, and exploits the disturbing possibilities latent in the conventions of language, conduct, dress, and the like, particularly when incompatible contexts are brought together and deliberately confused. Central to the burlesque manner is the presence everywhere of parody that works upon a multitude of conventional and inflated styles of discourse. But this parody appears to have no clearly defined, immediate satiric purpose, or indeed any identifiable intention at all, save that of agitating the stylistic texture in such a way as to create in the reader a delightful unease, a disturbing but pleasurable sense of something vaguely out of joint.

It is nevertheless clear that the burlesque voice shares with its grotesque counterpart a studied confusion of realms by means of a systematic program of incongruous comparisons; and it will be found on close inspection that Dickens' grotesquerie is shot through with parody which serves no immediately present purpose. Moreover, the melodramatic voice, which includes all the pathetic, sentimental, and horrible materials as well as the blood-and-thunder of the nineteenth-century stage, is a no less impure mode. The most touching pathetic episodes in Dickens' novels are often riddled with grotesquerie or burlesque characterization, just as these latter modes frequently contend with melodramatic materials. The intermixture and juxtaposition of incompatible modes, in short, defines every level of Dickens' prose style in the same way that a similar incongruity characterizes the Victorian playbill. Furthermore, there is a special strain of dark grotesque that can be isolated in the novelist's melodramatic voice, a macabre mode that is somber and even horrifying, although it shares many stylistic features with his lighter grotesquerie.

Perhaps the element that links Dickens' grotesque, melodramatic, and burlesque voices together is their shared exploitation of the disquieting possibilities of the simile. In sophomore introduction-to-literature courses the simile is usually dismissed nowadays as merely the lowest form of imagery, at best a metaphor *manqué*. The reason for this small regard may lie in the simile's tentative equation between object and image, its reluctance as it were to propose the absolute identity of the two parts of the comparison, whereas metaphor, symbol, and archetype are thought to possess more poetic *virtu* in consequence of their more nearly total commitment to the formularies of the writer's imagination. In the simile, on the other hand, a timid and partial reordering of experience by the image-making faculty is offered: the object as object is not wholly absorbed into the figurative likeness. Instead, a limited resemblance is indicated between an object that retains its separate identity outside the comparison and a figure which has no more than a single dimension of likeness to the object. The existence of the bridging term serves to keep object and image apart on different levels of reference even while it connects them by nothing more than an isthmus of similitude.

In the hands of Dickens, whose perception of "relations in things not apparent generally" worked in his fiction to indicate the presence everywhere of discrepancy, incongruity, and incoherence, the modest simile was appropriated for the subversive purpose of creating burlesque and grotesque effects. To achieve his aim, Dickens had recourse to a special kind of manipulation. His similes are marked, first, by the deliberately wide discrepancy between the two orders of the comparison: as in the comic transformations of pantomime, context, realm, scale, and many other dimensions which form the terms of the similitude are extreme, though surprisingly apt. Second, the Dickensian simile enjoys the same proliferation accorded to concrete realistic details and their accompanying comparisons as that which characterized popular theatrical practice in scene and action: fantasy exists by virtue of quantity as well as quality. Third, Dickens positively insists on the tentativeness of his comparisons, on the disquieting partiality of his likenesses, by elaborating the middle terms that bridge object and image in the simile much as Grimaldi did visually with his hussar. Although he by no means dispenses with the usual "like" or "as" to link object and image, wherever possible he seems to prefer other, more extended terms and phrases

—"appeared to be," "had the appearance of," "reminded one of," "looked as if," "might almost have been," "seemed to have," "as if," and many more of the same kind.

The effects of this method of treating the simile, when the simile is the dominant kind of image, are twofold. First, this sort of simile insists on the strangeness of the familiar by stressing the external resemblance of one commonplace thing with another, quite incongruous thing, as if the ordinary world were being perceived for the first time by a total stranger, an alien, who has no grasp of the conventional identities or functions of things or types. The reader is implicitly required to adjust his perspective toward the familiar life around him: he must scrupulously adhere to external appearance, free his mind from customary associations and conventional identifications, and accept a mode of drawing extravagantly incongruous likenesses to commonplace things and people which ignores the coherence he assumes they have because he is accustomed to seeing them every day. He is asked, in short, to take up a spectatorial position toward "the pantomime of life" in which he is otherwise a "busy actor," and become instead a "passive looker-on," as though he were a member of an audience at a harlequinade or burlesque. Having by the form of the simile established the stranger's point of view toward conventional objects, scenes, types, and events, the novelist is then free to indicate the entertainingly lively incoherence of commonplace life by means of his fantastic proliferation of observed details and incongruous likenesses, a method which simulates the technique of pantomime and burlesque.

Second, the ambivalence of the figurative equation

established by the form of Dickens' similes further
estranges the world so described by refusing to commit the spectator unequivocally either to the reality
implied by proliferated concrete details or to the
fantasy suggested by equally proliferated fanciful
imagery. On the contrary, the commonplace object,
scene, or person and the discrepant thing it resembles
are held in parity; and discomfiture is achieved by
the novelist's bland, equable refusal to take a stand
on one side or the other of his comparisons. All
remains unfixed, tentative, prospective, much as in
pantomime and burlesque. The familiar object-
world is fully realized, documented and catalogued
so sharply and completely as to have a little of the
disturbing clarity of dreams; but interwoven with
these reassuringly recognizable features so thoroughly
as to be inextricable is the fantasy world of imagery
that the real world so uncomfortably but delightfully
resembles. In Dickens' similes these two worlds are
held together in a curious, tenuous, and unsettling
suspension.

It is thus in Dickens' imagery and rhetoric—and
particularly in the ambivalent simile—that the grotesque milieu of theatrical burlesque and pantomime
finds its fictional counterpart. Grimaldi's hussar,
with humble household objects incongruously yet
aptly supplying the place of a soldier's accoutrements,
and its incipient satire undercut by simple absurdity,
reappears in the novelist's habitual characterization
by typical but eccentric leitmotif, his rootless burlesque of convention in language, dress, and gesture,
and his deliberate improprieties between matter and
manner. The scenic transformations of pantomime,
comprising a joyous confusion of inanimate and

animate realms, of scale, function, shape, and context, find new life in Dickens' characteristic handling of the object-world outlined above. The subject matter of burlesque, extravaganza, and pantomime—the refurbishing of children's literature and folk mythology in a grotesquely anachronistic contemporary setting that encourages the exploitation of inappropriate parallel and variation—is brought over into Dickens' novels, not only as the framework for a realistic story, as we have already seen, but also to serve as textural materials of imagery. The antic, gestic modes of harlequinade, burlesque, and farce recur in the novelist's use of typicality, leitmotif, burlesquerie, parody, and incidental business. Even the rattling orchestra in the pit of a cheap melodrama playhouse has its counterpart in Dickens' employment of a host of rhythmic, musical, and poetic devices to define and heighten the dramatic atmosphere of episodes and, indeed, of entire works.

If the works of Dickens demonstrate that he was capable of appropriating the techniques of burlesque for the serious fictional purpose of engaging a realistic story in the universal dimensions of folk myth by imitating with variation and anachronism the action of a dramatic prototype, as we have seen he did in *Dombey and Son* and *Great Expectations,* it should come as no surprise to discover that his prose style is similarly premised on the devices of that same theater. Only with two provisos: first, that the machinery of the stage is transformed under the novelist's genius into the tools of prose fiction, into figurative language and rhetorical organization. And second, that everywhere his overriding strategy involves the alteration and readjustment of his reader's perspective toward the familiar life around him from that of blinding convention to one of illuminating detachment. His ultimate aim was to awaken his reader to the vital significance of his ordinary experience.

Chapter Eight
GROTESQUE SCENE

Dickens' grotesque voice, primarily a mode of scenic description derived from the transformations of early Victorian pantomime, shares with its theatrical prototype a world-distorting vision that suddenly, incongruously, yet convincingly transmutes commonplace objects and settings into quite dissimilar things, that juxtaposes realms, contexts, functions, scales, and shapes while yet indicating some arresting and unforeseen likeness, and that intermixes anachronistic materials without committing itself to wholehearted acceptance of either side of the equation. In particular the grotesque voice, like pantomime, deliberately confuses the human and material realms, the animate and the inanimate, the realistic and the fantastic; and it achieves this cheerful ambivalence by exploiting the equivocations of the simile within a framework of extravagantly proliferated concrete objects and verbal manipulation.

We may begin to see these techniques in operation in a typical scenic description of Mrs. Pipchin's establishment in *Dombey and Son,* where Paul and Florence are first sent to school:

The Castle of this ogress and child-queller was in a steep by-street at Brighton; where the soil was more than usually chalky, flinty, and sterile, and the houses were more than usually brittle and thin; where the small front-gardens had the unaccountable property of producing nothing but marigolds, whatever was sown in them; and where snails were constantly discovered holding on to the street doors, and other public places they were not expected to ornament, with the tenacity of cupping-glasses. In the winter time the air couldn't be got out of the Castle, and in the summer time it couldn't be got in. There was such a continual reverberation of wind in it, that it sounded like a great shell, which the inhabitants were obliged to hold to their ears night and day, whether they liked it or no. It was not, naturally, a fresh-smelling house; and in the window of the front-parlour, which was never opened, Mrs. Pipchin kept a collection of plants in pots, which imparted an earthy flavour of their own to the establishment. However choice examples of their kind, too, these plants were of a kind peculiarly adapted to the embowerment of Mrs. Pipchin. There were half a dozen specimens of the cactus, writhing round bits of lath, like hairy serpents; another specimen shooting out broad claws, like a green lobster; several creeping vegetables, possessed of sticky and adhesive leaves; and one uncomfortable flower-pot hanging to the ceiling, which appeared to have boiled over, and tickling people underneath with its long green ends, reminded them of spiders—in which Mrs. Pipchin's dwelling was uncommonly prolific, though perhaps it challenged competition still more proudly, in the season, in the point of earwigs. (XVIII, 115-116)

The originating idea of this passage resides in a preceding paragraph, in which Mrs. Pipchin is described as a "marvelous ill-favoured, ill-conditioned old lady, of a stooping figure, with a mottled face, like bad marble, a hook nose, and a hard grey eye"; in short, an ogress (XVIII, 115). Really resembling an ogress, then, Mrs. Pipchin becomes one in Dickens' imaginative conception; and her house in Brighton is made to accord with this conception by means of fanciful imagery that likens it to a castle. Throughout the remainder of this chapter, moreover, the same likeness is employed to describe the regimen that the formidable old lady imposes on her charges.

One might expect that the passage in question would be entirely and overtly given over to drawing the parallel between Mrs. Pipchin's house and the castle of an ogress, but that is not the case. On the contrary, the term "castle" is mentioned but twice, both times early in the paragraph. Dickens' intention seems to have been more subtle. He wished, apparently, to suggest the likeness between the brittle, drafty house on its dry, sterile site and the typical features of an ogress' castle in fairy story, without at the same time sacrificing a realistically detailed description of the house as it is. The effect of this ambivalence is to keep both orders of reference—the realistic and the fanciful—equally before the reader, who is expected to visualize the scene in all its concrete particularity while being amused by the ingenious propriety of its likenesses to a fanciful thing. The house and site are typical of Brighton, and the plants in the window are just the sort a woman such as Mrs. Pipchin would choose; and for the castle of an ogress it is altogether appropriate to find blighted soil, drafty rooms, snails, spiders, earwigs, and cacti that resemble hairy snakes and green lobsters.

The natural repugnance aroused by such details is modified not only by the fanciful imagery but also by Dickens' extraordinarily precise vision and happily apt choice of descriptive terms. He has an almost Flaubertian facility to hit upon *le mot juste*: "brittle and thin" houses, "creeping vegetables," "writhing cactus," and "uncomfortable flower-pot," for example. While such linguistic brilliance vividly sets the scene, its very adroitness calls the reader's attention away from the abhorrent things described. Then again, the scene is everywhere infected with Dickens' exuberant hyperbole, which further helps to make the repugnant tolerable if not amusing. Nothing in this passage observes normal limitations: the soil is "more than usually" poor; the houses "more than usually" jerry-built; the front gardens have the *"unaccountable* property of producing *nothing but* marigolds," snails are *"constantly* discovered" holding on to street doors "with the tenacity of cupping-glasses"; and the house is *"uncommonly* prolific" in spiders and earwigs. The reader looks through eyes that see everything, and see more brilliantly and intensely, than his own would normally do, as if the object-world were that portrayed by a scenic designer for a pantomime theater—multiplied, enlarged, brightened, exaggerated, and schematized.

At the same time, the terms that Dickens employs to link the object-world's proliferated details with their defining images imply the presence of a bemused spectator who perceives the scene in all its rich particularity but, seemingly, is unable to account for its self-evident phenomena on the basis of prior experience of the relative significance of things. The commonplace is heightened; but it is at the same time made to seem strangely unique, much as it is when subjected to the transformations of pantomime. Thus, the "small front-gardens had the *unaccountable property* of producing nothing but marigolds, *whatever* was sown in them," and snails "were constantly *discovered* holding on to the street doors, and other public places *they were not expected to ornament*." And again, the "uncomfortable flower-pot . . . *appeared* to have boiled over, and tickling *people underneath* with its long green ends, *reminded them* of spiders." Even when the usual form of the simile is retained, its comparison is both extreme and exotic and maintains a tacit spectatorial perspective. "There was such a continual reverberation of wind" in the house, for example, "that it sounded like a great shell, which the inhabitants were obliged to hold to their ears night and day, whether they liked it or no."

In this latter connection another feature of the Dickensian image emerges, the tendency he shares with the pantomime clown or designer to extend an incongruous or fanciful likeness to extravagant lengths, far beyond any practical need dictated by context alone, as if for its own grotesque sake. In the instance above, another writer might have been content to liken the drafty house to a great, echoing conch shell and let the matter drop. But Dickens' method requires exhausting the grotesque possibilities of an unlikely similitude, working out the details of the incongruous comparison to their last jot with a kind of mad, compulsive logic reminiscent of the attitudes of pantomime personnel toward their transformation scenes. Thus, here, the windy house is not only like a shell; but it is also a shell that must always be held to the ear, and further, whether one like it or not. Style itself takes on its own independent measure of grotesque disproportion to the subject at hand. In a similar vein, Mrs. Pipchin's potted plants are likened extravagantly and in surely excessive detail to a host of incongruous things, to "hairy serpents," "creeping vegetables," "green lobsters," and to a pot boiling over—just the sort of grotesque inventions that would have appealed to Grimaldi.

In spite of this extravagance, Dickens handles his similes so that the object-world is not obscured but rather held in uneasy parity with its embodying fantasy. As in the transformations of pantomime, where realms are transposed in the twinkling of an eye but are always linked by some striking visual aptitude, the novelist maintains a decorous propriety of his own in drawing remote similitudes. However widely separated the realms connected by the simile may be, there is always a surprising but convincing justness about them which makes the reader wonder upon reflection why he had not noticed the similarity before. If, for example, a cactus *writhes* about a bit of lath in such a way as to resemble a *hairy serpent,* and a hanging vine reminds one simultaneously of a pot boiling over and of spiders, these likenesses carry the reader's conviction along with them, in spite of their remoteness, if only because they are drawn from familiar life, for the most part. Where they depart from experience, as in the wholly unnatural invention of "hairy serpents," they remain highly descriptive of the object so described. Then, too, such gratuitous realistic details as the "bit of lath" serve to keep actuality firmly in place. As in pantomime transformations, the audience addressed by Dickens is asked to perceive the object and the thing it grotesquely resembles with equal clarity and force; indeed, it is in this very ambivalence that grotesquerie has its life, whether in the pages of a novel or in a Victorian playhouse.

Moreover, the implicit spectatorial perspective of this description insures the equivalence of realism and fantasy, especially since the point of view implied by the form of the similes is ratified by the governing organization of this passage according to the movements of a "camera eye" that supposes a hypothetical spectator. He approaches "up a steep by-street," perceives the barren front gardens, the brittle houses, the snails, enters the drafty house, proceeds to the front-parlor, and concludes by standing underneath the hanging flower-pot. In this manner the reader is brought inside the scene, as it were, from which position the particulars are observed in an order comparable to that of a visitor.

Another feature of Dickens' grotesque style—one more typical of the burlesque voice—may be briefly noticed in this passage: a vaguely parodic tone. This play with the stylistic surface makes use of satiric devices without any clearly definable satiric intention, much in the manner of the comic modes peculiar to theatrical burlesque. Here as in the theater this running parody seems to have no other purpose than that of adding a playfully exuberant quality to the passage. Behind the prevailing likeness of Mrs. Pipchin's establishment to the "embowerment" of an ogress there lies a light-hearted burlesque of the features commonly associated in children's literature with such a place. Beyond all this is the last sentence of the passage, which indicates that, although Mrs. Pipchin's house is "uncommonly prolific" in spiders, "perhaps it challenged competition still more proudly, in the season, in the point of earwigs." No function

germane to the description is served by this mocking-
ly inflated form of words. Indeed, the lofty and
elaborate diction and syntax are grossly out of keeping with their contemptible subject matter. In this
arch way another dimension of incongruity is introduced into the description that, however slightly,
further disconcerts the reader's attitude toward scene.

This description of Mrs. Pipchin's house in
Brighton is a comparatively modest instance of Dickens' grotesquerie, but it illustrates many of the main
features of this voice. As in its dramatic prototypes,
whose controlling intention was an entertaining intermixture of realism and fantasy through the scenic
transformations that bridged widely dissimilar realms,
contexts, and scales with striking visual aptness and
through the interpenetration of the animate and inanimate, human and non-human realms, so too in
Dickens' grotesque voice scenic description is made to
serve the pleasures of anachronism by keeping in
parity the elements of realism and fantasy. The
vehicle for achieving this unsettling equivalence is
the form of the Dickensian simile with its elaborately
extended bridging terms. Often, as in pantomime and
burlesque, the basis of the grotesque lies in the use
of legendary or folklore materials to describe the commonplace scene; but more particularly the grotesque
voice is found locally in the wide discrepancy between
the realms drawn upon to link image and object and
in the peculiar proliferation to which each side of the
larger comparison is subjected. This, together with
the habitual animizing and humanizing of the physical environment occupied by Dickens' characters,
defines the relationship of the grotesque voice to the
early Victorian world of pantomime and burlesque.

To call this technique pathetic fallacy, with all its sentimental overtones, is to miss the peculiar quality of Dickens' scenic descriptions by a wide margin; for in his novels the object-world is a projection of the moral environment inhabited by his characters and as such is full of curiosity and interest.

The justly renowned opening description of November weather that serves as an overture to *Bleak House* may put this matter in clearer perspective.[1] In essence it is an elaborate expansion of the methods already isolated: naturalistic materials of setting—fog that obscures vision and mud that simultaneously clogs the way and makes footing treacherous—are made to serve a number of atmospheric and figurative purposes for the remainder of the novel. By means of extravagant parallelism and repetition, mud and fog are shown penetrating to every corner of England, often in terms of vividly grotesque images: flakes of soot as big as full-grown snowflakes, "gone into mourning, one might imagine, for the death of the sun" (XXII, 1); and people on bridges with fog all around them, "as if they were up in a balloon, and hanging in the misty clouds" (XXII, 2). The shops have been lighted two hours early, "as the gas seems to know, for it has a haggard and unwilling look" (XXII, 2). There is as much mud in the streets, indeed, "as if the waters had but newly retired from the face of the earth, and it would not be wonderful to meet a Magalosaurus, forty feet long or so, waddling like an elephantine lizard up Holborn Hill" (XXII, 1). Altogether, these heaped-up realistic details and fanciful imagery—not omitting pathetic fallacy—derived from the Biblical account of the Deluge and from scientific reconstructions of the primordial past combine to suggest, in Morton Dauwen Zabel's words, "frustrations that cast humanity back into the darkest abysses of ancient blindness and primitive futility."[2]

This extravagant likeness is made operative in the rest of the novel by an explicit connection between mud and fog and the obsolescent obscurantism of the High Court of Chancery, "mistily engaged in one of ten thousand stages of an endless cause, tripping one another up on slippery precedents, groping knee-deep in technicalities, running their goat-hair and horse-hair warded heads against walls of words, and making a pretence of equity with serious faces, as players might" (XXII, 2-3). But Chancery is only the creature of the aristocracy represented by the Dedlock family, a moribund contemporary institution also defined by imagery reminiscent of the remote geological past and the Deluge. The equation between mud and fog and Chancery is drawn in the first chapter, while that of the Dedlock family occupies the whole of the second: altogether, they comprise some sixteen full pages in my edition. The two chapters develop an extended and complex likeness between certain features of setting and political, social, and moral inadequacies which govern the mood and metaphorical structure of the remainder of the novel.

Yet the key to this elaborate superstructure rests in a simile that refuses to commit itself either to its naturalistic or figurative dimensions of meaning: "Never can there come fog too thick, never can there come mud and mire too deep, to assort with the groping and floundering condition which this High Court of Chancery, most pestilent of hoary sinners, holds, this day, in the sight of heaven and earth" (XXII, 2). A single, if many-faceted, similitude has been drawn between the mud and fog, simultaneously if contradictorily remindful of the Biblical and geological accounts of the primordial past and of the "dead hand of the past" embodied in Chancery and the aristocracy. Involved in this extravagant likeness are a host of incongruous ideas which are exploited later in the novel through a richly orchestrated system of analogies between obsolescence and divine judgment, extinction and damnation, pestilence and irresponsibility, and death by fire and water, together with the suggestion of a world suspended between two apocalyptic events. Refusal to change with the times is shown as contrary both to the natural order and to Divine Providence, and the idea of total innate depravity is equated with the view that inherited institutions are sufficient unto the day. This catalogue of analogies might be extended indefinitely, only to arrive at the same conclusion: the initial scenic description that quite literally raises the curtain on *Bleak House,* much in the manner of a pantomime, is both grotesquely proliferate in its original depiction of atmosphere and in its figurative elaboration throughout the body of the novel. But in the final analysis it is in no significant way different from the description of Mrs. Pipchin's establishment, in which an extravagantly detailed scenic conception becomes the vehicle for an equally extended comparison. Textural imagery is incongruous in its own right, and the larger similitude drawn across the first two chapters is no less fancifully elaborated than the proliferate analogies mined from it in later chapters.

An equally famous, if briefer, description of the bedroom furniture in a cheap overnight lodging-house in *Great Expectations* reveals a similar conception and technique: "It was a sort of vault on the ground floor at the back, with a despotic monster of a four-post bedstead in it, straddling over the whole place, putting one of its arbitrary legs into the fire-place, and another into the doorway, and squeezing the wretched little washing-stand in quite a Divinely Righteous manner" (XXIX, 392). Here a patently grotesque effect is achieved with Dickens' customary— by now—devices. As in the description of Mrs. Pip-chin's establishment, realistic details of setting take on the moral qualities of their defining imagery in order to demonstrate how scene reflects the character of its inhabitants or of its enrounding society. The description of Temple Bar at the beginning of *Bleak House* is really no more than a projection into the object-world of the moral qualities of the moribund institutions located there. In this depiction of a room at Hummum's, one identifies the proliferation of physical detail within a short space together with a prevalent hyperbole. Above all, the passage is organized around the pathetic fallacy of investing the bedstead with the sanctimonious despotism of a religious who is incongruously engaged in persecuting a wash-stand. The ruling conception behind this pas-sage is, as in pantomime, the mixture of animate and inanimate realms.

It does not necessarily follow, however, that this technique argues Dickens' existential estrangement before the vision of a dehumanized humanity and a sinister life in things.[3] Rather, the grotesque anima-tion granted to the furnishings in this passage has a certain fanciful propriety to one of the major themes of *Great Expectations:* the sort of complacent and superior moral oppression of the defenseless which Mrs. Joe, Pumblechook, Mr. and Mrs. Hubble, and Mr. Wopsle visit upon Joe and the young Pip, and which Pip himself, when he once comes into his "expectations," employs in turn against his old friends, Joe and Biddy. "Divinely Righteous" oppression of the weak and vulnerable, like that of the four-post bedstead toward the wretched little washing-stand, is the besetting sin of the human world of *Great Expectations*; now it reappears at a decisive moment in the plot of the novel, infecting the object-world. In Dickens' novels, as in pantomime and burlesque, the animate and inanimate realms, society and scene, people and their things, are all of a piece, are all interdependent parts of a larger living fabric. The physical setting in Dickens' works from the time of *Sketches by Boz* is touched and enlivened everywhere by the implied presence of some associated humanity, however grotesque or even terrifying that life may be; but the novelist's scenic descriptions do not suggest any usurpation of human life. Rather, scene in Dickens' works involves the extension of human vitality throughout the whole texture of things, just as, in theatrical pantomime, setting and character interpenetrate each other for ends entirely frivolous. Far from suggesting any dehumanization of people by urban industrialism, Dickens' handling of setting indicates that, to him, nothing among the works of man is without some tincture of his moral being.

Elsewhere, Dickens' grotesquerie demonstrates similar techniques and similar objectives, often in curiously unexpected places. The description of Miss Havisham's deserted mansion in *Great Expectations,* for example, is a *locus classicus* of Dickens' grotesque mode, especially in light of the fact that the scene is viewed through the eyes of a young and inexperienced country boy, Pip. The scene is depicted in the following manner:

I crossed the staircase landing, and entered the room she indicated. From that room, too, the daylight was completely excluded, and it had an airless smell that was oppressive. A fire had been lately kindled in the damp old-fashioned grate, and it was more disposed to go out than to burn up, and the reluctant smoke which hung in the room seemed colder than the clearer air—like our own marsh mist. Certain wintry branches of candles on the high chimneypiece faintly lighted the chamber; or, it would be more expressive to say, faintly troubled its darkness. It was spacious, and I dare say had once been handsome, but every discernible thing in it was covered with dust and mould, and dropping to pieces. The most prominent object was a long table with a table cloth spread on it, as if a feast had been in preparation when the house and the clocks had all stopped together. An épergne or centre-piece of some kind was in the middle of this cloth; it was so heavily overhung with cobwebs that its form was quite undistinguishable; and, as I looked along the yellow expanse out of which I remember its seeming to grow, like a black fungus, I saw speckled-legged spiders with blotchy bodies running home to it, and running out from it, as if some circumstance of the greatest public importance had just transpired in the spider community.

I heard the mice too, rattling behind the panels, as if the same occurrence were important to their interests. But, the blackbeetles took no notice of the agitation, and groped about the hearth in a ponderous elderly way, as if they were short-sighted and hard of hearing, and not on terms with one another. (XXIX, 89)

A distinction between grotesque subject matter and grotesque style appears to be in order at this point. Clearly, the setting of Miss Havisham's room is grotesque in its own right, whereas Mrs. Pipchin's establishment is made to appear so by virtue of Dickens' handling of figurative comparison. In the passage immediately above, however, little need be done to achieve a grotesque effect, since the materials are themselves weird and incongruous: a dark, dank, airless room in which nothing has been touched since Miss Havisham was abandoned at the altar, and everything covered with dust and mold and falling into rot.

But this passage also reveals a grotesque dimension of style that is separate from though it augments the grotesquerie of its subject matter. One may identify this grotesque style in several devices: loose verbal play quite out of keeping with the strangeness of the setting, an incongruous pathetic fallacy applied to the more repugnant features of the scene, and a strain of curiously apt descriptive terms. Of these latter perhaps the most telling phrase—"certain wintry branches of candles" which "faintly troubled" the darkness of the chamber—strikingly underlines the grotesque quality of the scene with a single, vividly realized detail. To this must be added that quite unrealistic microscopic sharpness of vision which enables Dickens to remark the "speckled-legged spiders with blotchy bodies" who run in and out of the "fungus-like" epergne, the mice "rattling behind the panels," and "blackbeetles groping about the hearth."

Against these devices calculated to emphasize the abhorrent strangeness of the setting, there is a strain of incidental stylistic play in the manner of theatrical burlesque which somehow makes the disgusting seem tolerable, if not amusing. The new fire in an old grate "was more disposed to go out than to burn up," for example. But this device usually joins with pathetic fallacy for the same ends. Thus the fire is *"disposed* to go out," its smoke is *"reluctant,"* the epergne "seemed to *grow,* like a black fungus," out of the yellow expanse of the tablecloth, and the horrible spiders run in and out of the center piece "as if some circumstance of the greatest public importance had just

transpired in the spider community." The decided
ambivalence of the similes in this passage is ratified
by Dickens' apparent effort, first, to stress abhorrent
qualities of the spiders' speckled legs and "blotchy
bodies," and then, immediately thereafter, to render
them innocuous by means of fanciful pathetic fallacy.
This simile-cum-pathetic fallacy is made even more
ambiguous in tone by a pervasive hyperbole, by a
faint breath of rootless burlesque in the inappropriately inflated tritenesses, and by the extravagant
elaboration of the figure so as to include the mice and
blackbeetles in its formulary. And the blackbeetles
are subjected to a wholly gratuitous redundancy:
they grope about on the hearth "in a ponderous
elderly way, as if they were short-sighted and hard
of hearing, and not on terms with one another."
Grotesque materials are subverted, so to speak, by
another, lighter dimension of grotesquerie, through
inappropriate comparisons, pathetic fallacy, and an
incommensurate burlesque.

Another passage, this time from *Dombey and Son,*
demonstrates Dickens' exuberant grotesquerie at its
full maturity in the description of a scene similar
to those in "Meditations in Monmouth Street" and
"Brokers' and Marine-Store Shops" of *Sketches by
Boz.* But now the novelist's skill at mixing animate
and inanimate realms as in theatrical pantomime has
achieved sophistication and subtlety:

> There lived in those days, round the corner—in Bishop-
> gate Street Without—one Brogley, sworn broker and
> appraiser, who kept a shop where every description of
> second-hand furniture was exhibited in the most uncom-
> fortable aspect, and under circumstances and in com-
> binations the most completely foreign to its purpose.
> Dozens of chairs hooked on to washing-stands, which

with difficulty poised themselves on the shoulders of sideboards, which in their turn stood upon the wrong side
of dining-tables, gymnastic with their legs upward on the
tops of other dining-tables, were among its most reasonable arrangements. A banquet array of dish-covers, wine-
glasses, and decanters was generally to be seen, spread
forth upon the bosom of a four-post bedstead, for the
entertainment of such genial company as half a dozen
pokers, and a hall lamp. A set of window curtains with
no windows belonging to them, could be seen gracefully
draping a barricade of chests of drawers, loaded with little
jars from chemists' shops; while a homeless hearthrug
severed from its natural companion the fireside, braved
the shrewd east wind in its adversity, and trembled in
melancholy accord with the shrill complainings of a cabinet piano, wasting away, a string a day, and faintly
resounding to the noises of the street in its jangling and
distracted brain. Of motionless clocks that never stirred
a finger, and seemed as incapable of being successfully
wound up, as the pecuniary affairs of their former owners,
there was always great choice in Mr. Brogley's shop; and
various looking-glasses, accidentally placed at compound
interest of reflection and refraction, presented to the eye
an eternal perspective of bankruptcy and ruin.

(XVIII, 133)

Here, as so often in *Sketches by Boz* and theatrical
pantomime, scene is permeated by an organic dyna-
mism and associated human life and motive; but in
Dickens' mature hands these materials are sublimated
into certain tacit figurative assumptions which underlie the organization of the imagery. All the characteristic features of the theatrically oriented grotesque voice are present. Precisely observed and
proliferate realistic details (altogether at least sixteen
different objects are named) contend with a pervasive
hyperbole ("every," "most uncomfortable," "most
completely foreign," "eternal perspective," for example) ; and a strongly implied spectatorial position

coexists with an elaborate verbal mannerism in diction and syntax.

Several features are worthy of more particular notice. To use George Orwell's excellent phrase, one detects in this passage the presence of the "unnecessary detail," together with a certain near-redundancy, that fits in well with the superlatives. This gratuitous exactitude, such as the earlier references to minute descriptive details of Miss Havisham's house, finds expression here in such purposeless precision as "cabinet" piano, little jars "from chemists' shops," and "four-post" bedstead. "Near-redundancy" is a singular device all its own and consists in using two or more terms where one would do as well, as if in token of a kind of exuberant stylistic filigree work. This lily-gilding may be found in the phrase, "under circumstances and in combinations," in "jangling and distracted" brain, and in compound interest of "reflection and refraction," which illustrates an extravagant state of "bankruptcy and ruin." Such constructions add greatly to the impression of crowdedness and liveliness that Dickens' scenic descriptions communicate: they keep his narrative surface "busy" in the theatrical sense of that term.

An equally gratuitous word play found here also typifies the Dickensian handling of scene, as in the case of the motionless clocks that "seemed as incapable of being successfully wound up, as the pecuniary affairs of their former owners," which plays upon two different senses of "wound up." A fondness for punning—an inescapable feature of the Victorian sensibility—is peculiarly appropriate to Dickens' scenic descriptions, where discrepant likenesses, similarities, and congruities are the rule: punning supplies this on a purely stylistic level and for no relevant purpose save that of vivacity.

The passage in question also reveals with special clarity that directionless parody which so often invades Dickens' grotesquerie, even though it is more definitively a part of his burlesque mode. It appears in that vaguely derisive note sounded by the introduction of a banal and indecorous grand style to describe humble and commonplace objects. In this case, we encounter a "homeless hearthrug severed from its natural companion the fireside," which "braved the shrewd east wind in its adversity, and trembled in melancholy accord with the shrill complainings" of a cabinet piano's "jangling and distracted brain." For lack of any better term culled from a rhetorical dictionary, this device might be dubbed "irrelevant parody" or "rootless burlesque." But it is neither irrelevant nor rootless, through it employs satire for unsatiric ends, for this deployment of language makes the utterly commonplace and vulgar seem amusing by virtue of the impropriety of the grandiose clichés that describe it. Banality is thus consciously employed to reorganize the reader's view of the familiar object-world.

At the same time, Dickens deliberately exploits awkwardness in syntax to achieve certain desired effects. The second sentence in the quoted passage is a pointed instance: "Dozens of chairs hooked on to washing-stands, which with difficulty poised themselves on the shoulders of sideboards, which in their turn stood upon the wrong side of dining-tables, gymnastic with their legs upwards on the tops of other dining-tables." Admittedly an awkward sentence; but it appears to have been made so in order to embody the essential qualities of its subject matter. The angular succession of "which . . ." clauses, each dependent from the last term of the previous clause, very well reproduces in syntactical organization the awkward and unstable jumble of furniture in Brogley's window that it was created to describe. The reader's attention is led further away from the first element with each succeeding clause until the final predicate—"were among its most reasonable arrangements"—makes its belated appearance. A consciously topheavy and wayward syntax, then, appropriately recreates the disorder and instability it seeks to describe; rhetorical structure embodies the structure of the objects it depicts.

The transposition of animate and inanimate realms, so prominent a feature of this passage through its extended pathetic fallacy, has a tacit principle of organization that is typical of Dickens' grotesquerie as of that of the early Victorian theater. In this case, imagery drawn from the animate realm endows the scene in Brogley's shop with the attributes—indeed, with an abbreviated life-history—of its former owners. The progression of pathetic fallacy traces the stages in the downfall of a man in financial difficulties. The second sentence suggests the growing imbalance of a tottering, makeshift structure of debt; the third implies luxury brought low; the fourth erects a barricade—presumably to keep out process-servers—and then proceeds through a succession of disasters: orphanage, dispossession, physical suffering, fear, melancholy, complaint, and final insanity. The concluding sentence deals with decay, futility, passive disuse, and the hopelessness of a bleak perspective of ever-deepening ruin. Characteristically, a single, simple, dramatic conception—the scene's mute testimony

to the lives of ruined men—organizes and gives
coherence to proliferated concrete objects and fanciful imagery. A number of subsidiary grotesqueries
support this presiding incongruity, as we have already
seen. The total effect of these several discrepancies is
a multiple elusiveness of tone. Matter is grotesque
in and of itself, as in the dishes piled atop a bed; and
this suggests a figurative grotesquerie in which the
objects indicate a likeness to a banquet spread for
some pokers and a hall lamp. Or the accidental—we
may suppose—conjunction of a hearthrug and its
modifier, "homeless," embarks the novelist on an
extended figurative *jeu d'esprit* that would have
warmed the heart of John Rich.

A close look at the concluding metaphor, in which
the looking-glasses are "accidentally placed at compound interest of reflection and refraction" and so
present "an eternal perspective of bankruptcy and
ruin," is in order at this point. This is an exceed-
ingly complex and many-faceted metaphor, apparently
based on a pun on at least two contrary senses of
"wound up": to set going and to conclude. But
another pun—this time on "placed"—intervenes to
complicate and extend the comparison. The point
is, of course, that the affairs of a bankrupt under
Victorian conditions were not concluded with his
bankruptcy but continued long after, putting him
deeper in debt even while he became increasingly
less capable of paying his debts, so long as his notes
continued to circulate among the discounting trade.
At the center of this metaphor is a calculated anachronism. The opposing mirrors present an "eternal"
perspective of debt, although eternality or perpetuity
is impossible in matters visual. For them, "infinite"
is the correct word. But the temporal overtones of

"eternal" interject human associations appropriate to the metaphor of a bankrupt which would not be engaged by the purely spatial connotations of "infinite." The precise effect of this relatively sophisticated stylistic management is to carry the confusion of animate and inanimate realms to the last jot. It is Dickens' practice to do this at every turn: by so doing he makes his interpenetration of discrepant referential orders strike with telling effect throughout the entire fabric of his descriptions.

Elsewhere Dickens' scenic descriptions employ other kinds of fanciful imagery to define realistic settings, chief of which is that characteristic use of materials drawn from fairy tales, children's literature, legend, and folk mythology, much in the manner of Victorian pantomime, burlesque, and extravaganza. In the sixth chapter of this study we saw how Dickens appropriated theatrical folklore materials in the structure and themes of *Dombey and Son* and *Great Expectations,* thereby invoking universal mythic patterns of action and character relationships with which to play an ironic game of parallel and variation. And in the discussion of the passage describing Mrs. Pipchin's house it has been shown how the enumeration of realistic details was governed by a fanciful similarity of the setting to the castle of an ogress. The same techniques are to be found extravagantly extended in those descriptive set-pieces of which Dickens appears to have been so fond, as in the three-page evocation of the lonely life led by Florence Dombey in her father's deserted mansion. Although the entire passage is far too long to quote here, some sense of its grotesque extravagance in working out the detailed parallels between the great empty house and a "magic dwelling-place in magic story, shut up in the heart of a thick wood," where the "king's fair daughter" lives, may be gained by citing a typical paragraph, the second:

There were not two dragon sentries keeping ward before the gate of this abode, as in magic legend are usually found on duty over the wronged innocence imprisoned; but besides a glowering visage, with its thin lips parted wickedly, that surveyed all comers from above the archway of the door, there was a monstrous fantasy of rusty iron, curling and twisting like a petrifaction of an arbour over the threshold, budding in spikes and corkscrew points, and bearing, one on either side, two ominous extinguishers, that seemed to say, "Who enter here, leave light behind!" There were no talismanic characters engraven on the portal, but the house was now so neglected in appearance, that boys chalked the railings and the pavement . . . and drew ghosts on the stable door. . . .

(XVIII, 365)

For all its fanciful imagery, reality and fantasy are here kept in that disconcerting balance typical of theatrical practice by means of ambivalent likenesses linking disproportionate things: "dragon sentries" and gargoyles, a wrought-iron lantern and an impenetrable thicket, "talismanic characters" and chalked ghosts, and, in later paragraphs, innumerable other likenesses. The special character of the comparisons is worthy of notice, for Dickens refuses to admit any absolute equation between fact and fancy, preferring instead to draw a parallel construction, "There were no . . . but there was . . . ," as if he wished equally to indicate the limits of the similitudes he drew and to stress their aptness to the quality of the scene. If, for example, there are no dragon sentries at the gate, there is a hideous gargoyle over the door. There is, further, a wrought-iron lighting fixture nearby that is subjected to its own fanciful imagery: it becomes a grotesque iron plant "like the petrifaction of an arbour," "budding in spikes and corkscrew points."

The same procedure is followed throughout subsequent paragraphs, thereby integrating with elaboration what is at bottom a single, simple likeness. The two sides of the comparison, however different their realms may be, have a certain propriety nevertheless, for they embody in scenic description the way a young girl such as Florence might very well view her situation: fairy-tale imagery infects physical setting with the forms of the human imagination which inhabits it. In another and a different way, then, scenic description becomes a mode of embodying and expressing an associated humanity. This is a far cry from the simple transposition of realms that occurs in theatrical pantomime when a property suddenly reveals the clown inhabiting it, or when grotesque transformations of character and setting are signaled by a wave of Harlequin's magic wand. But the underlying sense of an object-world pregnant with informing human life and motive in Dickens' novels is similar in spirit if not in intention to the liveliness and ease engendered by surprising, incongruous, but apt scenic revolutions of the popular theater.

Dickens' exploitation of a scrupulously ambiguous figurative methodology maintains the truth-status of both the concrete particulars of physical setting and their fanciful likeness to incongruous things drawn from familiar but unlikely realms. In this practice he was but following the lead of English comic mimes since the days of *commedia dell' arte,* who had been accustomed to taking advantage of the visual similarities between inappropriate things as the springboard for some extravagant comic sequence. At the same time, Dickens' insistence on the bridging terms of his similes implies a spectatorial position within but not of the commonplace world, rather like that of an audience at a pantomime, so that the "categorical determinations of the relative significance of its parts" are gaily estranged. With an attention to hyperbole and proliferation in his description of setting that approximates the gas-lighted, antic, and stylized theater he knew, Dickens' figurative manipulation that balances but refuses to reconcile discordant but not opposite qualities—to trifle with Coleridge's formulary—manages to imbue scene with a grotesque life in part supplied by the novelist's own theatrical vision and in part a projection of the personages who inhabit it. Capitalizing on the interpenetration of scene and setting with the manic life of pantomime clowns and burlesque comedians, Dickens animized and humanized the object-world of his novels without sacrificing the identity of either realm, just as he followed theatrical exploitation of the charms of anachronism by employing folkloristic and fairy-tale materials in describing contemporary environment. And over everything there blows the breath of burlesque and parody, a spirit alive to the subversive possibilities contained in the patterns of conventional and typical language when their use evades the clear determination of satiric purpose. This too has its counterpart in the early Victorian theater.

The grotesque voice, for all its multiple facets, remains a mode that is characterized by its transposition of realms. On the stage of Dickens' time, grotesquerie was epitomized by the scenic transformation and the mixture of animate and inanimate realms; in Dickens' prose style, theatrical grotesquerie consists in the equivocal management of the relationship between object-world and image-world by way of the simile, proliferation, hyperbole, and the mixture of incompatible realms. The novelist's descriptions do indeed treat of disintegration and incoherence, but only insofar as they mediate a vivid and viable way of perceiving the commonplace and convention-deadened world. Put into the terms of "The Pantomime of Life," Dickens sought by the idioms of theatrical pantomime and burlesque to isolate the discordant, disproportionate, and incongruous in familiar things that he might get at a deeper reality within them—that he might indicate their arresting consonance with the human life located among them. As the novelist conceived of the mode, grotesquerie is real.

Chapter Nine
BURLESQUE
PEOPLE

DICKENS' burlesque voice seeks to do for character and action what his grotesque mode does for the object-world: that is, by rendering conventional human categories alien or incoherent to make them appear full of surprising interest and unsuspected new meaning. The kinship between Dickens' grotesque and burlesque modes has already been suggested by the presence in scenic description of a peculiar kind of rootless burlesque, a vaguely parodic use of inflated diction and mannered syntax disproportionate to subject matter. In addition, scene is commonly handled as a projection of some associated human life and motive. The general contention has been that these stylistic techniques were appropriated from the theater's habitual confusion between character and setting in Dickens' time, a feature especially prominent in pantomime and burlesque.

But this formula may be read backwards. It is equally possible to demonstrate that Dickens em-

ployed the object-world to reveal character—after all,
a widely recognized feature of his characterization—
without concluding that his personages are in any
way dehumanized in the process. They are indeed
defined in terms of an undeviating repetition of
external trait, gesture, mode of speech, article of
clothing, or object; these leitmotifs are commonly
eccentric or are likened to incongruously discordant
realms; and the characters behave inside this framework with a puppet-like consistency and extravagant
typicality which we associate more with farce, harlequinade, pantomime, burlesque, and humors comedy
than with the novel. Dickens' characters are flat,
stereotyped, vivid eccentrics who ever move in antic,
gestic modes and are never "out of themselves," as it
were, nor gifted with that element of convincing
surprise which E. M. Forster thought essential to a
"round" character. They have, instead, a factitious
quality appropriate to the "phenomena of hallucination," in Lewes' phrase. Yet even so astute a critic
as Forster, while recognizing their artificiality, concludes that Dickens' characters are nevertheless alive
—even though their vitality may only be a conjuring
trick of the author's—and that there must be much
more to such characters than severer critics are willing
to admit.[1]

To be a mere mechanical contrivance, a puppet
that ingeniously simulates life, and yet to give a vivid
impression of vitality—this is the Dickensian character, a perplexing amalgam of contradictory qualities. Theatrical practice, of course, has always had
to rely on the exploitation of strikingly apt external
traits to depict character, and in the nineteenth
century this limitation of drama was turned into
comic advantage. In harlequinade, for example, the

characters of all the principal roles were wholly conventional, stereotyped, and traditional; and they were
indicated by no less ancient and inevitable costumes,
properties, gestures, and actions. Harlequin, the
clever rogue and lover, had a magic wand to foil his
pursuers; Columbine, his beloved, was as witty and
clever as he and not altogether a lady; Pantaloon, a
lecherous, gluttonous, fat old man, was usually in
amorous pursuit of the teasing but unwilling Columbine; and the clowns were all rogues, pranksters,
thieves, and swindlers, whose usual occupation was
cheating shop-keepers and in turn being cheated.
Their ties to the real world were not altogether
broken, thanks chiefly to the domestic drama of
lovers and parents that preceded the transformation
scene which ushered in the pantomime. Because
English pantomime was for the most part mimed,
look, gesture, dress, and properties were required to
carry the burden of conveying motive and meaning,
a tendency which throughout the century carried
over into other forms of drama. And thus it is that
we have the "elderly gentleman" of *Sketches by Boz,*
with a "large face and strongly marked features,"
who is "richly, not to say gaudily dressed." He is, of
course, the Pantaloon, "and that he indulges to a
reasonable extent in the pleasures of the table may
be inferred from the joyous and oily manner in
which he rubs his stomach" (II, 428). An extravagant exploitation of surfaces was the order of the day
in the theater Dickens knew, if only as a means of
overcoming the difficulties posed by huge, disorderly
playhouses.

Dickens' view of the chronic histrionism at the
heart of bourgeois codes of genteel respectability—
indeed, at the core of any and all conventionalized

patterns of attitude and conduct which stress form over function and appearance over reality—no doubt turned the novelist toward the devices of the theater. It is no accident that, in "Shabby-Genteel People," the title character is invidiously discriminated from out-of-work actors and then depicted projecting his identity by means of futile attempts to maintain the outward appurtenances of respectability.

We have already seen how, in *Sketches by Boz, Pickwick Papers, Oliver Twist,* and even, in subtle ways, in *Dombey and Son* and *Great Expectations,* Dickens envisaged his time in terms of the traditional modes of pantomime, farce, burlesque, and melodrama. But on a more esoteric level of sublimation the stage reappears in Dickens' characterization, and not simply in the form of leitmotif. I have called this the burlesque voice because its presiding trait corresponds to that of theatrical burlesque in Dickens' time: that is to say, the use of comic, satiric, farcical, and humorous elements together in a mixed mode in such a way as to evade classification according to the usual categories. The burlesque mode is a deliberately ambiguous voice, the tone of which may best be described by the term "ludicrous" or "ridiculous," particularly if the latter term is robbed of the pejorative overtones associated with ridicule. It seeks its partly comic, partly satiric effects chiefly through the play of typicality within a single character or between two or more personages. It achieves its peculiar tone by means of an extravagantly persistent repetition with variation of some distinctive leitmotif, frequently in surprising or disconcerting contexts and/or likened to incongruous things. More particularly, the leitmotif is characterized by grotesque verbal play, as the purely verbal implications of a similitude become the starting point for an endlessly inventive series of new and different incongruous likenesses. Dickens' characters approximate automata precisely because they are always so astonishingly themselves. The same peculiar crotchet, the same odd detail, the same eccentric gesture, phrase, or expression, the same summary object, recur with a mad but luminous consistency that both delights the reader and, when it becomes the germ of a host of grotesque wordplays, disconcerts him. It is, of course, the technique of pantomime, burlesque, and farce carried over from visual terms into the grammar of comparisons.

Along with this extravagant deployment of incongruity and typicality, however, go two devices that emphasize the ways in which the commonplace figure is odd, curious, singular, or grotesque. The first of these devices is the Dickensian simile, which has already been examined as it operates in the grotesque mode; in the burlesque voice, too, the ambivalence of the similitude is stressed by an elaboration of the terms that bridge the two remotely dissimilar elements of the comparison. When Mr. Pickwick encounters "a strange specimen of the human race, in a sackcloth coat, and apron of the same, who with a brass label and number round his neck, looked as if he were catalogued in some collection of rarities," the reader is later reassured that this "was the waterman" (III, 3), but not until the commonplace has been alienated. It is thus that the typical is rendered incongruous. The form of the simile, moreover, creates a spectatorial detachment which further heightens the sense of incongruity.

The second device is a pervasive but pointless parody, travesty, or burlesque of a multitude of prose styles. Whatever form this rootless burlesque may take, it betrays an exuberant fondness for cliché, banality, and the inevitable form of words that infects style with a gratuitous raillery which further complicates the question of tone. This studied irrelevance or disproportion between substance and surface, which corresponds in prose to the visual discontinuity of Grimaldi's hussar, lends to Dickens' style its own disturbingly independent energy, a manic life that parallels and supplements the vitality of the personages.

Nowhere else in fiction, with the possible exception of Laurence Sterne, does one encounter quite this kind of rootless, inconsequential burlesque of conventional prose styles and modes of discourse, nor the hard, rattling excitation that this device imparts to narrative surface. Such a management of tone does reappear, however, in the texture of much nineteenth-century musical drama. Incidental stylistic play with cant and jargon, parody and travesty of received vocabularies, anachronism in speech patterns, and the discontinuous potentialities of language were exploited there without any necessary relevance to dramatic concerns or even to immediate context. There too one finds the same brilliant, brisk pace which is so marked a feature of Dickens' style, the same antic surface that gives his pages their peculiar impression of liveliness. This method of concealing the deadness of stock types beneath a spurious vitality that belongs more to style than to character is indeed all a conjuror's trick, as E. M. Forster suspected; but for Dickens it had the important virtue of making rich and strange what would otherwise be commonplace and lackluster.

Dickens' largely stylistic management of characterization seems calculated to dislodge the common reader from his comfortable acceptance of the conventional relations between things and discriminations between categories. By means of the distortions involved in the ludicrous and the confusions latent in his language, Dickens sought to uproot his readers and plant them down in an unaccustomed detachment, like that of a stranger, from familiar types and events; it is as if the readers had suddenly become members of an audience witnessing the arbitrary impersonations of a pantomime troupe. Just as an audience has a lively sense of the contrivances of a clown or Pantaloon, Dickens' readers are asked to view the conventions of the life around them, through the medium of linguistic play, as though they were new and strange, as if the customary determinations of realms were no longer in force. If to Coleridge stage allusion requires a "willing suspension of disbelief," to Dickens a fictional representation of commonplace life involves a willing suspension—if not of belief, then—of the sense of coherence, of recognizable identities and relationships, of customary modes of comprehension.

We have already seen how in the *Sketches, Pickwick Papers,* and *Oliver Twist,* a multitude of burlesque linguistic devices were employed in characterization, from Stiggins' pantomime and Jingle's egregious impostures to the many varieties of parody employed in the discourse of the Pickwickians, their friends, and the Wellers. Even the interpolated tales, like the "Mudfog Papers," are tainted with burlesque, and Fagin and Bumble are serious travesties of experimental philosophers.

Elsewhere, the exploitation of convention, leitmotif, and burlesque for purposes of characterization is so well known as hardly to require further attention. In *Dombey and Son,* for example, Captain Cuttle is defined eccentrically by means of several associated objects, chiefly his hard, patent-leather hat and the iron hook that takes the place of a severed hand; but he is principally characterized by his habitual confusion between popular songs and the Anglican prayer book, which he is indiscriminately fond of quoting. The latter leitmotif is commonly linked to a repetitious form of words: after an incorrect ascription of a quotation, Captain Cuttle is in the habit of enjoining his auditor to look up the passage in question, and "when found, make a note of," in token of his fuzzy-minded certainty. Yet this same kind of device—ordinarily satiric in intention, but here employed humorously—may in another context contribute to pathos. An example is Captain Cuttle's confidently repeated prediction that Walter Gay will follow in the footsteps of Dick Whittington, a prophecy usually couched in the form of a quotation of the Bow Bells' message to the apprentice: "Turn again, Whittington, thrice Lord Mayor of London." When it appears that Walter has been lost in the wreck of the "Son and Heir," however, "Richard Whittington was knocked on the head" to the captain: the motif arouses our compassion for the old sailor, even though the language employed to invoke the reference to Whittington is flippant (XIX, 25). This tonal versatility and exploitation of the characteristic resources of language we call burlesque.

The same technique is used to characterize Walter Gay, the "Dick Whittington" of *Dombey and Son,* who is also a type of the hero of Victorian nautical melodrama, the stock figure of the "Jolly Jack Tar" or brash young midshipman. In Gay's case his character is embodied in the exuberant cockiness of the sign in front of Sol Gill's ships-instrument shop, "The Wooden Midshipman," to which the young apprentice is linked (XVIII, 37-39). In the same manner, the shop itself fancifully becomes a figurative vessel, Sol Gills its captain, and Captain Cuttle his mate. It is the captain's task to keep these nautical parallels before the reader's eyes; Dickens' task in Walter Gay's characterization is thus the relatively simple one of stressing the boy's midshipman-like qualities—his fresh, loyal, brash, active nature, his thoughtless acts of kindness and bravery, and his eagerness to do whatever is asked of him. Into this scheme Florence Dombey is fitted as the midshipman's shore-bound beloved. Thus the stereotypical as much as the banal is made the seed of extravagant characterization.

At the same time, many other characters, like Captain Cuttle, are depicted largely in terms of linguistic motifs that appear satiric but are not necessarily so. One of Dickens' most-used devices of characterization, the exploitation of banality, cliché, and conventional forms of discourse, is particularly evident in *Dombey and Son*. Mrs. Chick, for example, brings her complacent sense of superiority as a Dombey before the reader primarily in terms of the inflated genteel clichés she employs to describe her brother and his child; and her sycophantic but good-hearted friend, Miss Tox, is set off by her more perfect command of banality. Their best passages together occur when Mrs. Chick fails to find a fitting cliché and the lack is supplied by Miss Tox, often incorrectly: the comedy of farce and burlesque all over again. Mr. Chick is their foil. Perfectly word-less, he whistles snatches of street songs, puts his hands in his pockets, and stares at the ceiling. The crazy-legged Cousin Feenix is another instance of the same type, a character with a penchant for stale phrases which just elude his memory. Mrs. Skewton, again, is ruthlessly exposed by means of parody, not only of her "Cleopatra" pose, but also of the mean-ingless formularies of romantic sensibility; and the brilliant *tour de force* of the Dombeys' ill-assorted dinner party is a pastiche of contending banalities. Major Bagstock's consummate hypocrisy is every-where indicated by his too-ready command of bluff-hearty cliché. On the other hand, Mr. Toodle's good-hearted simplicity is consistently embodied in railroad metaphors, tokens of his employment; and Susan Nipper's constitutional belligerence is keyed to her use of defiant but inconsequential hyperbole. The leitmotif, whether verbal or material, is thus employed for a wide range of different effects, from simple identification to sarcasm, much as it was em-ployed visually in pantomime and linguistically in burlesque and farce.

The versatility of this device of characterization may be seen particularly clearly in *Bleak House,* where burlesque verbal techniques abound, and where a trite or conventional phrase or metaphor often becomes the starting point for extravagant linguistic play far in excess of the actual needs of context. Mr. Jarndyce's "East wind" motif is justly famous as a "pretence to account for any disappoint-ment he could not conceal, rather than he would blame the real cause of it, or disparage or depreciate anyone" (XXII, 90); throughout the novel he is depicted in the light of this crotchet. Elsewhere, more purely verbal devices embody character and/or comment satirically upon character, as in the case of Esther Summerson's ruthless paraphrase of Harold Skimpole's expressions of child-like irresponsibility.[2] The entire Dedlock ménage is dramatically presented in terms of parody, from Sir Leicester's pomposities and the clichés of conservative politics to Bob Staples' "horsey" vocabulary and the "debilitated cousin"'s outrageously burlesqued upper-class accent. All of them seem more at home in a burlesque or a farce than in a social novel. "Conversation" Kenge is very aptly named in the light of Dickens' amused but scrupulous burlesque of lawyers' talk. Indeed, legalese appears to have been as irresistible a temptation for the novelist's parodic imagination in *Bleak House* as for the writer of burlesques and farces: the scenes in Chancery figure prominently and the author does not scruple to make fun of clerk's style in a letter to Esther. And the novel is filled with memorable dark grotesques, like the spectral figure of Lawyer Vholes, a "black figure" who "secretly picked at one of the red pimples on his yellow face with a black glove (XXIII, 197). In addition, there is Inspector Bucket's ingratiating but implacable manner and his probing finger, and Mr. Snagsby, the abject little law-stationer with the apologetic cough and the habit of passing out half-crowns to the oppressed to ease his conscience. The crazy Miss Flite carries a reticule of "documents" in Chancery and keeps an aviary of imprisoned birds in her lodgings. And the inhuman Smallweed family is uniformly depicted in terms of lower animals, loathsome insects, or unnatural survivors of some primordial past.

It is with Chadband, the evangelical preacher, however, that the peculiar features of Dickens' burlesque mode are best displayed. To begin with, Chadband is uniformly characterized by travesty—in this case, of the conventional mode of dissenting pulpit oratory. When the reader first meets him, he is delivering a sermon over the head of the unfortunate crossing sweeper, Jo, in Mr. Snagsby's parlor:

For what are you, my young friend? Are you a beast of the field? No. A bird of the air? No. A fish of the sea or river? No. You are a human boy, my young friend. A human boy. O glorious to be a human boy! And why glorious, my young friend? Because you are capable of receiving the lessons of wisdom, because you are capable of profiting by this discourse which I now deliver for your good, because you are not a stick, or a staff, or a stock, or a stone, or a post, or a pillar.

> O running stream of sparkling joy
> To be a soaring human boy!

And do you cool yourself in that stream now, my young friend? No. Why do you not cool yourself in that stream now? Because you are in a state of darkness, because you are in a state of obscurity . . . because you are in a state of bondage. My young friend, what *is* bondage? Let us, in a spirit of love, inquire. (XXII, 307)

Redundant rhetorical questions, fatuous periodicity, insipid religiosity, and factitious enthusiasm—these are the features of pulpit oratory held up to ridicule. But this burlesque is not merely comic, for in the last chapter of the previous installment Dickens has demonstrated that Jo is indeed a "beast of the field" in his ignorance and misery and by no stretch of the imagination a "running stream of sparkling joy." Indeed, the illiterate boy cannot even understand

Chadband's fulsome rhetoric, which is in any event more for the edification of the others than for the boy. In consequence, we are meant to realize that Chadband is not merely foolish and contemptible but vicious as well. The use of travesty in this case achieves more than mere burlesque comedy; in the larger context of the novel it is a means of tacit ironic commentary. It is nevertheless ludicrous in the manner of Fagin, Bumble, or any other *farceur*.

This burlesque use of typicality and cliché is very flexible, however, and often aims at simple farce. For example, when Chadband poses the question, why is it that human beings cannot fly, Mr. Snagsby, in all the innocence of a profoundly literal mind, answers, "No wings" (XXII, 299), thus bringing down upon his luckless head the indignation and contempt of his wife and the orator.

As we have seen in *Pickwick Papers'* play with the discontinuous potentialities of transposing the figurative and literal dimensions of language, the staple of Victorian theatrical comedy, burlesque style typically exploits the resources for chaos contained in words themselves. In the case of Mr. Chadbrand, characterization and commentary in the burlesque mode have their source in parody. When the preacher appears, he is inseparable from the verbal formularies of the pulpit, and these images and motifs become the materials for fanciful exploitation to depict and condemn the man. Burlesquerie, then, *is* characterization in that the resources of language itself are mined for banal typicalities and extravagant incongruities.

Thus at the outset, "Being much given to describe himself . . . as a vessel, he is occasionally mistaken by strangers for a gentleman connected with navigation. . . . Mrs. Snagsby has but recently taken a passage upward by the vessel, Chadband . . . that Bark A 1 . . ." (XXII, 296). By punning on the banal religious and nautical senses of "vessel", or rather, perhaps, by confusing the literal and metaphorical levels of the word's meaning, Dickens contrives to identify Chadband—he is the sort of bogus pietist who tritely speaks of himself as a "vessel of the Lord"—and to comment indirectly on him—he is tainted with overtones of trade and commerce. The satiric tone of this passage is complicated, however, by the introduction of an extravagant parody of the language employed in shipping bills to describe Mrs. Snagsby's attachment to Chadband's pulpit style. This entirely fanciful burlesque grace note undercuts the satire with a touch of absurd fantasy that is wholly in keeping with the kind of visual punning which marked the early Victorian theater.

Furthermore, later appearances of Chadband exploit all the grotesque potentialities of the original burlesque pun into a rich system of fanciful similitudes. Thus when he first appears *in propria persona,* he is described as

a large yellow man, with a fat smile, and a general appearance of having a good deal of train oil in his system. . . . Mr. Chadband moves softly and cumbrously, not unlike a bear who has been taught to walk upright. He is very much embarrassed about the arms, as if they were inconvenient to him, and he wanted to grovel; is very much in a perspiration about the head; and never speaks without first putting up his great hand, as delivering a token to his hearers that he is going to edify them.
(XXII, 297-298)

A number of new features are introduced here for later incongruous development with the "vessel" pun, of which the most prominent is the man's unhealthily oily obesity and tendency to sweat. At the same time, Dickens indicates Chadband's likeness to a bear, or some other lower animal with an instinct to grovel, in a catalogue of emphatic similes that suggests the point of view of a detached spectator.

One other characteristic remains to be sketched in —Chadband's affected habit of keeping a "sort of debtor and creditor account in the smallest items, and to post it publicly on the most trivial occasions" (XXII, 299). This is added in a ludicrous little scene with a cabman whom Chadband has short-changed, and who now appears to demand another eightpence. " 'My friends,' says Chadband, 'I remember a duty unfulfilled yesterday. It is right that I should be chastened in some penalty. I ought not to murmur. Rachel, pay the eightpence' " (XXII, 299). The picture of the evangelist is now complete, and the process of mixing its elements in new and incongruous combinations may begin.

Indeed, it has already begun, for when Chadband settles up his ethical account he is shown "glowing with humility and train oil." That the preacher is not only a vessel of shipping and trade but a vessel of train-oil as well—possibly a smoking oil lamp— quickly becomes apparent. When Chadband adjourns to the Snagsbys' tea-table, the source of his oiliness is revealed:

The conversion of nutriment of any sort into oil of the quality already mentioned, appears to be a process so inseparable from the constitution of this exemplary vessel, that in beginning to eat and drink, he may be described as always becoming a kind of considerable Oil Mills, or other large factory for the production of that article on a wholesale scale. On the present evening . . .

he does such a powerful stroke of business, that the ware-
house appears to be quite full when the works cease.
(XXII, 300)

Faced with such an extravagant instance of Dickens'
variant repetition and expansion of burlesque motifs
as this, the earnest analyst of style hardly knows
where to begin. Two immediate observations may
be made, however. First, Dickens has fixed on
Chadband's leading trait, his oily fatness, for exploitation of the "vessel" pun as a type of his pretension
to religious unction. Second, this single, simple
element of his appearance—as of his character—is to
be the pretext of a complex, grotesque burlesquerie.
The connection between "vessel" and "train oil" on
the one hand, and Chadband's fat on the other lies
in the fact that train oil was obtained by boiling
down the blubber of whales for use in cheap oil
lamps. The man's gluttony here becomes the vehicle
of an elaborate simile—"he may be described as
always becoming a kind of"—which likens his eating
to an oil mill, his oiliness to its originating fat, his
perspiration to the action of a train-oil lamp flame,
and most of all, his unction to lard. In this grotesque
application, Chadband becomes a "vessel" indeed, a
vessel that burns low-grade fat. What we are witnessing is a fanciful verbal transformation comparable in its grotesque effect to its visual counterpart
in a pantomime.

Quite apart from the sheer verbal audacity of such
a comparison, however tentative it may seem in
consequence of Dickens' insistence on the bridging
terms of the similitude, a number of complex overtones are engaged in an ill-assorted union of dissonant
realms. The vessel as ship is suggested by the mari-

time origin of train oil; the vessel as container in one context means quite literally the chamber that holds train oil in a lamp; and, finally, as a "vessel of the Lord" Chadband is shown to be a pot of fat. The gluttony that produces this train oil is likened to a factory, thereby picking up earlier implications of trade and commerce involved in Chadband's ministrations. But what dominates one's impression of this passage is the grotesque extravagance of the length to which this unlikely comparison is drawn, the burlesque flavor imparted to it by its inappropriately grand style, and the spectatorial position of the observer implied by the repeated "appears to be." Furthermore, we are witnesses of a rapid succession of audacious verbal transformations as a host of incongruous but apt kinships in language are exploited.

What links this passage to Grimaldi's hussar is their common use of incongruous visual—for Dickens read linguistic—materials in ramified form. Their shared burlesque consists precisely in the recognition of an apt "relation in things not apparent generally." In Dickens case, however, this recognition identifies the moral relevance of a man's actions by means of a burlesque misappropriation and elaboration of the banal terms he uses to describe himself. He takes Chadband's trite metaphor and, like the Wellers, applies it with rigorous logic to his actions and appearance; to reconcile the two requires a remarkable degree of verbal legerdemain with multiple senses of unction, vessel, and oil.

This being Dickens, the ramifications do not cease at the end of the passage quoted above. They reappear in even more variant form whenever Chadband reappears. For example, after a page or two devoted to other matters, Dickens reminds us of the pious fraud's continued presence at the tea-table: "During the progress of this keen encounter [between Guppy and the unfortunate Jo] the vessel Chadband, being merely engaged in the oil trade, gets aground, and waits to be floated off (XXII, 306). Presumably, he has eaten his fill. But is he, in this guise, a ship or a whale?

When Chadband returns to stage center a page or two later to address the luckless crossing-sweeper, he "rises with a smoking head, which he dabs with his pocket-handkerchief" (XXII, 305), as if he were indeed a burning train-oil lamp. In the course of his sermon, Jo yawns in the preacher's face, and Chadband is shown "with his persecuted chin folding itself up into its fat smile" (XXII, 307), in the process of making a further adjustment in his moral bookkeeping. This image is particularly dense, since it combines suggestions of Chadband's bogus humility, his pretended persecution at the hands of sinners, and his obesity with mechanical overtones that square with earlier references to the oil works. That Chadband's unction is nothing more than fat is reiterated near the end of this chapter when he "retires into private life until he invests a little capital of supper in the oil-trade" (XXII, 308).

But the evangelist once again is not to be allowed to escape with simple ridicule; for as he gorges over dinner, Dickens gives the reader a brief but stunning glimpse of Jo, huddled in a corner of Blackfriars Bridge munching table-scraps from the Snagsbys' tea and staring up uncomprehendingly at the great spire of St. Paul's Cathedral. This final contrast turns into scathing irony all the high farce and burlesque of Chadband's meeting with the law stationer, his wife, Guppy, and Jo. With such sudden twists and alterations, typical of Dickens' management of a wide range of tones in his burlesque, the novelist's versatility forces the reader to perform a disturbing adjustment of his perspective toward the preceding scene and its actors that creates a profoundly ambivalent tonal effect.

Later appearances of Chadband in the narrative[3] find him presented in terms of the same burlesque motifs as those by which he was introduced. He is, for example, a "gorging vessel" with a "fat smile" and "oily exudations" from his forehead (XXII, 405), which "smokes to such an extent that he seems to light his pocket-handkerchief at it . . . after every dab" (XXII, 408). On his next appearance some nine months later, Chadband is one of a gang of extortionists swarming around the stricken Sir Leicester Dedlock following the flight and death of his lady. There he comes forward "with a little sleek smiling and a little oil-grinding with the palms of his hands" (XXIII, 331). The same motifs appear as heretofore, but now they combine to show a vicious, fawning blackmailer where before Chadband had been nothing more than a stupid, insensitive clod. Yet they all arise out of an initial burlesque play on a trite form of words, out of an extravagant elaboration of the possible senses of vessel, unction, fat, and oiliness.

It may be well at this point to examine an entire scene, in order to see how Dickens deploys these devices variously for the creation of many different tonal effects within a unified context that contains quite incongruous elements. A typical instance is the chapter in *Bleak House* that recounts the dis-

covery of and the inquest over the dead body of
Nemo, the law-writer.[4] The episode begins grimly
enough with the discovery of the corpse by Tulkinghorn and Krook in Nemo's room. Doctors are
summoned—including Allen Woodcourt, as we later
learn—and a page or two later Snagsby, whose presence lightens the mood of a scene that is otherwise
somber. When the witnesses realize that identification of the dead man is impossible, the beadle is sent
for and Nemo's room shut and locked.

What follows is, from the point of view of its tone,
an extraordinarily diverse set-piece which nevertheless achieves its effects through essentially similar
means. These means consist of the rapid alternation
of mood and tone, or their mixture together in a
single context, which as we have seen constitutes
one way of describing the burlesque voice. So thoroughly are incongruous tonal elements juxtaposed
or mingled in this passage that it is impossible to
define its overall quality by reference to the usual
categories. At the same time, Dickens' total intention
seems clear. In the alternations between the broad
types comedy of the Cook's Courtiers and the inquest, on one hand, and the somber preparations of
Nemo's body for burial, together with the mingled
social satire, outraged sarcasm, and pathos prompted
by neglect of such outcasts as Nemo and Jo, on the
other hand, Dickens achieves a complexly orchestrated piece of dramatic irony which is at once
pathetic, savage, solemn, and yet hugely comic. The
reader is implicitly urged to note the gaiety occasioned in Cook's Court by another's tragic fate and
the carelessness of society toward its forgotten. The
court makes a carnival of Nemo's death.

While the stylistic techniques employed to evoke the pathetic and melodramatic qualities of this scene must await treatment in the next chapter, the remainder of this passage offers a *locus classicus* of Dickens' burlesquerie. Burlesque is pandemic in these pages, ranging from outright parody, through the play of cliché, to sheer farcical bustle and the interaction of many kinds of typicality. The comedy of types is the strongest opening note. Once the "news has got into the court," the Cockney types emerge in great profusion. A policeman is called to guard the premises. He is tall, magesterial, contemptuous of the futile beadle who is rounding up witnesses for the inquest, and yet intent on keeping order—the law in all its humanly fallible dignity. The neighborhood children are characteristically torn between curiosity, excitement, fear of the law, and impertinence—archetypal Cockney urchins. The beadle is the universal beadle, officious, stupid, vainglorious, and bumbling, and Mrs. Perkins and Mrs. Piper the Cockney housewives par excellence. The potboy on the corner is a conscious insider with "official" status. Later, at the inquest, the coroner is all brisk, brusque business. And there are many minor types to fill out the *dramatic personae*: a pieman selling brandy-balls, the proprietor of the Sol's Arms, the "gentleman of professional celebrity" and Little Swills, who chair the "Harmonic Meetings," the jury, the members of the beadle's burial party from the parish workhouse, and many more.

Dickens' use of the present tense, coupled with his tendency to truncate verb-forms and sentence structure, lends to the Cook's Court portion of the narrative a certain sprightly brightness and breathless hurry appropriate to the depiction of a bustling, crowded scene much like those to be found in farce or pantomime.

At the same time, Dickens exploits his omniscience brilliantly, but in a manner, I believe, peculiar to himself. Although point of view moves freely among the various characters, the presence of an observer reporting what he sees is stressed. This characteristic effect is achieved through a number of devices, chiefly the emphatic form of the similes, the use of passive verbs, the habit of interpreting external details in parenthetical asides, and—most particularly —the tendency of the language of the characters to infiltrate narrative without formal quotation. Thus the "potboy on the corner . . . *has the appearance of* an impregnable youth"; *"The general feeling seems to be* that *it's a blessing Mr. Krook warn't made away with first";* and the beadle *"is understood in the neighborhood* to be a ridiculous *institution."* Indeed, the beadle *"is understood to be* in want of witnesses. . . . *Is* immediately *referred.* . . . *Is made* more imbecile. . . . Policeman *seen to smile* to potboy. *Public* loses interest, and *undergoes reaction. Taunts the beadle* . . . with having boiled a boy; choruses fragments of a popular song to that effect. . . . Policeman *finds it necessary to support the Law,* and seize the vocalist; who *is released* . . . on condition of his *getting out of this then, come! and cutting it*—a condition he immediately observes."

The receptive consciousness at the center of this scene, receiving and communicating the observed data to the reader, projects an attitude that is difficult to pinpoint. The scene is realized with genuine dramatic objectivity: the reader is thrust into the midst of the Cook's Courtiers with remarkably vivid

immediacy of impression, as if he were an alert consciousness actually on the ground. Or more to our
present purpose, he witnesses the animated doings of
types as though he were a member of a audience
at a pantomime or farce. On the other hand, the
observing consciousness asks the reader to adopt an
attitude toward the actors and events which is poised
ambiguously between the comedy of types and simple
ridicule, between amused sympathy and contempt.
This latter effect is heightened by a burlesque play
with the grand style—an incongruous inflation of diction and image which just misses being arch—that
keeps tone ambivalent. The potboy on the corner,
for example, is "a *privileged amateur,* as possessing
official knowledge of life, and having to deal with
drunken men occasionally." He "has the appearance
of an *impregnable youth, unassailable by truncheons,*
and *unconfinable in station houses."* The beadle is
"a ridiculous institution," an *"imbecile civilian"* and
"remnant of the barbarous watchmen-times," "who
must be borne with until *Government shall abolish
him." "Public* loses interest, and *undergoes reaction."*
And so on. The effect of this technique is to make narrative simultaneously depict action and suggest character through implied attitude at the same time that
it indicates a complex response to event and type.

The central portion of the episode, the Coroner's
inquest in the "Harmonic Meeting Room" of the
Sol's Arms, incorporates the prevalent parody, burlesque, and types-comedy, but moves beyond them to
that point at which dialogue and formal narrative
collapse into direct, objective, dramatic rendering.
In Mrs. Piper's hilarious testimony, the burlesque
ironies of the cross-examination of Jo, and the darker
tones of the return of the verdict, direct transcription

of idiosyncratic and stereotypical patterns of speech and dialect displaces the conventional methods of third-person narration with scenario, and burlesque- and parody-like devices effect a realization of the scene in dramatic terms.[5] Technically, the handling of this episode remains burlesque in our special sense of that term. Directly rendered paraphrase is so ordered as to achieve a diverse breadth of tone, from Mrs. Piper's irrelevant, ungrammatical, and asyntactical cockney and the curiously pathetic tone of Jo's illiterate evidence, to the ironic inhumanity of the coroner's examination of the crossing-sweeper and his charge to the jury, and the burlesque horror he registers at the boy's lack of religious knowledge. All the categories are represented, mingling and alternating with infinite variety and complexity, but the overall tone remains elusive, disturbing, yet richly satisfying. The passage is marked by a strongly implied spectatorial perspective within the scene; the narrator dispenses with his customary omniscient, third-person point of view in order to report anonymously, in the manner of a stenographer, court-reporter, or dramatist, what is said. Indeed, the scene is not reported at all, but realized, as it would have been in one of Renton Nicholson's satirical "Judge and Jury" improvisations. The shorthand effect is further enhanced by the same truncated sentence structure and paraphrase that mark the earlier account of the Cook's Courtiers' reaction to Nemo's death.

Two instances of burlesque techniques of a variant but by now familiar kind occur during the inquest with the introduction of Little Swills, the comic vocalist, and the "Harmonic Meeting Room," on one hand, and on the other hand the beadle's solicitous

interest in "two gentlemen not very neat about the
cuffs and buttons"—penny-a-liners. The first of these
derives its strong burlesque flavor from the introduction of the two entertainers in language that
parodies their wafered advertisement in the window
of the Sol's Arms. The chair, it reads, will be "filled
by a gentleman of professional celebrity, faced by
Little Swills, the comic vocalist, who hopes (according to the bill in the window) that his friends will
rally round him, and support first-rate talent" at that
night's Harmonic Meeting. Later appearances of the
two music-hall types find them imbedded in the terminology of their introduction. Thus, "The Harmonic Meeting hour arriving, the gentleman of professional celebrity takes the chair; is faced (red-faced)
by Little Swills; their friends rally round them, and
support first-rate talent." And a line or two later,
Little Swills "comes in as the Coroner (not the least
in the world like him); describes the Inquest, with
recreative intervals of piano-forte accompaniment to
the refrain—With his (the Coroner's) tippy tol li
doll, tippy tol lo doll, tippy tol li doll, Dee!" Or,
finally, "The jangling piano at last is silent, and the
Harmonic friends rally round their pillows." Here
burlesque repetitions of banal motifs, together with
grotesque variations on them, have the appearance
of indicating the ridiculous. But the phrase, "Harmonic Meeting Room," has been used throughout
the scene to refer to the place where the inquest is
held, thus pointing to the deeper ironic intention of
the entire chapter in contrasting the festivities of
the court with the image of Nemo's lonely corpse.

The same unsettling ambiguity of tone is achieved
with the motif of "the active and intelligent" beadle,
the conventional newspaper phrase employed by the

"two gentlemen not very neat about the cuffs and buttons." Already knowing as we do that the beadle is not particularly active and certainly not intelligent, we respond to this term derisively when we first meet it. But later, when it becomes a substitute for the beadle's proper name and correct title—when, in short he is identified simply as "the active and intelligent"—the use of the term is complicated in several ways. In the first place, it often reappears in conjunction with the motif employed to describe the newspapermen, notably near the middle of the novel, when they and the beadle come upon the scene again following Krook's death by spontaneous combustion. At that point, much more is made of the journalists, whose style is appropriated for narrative purposes by the novelist in a brilliant short parody.[6] In this Dickens is simply extending an ironic narrative device he has used elsewhere in *Bleak House* to comment on the Dedlock family by describing them in language that parodies the Court Bulletin and the London Gazette. There too cliché becomes a definitive motif, as the "brilliant and distinguished circle" of the Dedlock entourage and their "Fashionable World" come to stand for the aristocracy and to displace their proper names. These terms are also repeatedly contrasted with the great wheeling movement of the cosmos, of which the vain and puny "Fashionable World" is unaware.[7] Burlesque journalese, like that of a host of other styles in *Bleak House,* is a means of characterization and commentary as much as of narration. Like theatrical burlesque, again, it cuts in more than one direction: toward character as well as toward the thing parodied.

Similarly, the same technique may not always be employed toward a character in the same way. Upon

the second appearance of "the active and intelligent,"
for example, the reader encounters the phrase in a
bitterly sarcastic passage describing Nemo's burial in
the parish cemetery. There its derisiveness is overlaid
by Dickens' indignant parody of the Anglican burial
service in the phrase, "our dear brother here departed . . . sown in corruption," that is used in an
all-out indictment of official neglect of the poor and
oppressed. Burlesque in Dickens' hands may take
any materials, even holy writ, to achieve a wide
variety of effect, ranging from the "unreflective guffaw" of simple farce to the savage gorge of Menippan
satire. Yet an extraordinary sense of familiarity and
intimacy is communicated by these devices as, repeated and varied in a kind of rough shorthand, they
take on the qualities of nicknames. Taken together
with Dickens' dramatic rendering of scene, this burlesque technique projects the reader ever more completely within a realized fictional world, there to
identify a character through a banal form of words
that at the same time derides the context and system
of values from which the words are drawn. Gaiety
and solemnity, comedy and irony, are so inextricably
mingled, so incongruously juxtaposed, as to create
that special grotesque mode we have named burlesquerie, after its more frivolous theatrical prototype.

It is in the light of this latter subject that one final
variety of burlesque may be distinguished, a special
kind of simple incongruity, the aim of which appears
to be the creation of farcical grotesquerie and contretemps that was the basic stuff of the popular theater.
The very idea of holding a solemn inquest in the
public room of a tavern is grotesque by its very nature, but Dickens stresses and elaborates all the discrepant possibilities of the setting, apparently for no

loftier purpose than the establishment of a frolicsome tympany to play with and against the other rhythms of the chapter. The effect of this technique is to invest the scene with irrelevant business, in the dramatic sense of that term, with an aimless sport that takes its pleasure in ludicrous juxtapositions of incongruous and ill-assorted contexts, much in the manner of the incidental comedy of a clown. For example, when the coroner enters the Harmonic Meeting Room, he "puts his hat on the piano, and takes a Windsor-chair at the head of a long table, formed of several short tables put together, and ornamented with glutinous rings in endless involutions, made by pots and glasses." Those of the jury who cannot find places at the table, again, "get among the spittoons and pipes"; and "Over the Coroner's head is a small iron garland, the pendant handle of a bell, which rather gives the Majesty of the Court the appearance of going to be hanged presently." "Mr. Tulkinghorn is received with distinction, and seated near the Coroner; between that high judicial officer, a bagatelle-board, and the coal box." And the coroner enjoins the jury that "You will give your verdict according to the—skittles; they must be stopped, you know, beadle! —evidence, and not according to anything else." While the reader readily identifies the rather heavy-handed irony of "that high judicial officer" and "Majesty of the Court," he is by no means so sure of the aim of suggesting that the coroner appears to be about to hang or of seating Mr. Tulkinghorn between a bagatelle-board and the coal box; and the incongruity of giving evidence according to the skittles is obvious. The shifting and elusive object of the use of these incidental grotesqueries, however, remains to confirm the presence of the burlesque voice in this continuous antic business.

At the heart of Dickens' burlesque, in sum, lies a spirit of unremitting parody, travesty, and incongruity directed upon the typifying external norms of speech of conventional characters. This play with typicality and cliché at its most extreme point invades narrative and description to foster a curious kind of direct dramatic rendering of scene which implies the presence inside the scene of a detached if not alien perspective, a recording observer whose perceptions dictate style and technique. This burlesque characterization exploits all the leading traits of its theatrical counterpart. There one finds the same mixture of anachronism, incongruity, and fantasy with realism, the same play with grotesque incidental business and antic activity, the same preoccupation with the balance or juxtaposition of discordant realms. But where theatrical burlesque relies primarily on visual devices, Dickens' burlesquerie exploits the capricious elements contained in conventional language.

Dickens' style, for example, is consciously discordant to subject matter, thereby creating a kind of rootless burlesque texture which is in spirit close to its theatrical prototype in having no identifiable satiric object. Indeed, verbal play with cliché and convention forms the substance of burlesque motif and image for purposes of characterization, which is carried on through an extravagant process of variant repetition; and this is in essence the method of pantomime and burlesque, given the theater's greater emphasis on visual and gestic materials. In the same manner, we have earlier seen how Dickens exploited a kind of serious burlesque of literary and dramatic forms in *Great Expectations* to give shape and meaning to his novel, thereby turning to high artistic uses the presiding tactic of frivolous theatrical genres. Dickens' burlesque mode, like its progenitor in the popular theater, capitalizes on the confusion between discordant realms, particularly the animate and inanimate, together with the equivocations latent in the simile, to achieve versatile, tonally ambivalent effects.

An important consequence of these technical borrowings from the theater, whatever transmutations they must go through in making the jump from playhouse to novel, is that the reader's comfortable and detached relationship to the narrative is jarred. The reader is continually prevailed upon to adjust and then readjust his perspective and attitude; he is perplexed about overall tone or made uneasy by sudden shifts in tone from passage to passage. Ultimately, he is drawn into events and scenes as though he were a witness to them or a spectator. At the same time, style exerts a pull toward fantasy while subject matter draws him toward realism: the whole matter of the reader's relationship to the fiction and to its author, as well as the fiction's relationship to the commonplace world, is left up in the air, as Dickens manipulates the point of view of a conscious stranger.

Chapter Ten
MELODRAMATIC
NARRATIVE

CERTAINLY one of the most striking features of the early Victorian theater was the introduction into drama, as a result of the licensing acts, of music, verse, dance, song, and various rhythmic devices. Burlesque, extravaganza, burletta, revue, the several varieties of opera and operetta, and even pantomime, all employed music, song, or verse to a greater or lesser extent. Melodrama, of course, utilized musical background to establish and augment mood, and incidental songs and dances to relieve suspense and to provide a lighter counterpart to the pathetic or terrible concerns of the main plot. Melodramatic style was no less characterized by exploitation of rhetoric and rhythm. Under the influence of a bogus Elizabethan blank verse, playwrights labored to achieve a divine afflatus replete with periodic and parallel constructions, a consciously elevated diction, and a certain almost choral use of repeated motifs. More subtly, they sought a musical or poetic structure by manipulating analogy and contrast, double and triple plotting, and parallel variations in speech, characters, and scenes. At the same time, developments by stage designers and engineers, together with more conscientious staging by managers and directors, made more convincing theatrical productions of relatively fantastic theatrical forms.

In an earlier chapter we have indicated those areas of general melodramatic practice in Dickens' style and technique, such as his tendency toward scene-setting and tableaux and his outright expropriation of patterns of action and character relationships from melodrama and sentimental drama. He was as prone as a playwright to mix or alternate mood and tone and to use for broad structural purposes systems of analogy and contrast, extensive complexes of images, metaphor, and symbol, and repeated motifs. Nearer to home, we have examined how Dickens' texture is marked by many dramatic or "poetic" devices: the lapses into blank verse, the frequent invocations, apostrophes, direct addresses, soliloquies, and authorial "asides," and the theatrical way he handles scenes, defines character, and manipulates speech and dialogue. Rhetorical and stylistic analysis of typical passages has revealed a range of theatrical effects that touches on scenario at one extreme and at the other on a consciously melodramatic use of the musical and rhythmic resources of language.

Where the grotesque voice is primarily devoted to setting and scene in Dickens' novels, and the burlesque mode is largely confined to characterization and the interplay between characters, the melodramatic voice is predominantly located in narrative, where its aim is to perform for the novel what the orchestra does for melodrama: that is, to establish and reinforce mood, not only in individual scenes but across the whole extent of a narrative. Ultimately, the melodramatic voice seeks to achieve unity and coherence in atmosphere, feeling, and pace in the serial novel, whose mode of publication makes it especially difficult to unify, by the conscious and deliberate manipulation of prose rhythms and other rhythmic dimensions of language. In achieving these ends, the melodramatic voice underlines those moral polarities in Dickens' novels, which correspond to the polarities in setting and character, by endowing each with its appropriate emotional quality suggested by rhythm.

At the same time, however, the grotesque, burlesque, and melodramatic modes all share a common tendency to exploit the rhythmic and musical overtones of language. If we recall that extended passage in the last chapter of this study dealing with the response of Cook's Court to the death of Nemo, for example, we will be struck at once by the fact that at least one of its principles of organization is rhythmic. Those scenes devoted to the Cook's Courtiers, the inquest, and the Harmonic Meeting have a hard, bright, and erratic pace that in each case is hurried and heightened by increased truncation and fragmentation in sentence structure to a terminal crescendo— the dispersal of the urchins, the return of the verdict, and Little Swills' imitation of the coroner. Against the rattling tympany of these farcical episodes stand the glimpses of Nemo's corpse, each with its own contribution to make toward creating an alternative rhythmic mode with its own climactic form. Opening with the discovery scene, which is mainly narrative in character, this strain of rhythm is briefly invoked just prior to the inquest in two quiet paragraphs devoted to the preparation of the body for burial by the beadle and his pauper crew, but it must await full orchestration in the pages following the return of the verdict and the quieting of the Harmonic Meeting. Then these rhythms swell up to dominance, first in the relatively quiet and regular if increasingly complexly organized apostrophe delivered over the body, culminating in the rising agitation of the prophetic meditations. Next comes the raw sarcasm of the paraphrased burial service, with its abrupt exclamations and hammering insistence of heavy punctuation and parallelism. This in turn gives way to the sonorous measures of the blank-verse invocation to night, and all is finally stilled in the looser rhythms of the concluding apostrophe to Jo, the crossing sweeper, who has come to mourn at the gate. On the one hand, then, the increasing speed and hurry of the farcical portions of this passage alternate with, or give way to the longer, more complexly organized, and abruptly interrupted periods of the somber paragraphs.

Elsewhere, rhythms function organically in the description of setting, in the relatively straightforward measures of the passage on Mrs. Pipchin's house in Brighton, and in the jangling pell-mell of the paragraph devoted to Brogley's shop, with its scrupulously trailing subordinate clauses and dying falls. *Bleak House,* again, is polarized not only by two different narrative points of view and tenses but by two narrative rhythms as well, each appropriate to the temporal and personal perspective of the narrator. Esther's portion of the novel is told from a point of view in time long after the events have happened and their consequences known, by a narrator who is—or was—deeply involved in the action and who is in character timid, tentative, and self-effacing. Her portion of the narrative is therefore marked by a generally tranquil and unmannered measure that derives from her *ex post facto* position in time and by her anomalous social position. There is a certain retrospective serenity and finality about Esther's narrative, a careful, reportorial deliberation in its pace, that on the one hand suggests a sense of some overriding order and direction inhering in events, and on the other hand implies a slow and gradual realization of the truth of things. The omniscient narrator's portion of the narrative, however, is told in a strident, raucous, rattling progressive present tense much like that depicted in the passage quoted in the last chapter. It rather suggests the forward tumble of time without that sense of proportion and order imparted to events by hindsight, the disorderly jumble of actual, present experience. Taken together, these two rhythms, narrators, and temporal perspectives coincide to give the novel a meaningful form. They tend to discriminate between the moral qualities associated with two circles of characters, each of which is centered on a particular locale—Bleak House as against Chesney Wold-Chancery—by investing the former with overtones of permanence and order and the latter with transience and disorder, which define the kinship of each to what is respectively eternal or ephemeral in life.

Within this general rhythmic framework, the more immediate significance of Dickens' use of musical devices borrowed from the popular theater lies in their deployment at those points in his novels at which some crucial issue is at stake or some decisive action occurs. A mode designed to narrate sensational or spectacular episodes, the melodramatic voice and measure dominate scenes of mob violence, escape and pursuit, confrontation and revelation, extreme psychological states, and those passages which describe how subterranean forces are building toward some later explosion.[1] Yet exactly similar stylistic devices, modified by the demands of less sensational materials, define gentler melodramatic episodes, such as the death of innocents, grief, hardship, or loneliness.[2]

Because melodramatic episodes occur at decisive points in Dickens' narratives, they assist in projecting the novelist's world view in important ways. Often a guilty person such as Carker attempts to avoid the consequences of his acts by flight; but his means of escape are fatally twisted into an ironic tool of his own destruction. Suspense in such passages depends upon the delay of an expected conclusion clearly prefigured in the narrative, as the subterranean forces of justice slowly but inevitably bring their strength to bear upon the fleeing villain. For this reason the use of rhythmic devices of style reinforces the novelist's larger structural employment of rhythm: together they suggest the outbreak of immanent superhuman ordering powers and processes after long suppression. The ever-heightening measures of the general narrative as it reaches toward critical moments manifests Dickens' belief in a Carlylean vitalism in the cosmos working in and under the apparently disparate quality of events to affirm a comprehensible moral order in all things. Those who set their faces against this integrative tendency put themselves in opposition to the order of nature and Divine Providence—the two appear to be congruent in Dickens' thinking—and cannot escape being overwhelmed by some culminating rush of events. Those whose lives have been led in consonance with this mysterious, universal ordering agency—those in short who value brotherhood, humility, love, and charity—similarly find themselves participating in these cosmic rhythms in ways which manage to work to their benefit, in spite of apparent adversity. Ultimately, the events which bring disaster to those who set their faces against the direction of life are the incidents which spell success for those in harmony with the rhythms of the universal order.

This being the case, Dickens' deployment of the potentialities for the rhythmic management of prose implicit in musical drama is calculated to reinforce theme and structure with a congruent atmospheric system that in some instances at least reaches across the full extent of a narrative. However rudimentary may have been the sources of this technique in dramatic prototypes, it is still to be found there. In melodrama as in its modern counterpart, the motion picture soundtrack, music and rhythm were and are used as Dickens employed them: to define the emotional quality of a scene, to identify and heighten an expectation, and to differentiate between the moral texture of characters or groups of characters. The foreboding "hurry" that ushered in a villain, the delicate cadences that provided the musical setting for the fair heroine, the brisk and strident measures that introduced the comic lead, the vigorous tempos that accompanied the entrance of the manly nautical hero and his band of true-blue shipmates, or the pensive or somber strains that opened a pathetic episode—these fixtures of theatrical melo-

drama have their counterparts in Dickens' management of motif, syntax, and rhetoric. The Cook's
Courtiers have their identifying measure as much as
do Esther Summerson, Chancery, and Chesney Wold.
Where Dickens departs from his theatrical prototypes
is in the pervasiveness of his rhythmic manipulation
and in the structural uses to which he puts it, a task
to which melodrama playwrights do not appear to
have set their minds. In another matter Dickens
also seems to stand alone, for the atmospheric system
he creates out of his handling of the musical and
rhythmic resources of prose has its origin in the
figurative patterns developed for each novel out of
its naturalistic materials of setting and action. It is
this which gives to Dickens' novels their extraordinary coherence.

A characteristic example of this exploitation of
melodramatic rhythms may be found in the justly
famous passage in *Dombey and Son* (Chapter XX)
which recounts the protagonist's journey by rail to
Leamington following the death of his son and heir,
Paul; he travels aboard a train stoked by Mr. Toodle,
the husband of the boy's beloved nurse, Polly, and
himself the father of a child who has recently died.
Dombey's proud rejection of Toodle's sympathy
establishes the merchant's moral position—his refusal
to accept the idea that he participates in a common
human mortality. The train trip to Leamington thus
becomes a dual symbol according to the different
moral perspectives of the passengers: for all of them,
it typifies the passage of time; for Dombey, the
swiftly passing scenery is a type of death and frustration; for Toodle and society generally, it is a sign
of progress. Moreover, these several meanings form

part of a larger scheme of ideas running throughout the novel that corresponds to a system of rhythms associated with the railroad and its polar opposite, the ocean.

The meanings and rhythms begin to accrue around the railroad from its introduction in Chapter VI, when Polly and Susan Nipper take Florence and the infant Paul to visit the Toodles' home in Staggs' Gardens, the site of the construction of Euston Station. Although the coming of the railroad has brought with it much destruction and disorder, its ultimate effect, as Dickens put it, will be "civilization and improvement" (XVIII, 74). Upon its next appearance at the time of Paul's death in Chapter XV, the work of building is complete, Staggs' Gardens has been replaced with model workers' housing, and the inhabitants' initial suspicion has given way to enthusiastic acceptance of the railway. Now it is seen as a potent creative force charged with life and purpose. The "conquering engines" are "dilating with the secret knowledge of great powers yet unsuspected in them, and strong purposes not yet achieved." The station is a "throbbing current" of "life's blood" and "fermentation"; and events there seem to be thrusting forward into a better future at locomotive-like speed (XVIII, 251-253).

The melioration promised by the coming of the railroad is epitomized by Mr. Toodle, who is now earning a comfortable wage as an engine-stoker and even learning to read. The railroad is by this point in the narrative invested with twofold meaning as a destroyer of old evil and a creator of beneficial change, and these two values are maintained and developed throughout the rest of the novel. The

train carries Dombey to his meeting with the woman
whose marriage to him will end in disaster for them
both; and much later the railroad is the agent of
retributive justice that strikes down Carker, Dombey's
betrayer and the would-be seducer of his wife. As
a temporal symbol the railroad benefits those who
work in consonance with the spirit of change; and
it destroys those like Dombey who seek an impossible permanence in transient, mundane things, and
those like Carker who seek to evade the consequences
of their evil. At the same time, the rail journey
stands for the oneness of mankind and society in
their participation in mortal life, with all the soli-
darity that requires.

In the long, melodramatically contrived passage
that narrates Dombey's trip aboard the train, Dickens
manages to make the narrative a projection of the
merchant's state of mind following the death of the
son on whom he had centered his impossible ambition of founding an eternal mercantile dynasty.
Thwarted and frustrated by the inescapable conditions that time and mortality place upon human life,
by limitations which his pride of wealth and position
prevent him from recognizing as applicable to himself, Dombey sees the journey by rail as a "type of
that triumphant monster, Death," insofar as death is
the ultimate fact of a life in time, a symptom of the
brevity, transience, and insignificance of human existence. Time symbolized by the train's rushing speed
is indifferent to man's personal desires and mocks
"the swift course of the young life [Paul's] that had
been borne so steadily and inexorably to its fore-
doomed end." It unifies all "classes, ages, and degrees" in the irresistible progress "that forced itself

upon its iron way—its own—defiant of all paths and roads, piercing through the heart of every obstacle" (XVIII, 323). To the thwarted and grief-stricken Dombey, the train's swift passage makes a world of change seem "a wilderness of blighted plans and gnawing jealousies"; but to those whose lives are governed by the eternal values of humility, love, and brotherhood, the journey through time shows "a rich and varied country" (XVIII, 323). The implacable momentum of the train ends at last in the hideous, ash-strewn immensity of the Birmingham slums, the "ruinous and dreary" end awaiting all such time-bound men as Dombey. But Dickens is careful to add that the railroad has merely "let the light in" on this awful scene; it did not "make or cause" the slums (XVIII, 325). The progress of time exposes old evils hitherto hidden by ignorance; but to Dombey, brooding on the death of his son, "All things looked black, and cold, and deadly. . . . He found a likeness to his misfortune everywhere. There was a remorseless triumph going on about him, and it galled and stung him in his pride and jealousy, whatever form it took . . ." (XVIII, 325). Further, "He knew full well . . . as he stood there, tingeing the scene of transition before him with the morbid colours of his own mind, and making it a ruin and a picture of decay, instead of hopeful change, and promise of better things, that life had quite as much to do with his complainings as death" (XVIII, 326).

The passage which narrates the journey by rail to Leamington, one of those brilliant set-pieces that Dickens appears to have been fond of contriving when he assumed the stance of melodrama, is a typical example of his manipulation of rhetorical schemes and motives to achieve a rhythmic and musical unity in the narrative of sensational episodes. It may be well to quote the passage in full:

He found no pleasure or relief in the journey. Tortured by these thoughts he carried monotony with him, through the rushing landscape, and hurried headlong, not through a rich and varied country, but a wilderness of blighted plans and gnawing jealousies. The very speed at which the train was whirled along mocked the swift course of the young life that had been borne away so steadily and so inexorably to its foredoomed end. The power that forced itself upon its iron way—its own—defiant of all paths and roads, piercing through the heart of every obstacle, and dragging living creatures of all classes, ages, and degrees behind it, was a type of the triumphant monster, Death.

Away, with a shriek, and a roar, and a rattle, from the town, burrowing among the dwellings of men and making the streets hum, flashing out into the meadows for a moment, mining in through the damp earth, booming on in darkness and heavy air, bursting out again into the sunny day so bright and wide; away, with a shriek, and a roar, and a rattle, through the fields, through the woods, through the corn, through the hay, through the chalk, through the mould, through the clay, through the rock, among objects close at hand and almost in the grasp, ever flying from the traveller, and a deceitful distance ever moving slowly within him: like as in the track of the remorseless monster, Death!

Through the hollow, on the height, by the heath, by the orchard, by the park, by the garden, over the canal, across the river, where the sheep are feeding, where the mill is going, where the barge is floating, where the dead are lying, where the factory is smoking, where the stream is running, where the village clusters, where the great cathedral rises, where the bleak moor lies, and the wild breeze smooths or ruffles it as its inconstant will; away, with a shriek, and a roar, and a rattle, and no trace to leave behind but dust and vapour: like as in the track of the remorseless monster, Death!

Breasting the wind and light, the shower and sunshine, away, and still away, it rolls and roars, fierce and rapid, smooth and certain, and great works and massive bridges crossing up above, fall like a beam of shadow an inch broad upon the eye, and then are lost. Away, and still away, onward and onward ever: glimpses of cottage-homes, of houses, mansions, rich estates, of husbandry and handicraft, of people, of old roads and paths that look deserted, small, and insignificant as they are left behind: and so they do, and what else is there but such glimpses, in the track of the indomitable monster, Death!

Away, with a shriek, and a roar, and a rattle, plunging down into the earth again, and working on in such a storm of energy and perseverance, that amidst the darkness and whirlwind the motion seems reversed, and to tend furiously backward, until a ray of light upon the wet wall shows its surface flying past like a fierce stream. Away once more into the day, and through the day, with a shrill yell of exultation, roaring, rattling, tearing on, spurning everything with its dark breath, sometimes pausing for a minute where a crowd of faces are, that in a minute more are not: sometimes lapping water greedily, and before the spout at which it drinks has ceased to drip upon the ground, shrieking, roaring, rattling through the purple distance!

Louder and louder yet, it shrieks and cries as it comes tearing on resistless to the goal: and now its way, still like the way of Death, is strewn with ashes thickly. Everything around is blackened. There are dark pools of water, muddy lanes, and miserable habitations far below. There are jagged walls and falling houses close at hand, and through the battered roofs and broken windows, wretched rooms are seen, where want and fever hide themselves in many wretched shapes, while smoke and crowded gables, and distorted chimneys, and deformity of brick and mortar penning up deformity of mind and body, choke the murky distance. As Mr. Dombey looks out of his carriage window, it is never in his thoughts that the monster who has brought him there has let the light of day in on these things: not made or caused them. It was the journey's fitting end, and might have been the end of everything; it was so ruinous and dreary.

(XVIII, 323-325)

Within this multifaceted symbolic configuration, Dickens manipulates his style in order to achieve an effect which simulates the rushing forward speed of an oncoming locomotive; and the means employed to this end are largely rhythmic and musical. The stylistic premise of this and similar passages of whatever quality, ranging from sentiment and pathos through sensation, involves parallel variation in motif. In this case, the immediate figure is the likeness of the rushing train to some frightful dragon or other monster typifying death, a motif that is repeated with appropriate variation at the end of each of the five paragraphs given over to the journey—a triumphant monster first, then twice a remorseless monster, next an indomitable monster, and finally and more simply a monster, as in the last two paragraphs more general animate imagery supplants the specific similitude.

A second motif—"Away, with a shriek, and a roar, and a rattle"—reinforces the animism of the train-as-monster figure and adds its own rhythmic element to the passage. Appearing first at the beginning of the second paragraph, this refrain recurs in the middle of the same paragraph, near the end of the third, where it is closely conjoined with the monster motif, and again in the opening line of the fifth paragraph, in addition to oblique echoes along the way. By the fifth paragraph, however, the union of these two motifs validates a fuller and more pervasive use of pathetic fallacy with the result that the train is given a general animism: its noisy way becomes a "shrill yell of exultation," it "shrieks and cries," it spurns "everything with its dark breath . . . pausing for a minute . . . and lapping water greedily" before "shrieking and roaring" on.

In the meantime, more specifically rhetorical manipulation of sentence structure, syntax, and verb forms contrives to add a rhythmic hurry and rush to the passage and to make it in effect a single parallel construction dependent from the initial motif, "Away, with a shriek, and a roar, and a rattle." Beginning in the second paragraph with a series of present participial phrases, it gives way to prepositional phrases continuing on into the third paragraph, until a succession of subordinate clauses marked by progressive present verbs supplants that rubric. The fourth, fifth, and sixth paragraphs are characterized by much more complex and less consistent syntactical contrivance, but the use of parallel, truncated sentence elements is still pursued in prepositional and participial phrases linked by the simplest of additive connectives and recurrent refrains. The entire passage, furthermore, is integrated by an overall climactic structure based upon rhythm. The speed and hurry of the rhetoric builds toward a peak that is reached in the fifth paragraph and the beginning of the sixth, where, after a pause to pick up passengers and take on water, the train reaches the concluding hell scene of the Birmingham slums, and the forward rush of the narrative is stilled by the description of that terrible setting and by a return to direct commentary. The same rise-peak-fall pattern of rhythm which unifies the entire passage so melodramatically also operates within its component elements, the paragraphs, which have their own little form. Based on the development of the parallelisms dependent from the opening "away" motif, each paragraph peaks near its end before rounding off with the dying fall of the extended simile, "like as in the track of the remorseless monster, Death," in the last line. This method in itself thus adds a further rhythmic dimension to an already highly mannered passage by reproducing in its parts the presiding scheme of the whole, and partial climaxes build toward the rhetorical crisis of the entire episode as they add their hurried measures each to the other.

Nor is this all, for these rhythms derived from the railroad contribute to the beat and measure of the whole novel, until they climax in the most brilliantly orchestrated and sensational episode of *Dombey and Son,* the flight of Carker from Dijon to his death, before the horrified gaze of his pursuer, Dombey, under the wheels of a locomotive—an episode that occupies the entire fifteen pages (in my edition) of Chapter LV, the first chapter of the eighteenth, or next-to-last installment of the novel. What follows thereafter is largely dying fall, aside from the melodramatic rescue of Dombey from suicide by his daughter Florence in Chapter LIX, which is organized on the same rhetorical principles that govern Dickens' melodrama everywhere.

The first theme of Carker's flight is introduced as a psychological phenomenon in the culprit's fevered brain following the double shocks of Edith's contemptuous rejection and the sudden arrival of his pursuers:

Some other terror came upon him quite removed from this of being pursued, suddenly, like an electric shock, as he was creeping through the streets. Some visionary terror, unintelligible and inexplicable, associated with a trembling of the ground,—a rush and sweep of something through the air, like Death upon the wing. He shrunk, as if to let the thing go by. It was not gone, it never had been there, yet what a startling horror it left behind.

(XIX, 377)

Although eleven months had gone by between the appearance of the installment in which Dombey journeys to Leamington in April, 1847, and the introduction here in the March, 1848, installment of the "rush of Death" motif, I doubt if there would have been much difficulty in identifying this theme as a fitting reminder and invocation of the railroad and as a prophetic hint of the fate in store for Dombey's fleeing manager. Certain it is at any event that Dickens did not intend to create any spurious mystification about Carker's doom by means of this motif but rather to adjust the reader's perspective toward the flight so as to see it in the light of an ironically "fore-doomed end." Indeed, Dickens employs precisely those words to describe the railroad at the time of its last appearance in the narrative (XVIII, 323), and the chapter in question is ironically entitled, "Rob the Grinder Loses his Place."

The prophetic irony of this "rush of Death" motif is repeated on the following page, together with a newly introduced motif, when Carker arranges for a phaeton to carry him in his flight:

Leaving word that the carriage was to follow him when they [the horses] came, he stole away again, beyond the town, past the old ramparts, out on the open road, which seemed to glide away along the dark plain, like a stream.

Whither did it flow? What was the end of it? As he paused, with some suggestion within him, looking over the gloomy flat where the slender trees marked out the

way, again that flight of Death came rushing up, again
went on, impetuous and resistless, again was nothing but
a horror in his mind, dark as the scene and undefined as
its remotest verge. (XIX, 378)

The image of the receding road "like a stream" and
the "whither" motif join with the "rush of Death"
theme to augment the sense of dark foreboding which
grips Carker's mind. This juncture of motifs and
images is carried on throughout the whole narrative
of his flight, giving unity and coherence to the episode
at the same time that the technique projects the
manager's state of mind. Rhythmically repeated,
varied, and joined with other motifs introduced
along the way, they add a powerful musical quality
to the narrative that functions much in the manner
of a refrain or theme in a piece of music. Certain of
these motifs and images, like that of the "rush of
Death," are repeated with variations throughout the
chapter, gaining new significance and added insistence
at each repetition; others, like the "whither" theme,
link up with later motifs and eventually drop out
of sight after serving to define a limited mood. However they operate, they serve the functions of the
musical accompaniment of a melodrama or a motion
picture soundtrack locally and of the latter's fully
orchestrated score as far as the novel as a whole is
concerned.

The mannered formality in diction and syntax
apparent in this passage ("Whither did it flow?" and
"Again was nothing but a horror") is typical of
Dickens' effort in the melodramatic voice to achieve
a certain high religious solemnity appropriate for
the narration of events in which the divine hand is
manifest. Sentence structure assumes a rhythmic

parallelism and periodicity which is to be exploited more fully in later passages, as in the construction that begins "He stole away *again, beyond* the town, *past* the old ramparts, *out on* the open road . . ." and "*Again* that flight of Death . . . *again* went on . . . *again* was nothing. . . ." Already, however, the reader senses a quickening pace and mounting momentum in the narrative rhythm, a gradually developing insistence and forward thrust, that reminds him of the measures used earlier to narrate Dombey's journey to Leamington. Through it all, he gains the feeling of some grand working-out of ultimate issues involved in Carker's flight, a more-than-human agency directing the manager's retribution.

Meanwhile, Carker appears to be escaping. The carriage he had ordered in Dijon arrives, and Carker begins his headlong flight toward Paris, the Channel, and England:

"Halloa! Whoop! Halloa! Hi!" Away, at a gallop, over the black landscape, scattering the dust and dirt like spray!

The clatter and commotion echoed to the hurry and discordance of the fugitive's ideas. Nothing clear without, and nothing clear within. Objects flitting past, merging into one another, dimly descried, confusedly lost sight of, gone! Beyond the changing scraps of fence and cottage immediately upon the road, a lowering waste. Beyond the shifting images that rose up in his mind and vanished as they showed themselves, a black expanse of dread and rage and baffled villainy. Occasionally, a sigh of mountain air came from the distant Jura, fading along the plain. Sometimes that rush which was so furious and horrible, came again sweeping through his fancy, passed away, and left a chill upon his blood.

The lamps, gleaming on the medley of horses' heads, jumbled with the shadowy driver, and the fluttering of his cloak, made a thousand indistinct shapes, answering to his thoughts. Shadows of familiar people, stooping at their desks and books, in their remembered attitudes; strange apparitions of the man whom he was flying from, or of Edith; repetitions in the ringing bells and rolling wheels, of words that had been spoken; confusions of time and place, making last night a month ago, a month ago last night—home now distant beyond hope, now instantly accessible; commotion, discord, hurry, darkness, and confusion in his mind, and all around him. —Hallo! Hi! away at a gallop over the black landscape; dust and dirt flying like spray, the smoking horses snorting and plunging as if each of them were ridden by a demon, away in a frantic triumph on the dark road—whither?

Again the nameless shock comes speeding up, and as it passes, the bells ring in the ears "whither?" The wheels roar in his ears "whither?" All the noise and rattle shapes itself into that cry. The lights and shadows dance upon the horses' heads like imps. No stopping now; no slackening! On, on! Away with him upon the dark road wildly! (XIX, 379-380)

The long, sensational narrative of Carker's flight may now be said to have fairly begun. The double task of recounting the destruction of a powerful but twisted mind under the impact of hysterical guilt and of narrating the course of the manager's flight and retribution is solved by the novelist's decision to make Carker's psychological condition embody and reflect external narrative. Dickens appropriates for the purposes of narration Carker's interior point of view, so that events are depicted only as they impinge upon or are interwoven with the frantic consciousness of the fleeing villain. Like the technique in the Cook's Court episode, where it is used for predominantly burlesque effects, narration and psychological dramatization are here fused together. Formal third-person narrative disappears as its functions are assumed by the working perceptions and interior monologue of the fleeing man, but with this difference: whereas in the inquest scene Dickens projected an anonymous consciousness at the center of events, from which vantage point they are depicted without formal narrative or identification of speakers, here point of view is lodged in the central conscious-ness of Carker himself, a mirror in which outside events are reflected. This is not a stream-of-conscious-ness technique, for the novelist never abandons the third-person point of reference nor otherwise gives up the narrative wholly to the informing conscious-ness; rather, Dickens' method here is an extreme in-stance of the use of a restricted third-person point of view. Carker's consciousness becomes Dickens' narrative surrogate for the duration of the episode.

To achieve this effect, Dickens transfers the outer scene into the thought processes of Carker, exactly as he had done with Dombey in the case of the Leamington journey. Sounds are not so much re-corded as heard, as "Halloa! Whoop! Halloa! Hi! Away at a gallop. . . ." The first sentence of the second paragraph very clearly bridges the gap be-tween narrative and psychological analysis and fuses interior and exterior scene. Parallelism, repetition, and formal syntactical devices tie the objective and subjective realms together and so give the presenta-tion of psychological states the functions of narrative, thus: "Beyond the shifting images . . . a black expanse of dread . . ."; or again, "The lamps . . . made . . . shapes, answering to his thoughts. Shadows of people. . . ." While Dickens was careful at first to distinguish between inner and outer realms, to say in effect, "This is how things would look from the fugitive's perspective," the tendency is always toward blurring this distinction as point of view absorbs the object-world. The novelist's effort throughout is to project the reader into the psychological center of the scene and action with the utmost realism and dramatic impact.

To this end, other syntactical devices like fragmented sentence structure and a loosely rhythmic, climactic form within sentence constructions, paragraphs, and longer passages encourage the reader to participate in the central consciousness. Fragmentation here involves a removal of verbs and verb forms, so that what remains are nominative elements —the effect is the creation of brief, vivid images that flash brilliantly out of the narrative for a moment, only to be replaced by others. The sense of discordant hurry suggested by this manipulation, by the numerous present participles, gerunds, and gerundives, contributes to the emphatic rush of the immediate progressive present, as in "scattering the dust and dirt," "rolling wheels and ringing bells," "fluttering cloak," "smoking horses snorting and plunging," and so on.

Local climaxes of emotional intensity built up by extended parallel and periodic constructions characteristically round off in some dying fall. Thus in paragraph three, there is a series of noun-prepositional phrases in ascending order of complexity and length, until, when the hurried measure can no longer be sustained by clause or phrase, a succession of intense nouns is introduced—"commotion, discord, hurry, darkness, and confusion"—to form a climax that in turn gives way to the easing rhythms of the phrase, "and all around him." But the next sentence —actually a fragment—rises to an abrupt new climax: "On, on! Away with him upon the dark road wildly!" The pattern of excitation and relaxation begins to emerge: climax, relief, new climax more intense than the first, as the management of rhythm accelerates or slackens.

Earlier motifs are repeated, varied, expanded, combined, or joined with new ones for greater meaning; together they contribute their own important rhythmic impulse to the driving pace of the whole. The coachman's cry mingled with the evocative sounds of the equipage add tempo to local measures. Their later repetition in conjunction with new images of "demon riders," "imps," and "frantic triumph" not only acts as refrain but expands ideas implicit in the motifs to include suggestions that Carker's flight is controlled by subterranean forces. In short, they subtly answer the question raised by the "whither" motif.

The "rush of Death" motif now appears allied with new imagery of the "ringing bells and rolling wheels," the imps, and the dark road. Prophetic hints of the bleak fatality driving Carker's escape are often managed by minor alterations of familiar motifs, as in the shift from "Away upon the dark road wildly" to "Away *with him* . . . ," which implies that the manager's flight is a means of disposing of him. The management of rhythm, then, whether it be in trope, figure, or scheme, aims at suggesting the presence of an ordering agency immanent in events that emerges as it drives them toward some rough justice. The manipulation of tempo serves not only the function of atmospheric control and augmentation, it has thematic overtones as well.

There follows the most extensive rhythmic passage in this chapter, in my text a three-page periodic construction that typically opens with a repetition of the "bells and wheels" refrain, but now modified and varied in order to suggest the despairing and agonizing montony of Carker's flight—"that made the journey like a vision, in which nothing was quite real but his own torment" (XIX, 382). Dependent from this initial simile of the vision, the entire passage is an extravagantly extended parallel construction:

It was a vision of long roads; that stretched away to a horizon, always receding and never gained; of ill-paved towns, up hill and down, where faces came to dark doors and ill-glazed windows, and where rows of mud-bespattered cows and oxen were tied up for sale in the long narrow streets, butting and lowing, and receiving blows on their blunt heads from bludgeons that might have beaten them in; of bridges, crosses, churches, post-yards, new horses being put in against their wills, and the horses of the last stage reeking, panting, and laying their drooping heads together dolefully at stable-doors; of little cemeteries with black crosses settled sideways in the graves, and withered wreathes upon them dropping away; again of long, long roads, dragging themselves out, up hill and down, to the treacherous horizon.

Of morning, noon, and sunset; night, and the rising of an early moon. Of long roads temporarily left behind, and a rough pavement reached; of battering and clattering over it, and looking up, among house-roofs, at a great church-tower; of getting out and eating hastily, and drinking draughts of wine that had no cheering influence; of coming forth afoot, among a host of beggars—blind men with quivering eyelids, led by old women holding candles to their faces; idiot girls; the lame, the epileptic, and the palsied—of passing through the clamour, and looking from his seat at the upturned countenances and outstretched hands, with a blurred dread of recognizing some pursuer pressing forward—of galloping away again, upon the long, long road, gathered up, dull and stunned, in his corner, or rising to see where the moon shone faintly on a patch of the same endless road miles away, or looking back to see who followed.

.   .   .   .   .

It was a fevered vision of things past and present all confounded together; of his life and journey blended into one. Of being madly hurried somewhere, whither he must go. Of old scenes starting up among the novelties through which he travelled. Of musing and brooding over what was past and distant, and seeming to take no notice of the actual objects he encountered, but with a weariness exhausting consciousness of being bewildered by them, and having their images all crowded in his hot brain after they were gone.

A vision of change upon change, and still the same monotony of bells and wheels, and horses' feet, and no rest. Of town and country, post-yards, horses, drivers, hill and hollow, wet weather and dry, and still the same monotony of bells and wheels, and horses' feet, and no rest. A vision of tending on at last, towards the distant capital, by busier roads, and sweeping round, by old cathedrals, and dashing through small towns and villages, less thinly scattered on the road than formerly, and sitting shrouded in his corner, with his cloak up to his face, as people passing by looked at him.

Of rolling on and on, always postponing thought, and always racked with thinking. . . . Of being parched and giddy, and half mad. Of pressing on, in spite of all, as if he could not stop, and coming into Paris, where the turbid river held its swift course undisturbed, between two brawling streams of life and motion.

A troubled vision, then, of bridges, quays, interminable streets; of wine-shops, water-carriers, great crowds of people, soldiers, coaches, military drums, arcades. Of the monotony of bells and wheels and horses' feet being at length lost in the universal din and uproar. Of the gradual subsidence of that noise as he passed out in another carriage by a different barrier from that by which he had entered. Of the restoration, as he travelled on towards the sea-coast, of the monotony of bells and wheels and horses' feet, and no rest.

Of sunset once again, and nightfall. Of long roads again, and dead of night, and feeble lights by the roadside; and still the old monotony of bells and wheels, and

horses' feet, and no rest. Of dawn, and daybreak, and
the rising of the sun. Of toiling slowly up a hill, and
feeling on its top the fresh sea-breeze. . . . Of coming
down into a harbour. . . . Of the bouyancy and brightness of the water, and the universal sparkling.

Of receding from the coast. . . . Of the swell, and
flash, and murmur of the calm sea. . . . Of steaming on
at last into smooth water, and mooring to a pier whence
groups of people looked down, greeting friends on board.
Of disembarking, passing among them quickly, shunning
every one; and of being at last again in England.

(XIX, 382-385)

Repeated employment of two refrains—"bells and
wheels, and horses' feet, and no rest," and "the long,
long road"—add a characteristic rhythmic organization to this passage. Now, too, the "whither" refrain
reappears in connection with the image of a "treacherous horizon" as a means of imbuing narrative with
the helpless dread of the fleeing manager.

The syntactical tempo has been steadily picking
up in the meanwhile, largely as a result of the long
periodic construction depending from the opening
"It was a vision . . ." which dominates the organization of this extensive passage. Three paragraphs of
prepositional phrases (only two are quoted above)
define and vary the quality of Carker's vision before
the main clause is repeated and modified in accord
with the manager's exact psychological state—"It was
a *fevered* vision. . . ." Within this framework, rhetorical management aims at accelerating the pace,
as the subordinate clauses of the first paragraph, with
their prepositional phrases, are held within the embrace of a single compound-complex sentence. The
second paragraph begins to break up the syntactical
units into fragments, principally prepositional phrases,
which are in their turn broken up by abruptly

punctuated interruptive elements. The same tendency is carried farther in the unquoted third paragraph, whose form is dominated by a series of relatively short prepositional phrases punctuated as sentence fragments.

The paragraph following—that which begins "It was a fevered vision . . ."—carries the same pattern forward: an initial main clause, followed by prepositional phrases dependent from it and handled as sentence fragments. The next paragraph dispenses with the opening clause altogether, being content simply to repeat the words, "A vision . . . ," at the beginning and again near the middle of the paragraph, in each case as a prelude to parallel prepositional phrases which extend over into the next paragraph. The paragraph that follows reiterates with a variation—"A *troubled* vision . . ."—the same motif together with the same arrangement of prepositional phrases; but these latter now are marked by internal modifying clauses, inserted to keep the reader informed of the progress of Carker's journey amid the welter of images. The passage concludes with two paragraphs which continue the phrases dependent from "A troubled vision" until Carker arrives in England, while at the same time gradually relaxing the tempo and ending this long, excited *tour de force* on a relatively quiet note.

The sheer repetition of such an extended parallel periodic construction, within which there are a number of local parallel and periodic constructions, is enough by itself to induce a certain relentless narrative tempo, quite aside from the iteration of its many motifs. The very length of the construction, because it separates dependent elements from their common referents and so gives them the autonomy of hallucinative images, puts the narrative squarely in Carker's consciousness while it invests the episode with an underlying insistent cadence. A dual effect is achieved thereby: the sense of frantic progress is suggested at the same time that a static condition of hysterical dislocation of vision is defined. The technique approaches that of the stop-action camera.

However that may be, to the mingled measures of parallelism, periodicity, and fragmented imagery must be added the effects of a host of other stylistic devices that contribute their share to the proliferated images and broken hurry of the tempo. Verbs are largely eliminated, and present participles and other progressive verb-forms are substituted for them. At the same time, punctuation is heavy and abrupt, and connectives are largely loose, indiscriminate, and seriatim. Extended prepositional phrases are broken in upon by interruptive constructions and dependent clauses; and sentence fragments are found within sentence fragments, whose subjects and verbs may be a paragraph or more away. By means of this rhetorical versatility, Dickens' total intention seems to have been the creation of a contradictory dualism: he wished to project a sense of the chaotic hysteria of the fugitive within an ordered, indeed mannered narrative progress. Put another way, Dickens mingles the static monotony of a frantically disorganized consciousness with a narrative framework that suggests a purposive if foreboding forward motion.

Diction and imagery augment the melodramatic intensity of narrative rhythms and purposefully disorganized syntax. The reader finds himself in the midst of a mass of precisely seen but grotesquely disquieting concrete details of the passing scene, as in the cattle market, the carriage-stages, the ceme-

teries, and the importunate beggars. The general
hyperbole of this melodramatic diction takes on a
certain propriety it might not otherwise have in
consequence of Carker's disordered state of mind, so
that terms like "parched and giddy," "lowering
waste," "torment," and "villainy" do not seem out
of keeping.

At a railway junction in the interior Carker pauses
to rest and await a train connection, and Dickens
abandons the rhythmic pattern he had established
earlier in favor of a quieter and less "musical" formal
narrative and psychological analysis as he resumes the
role of omniscient author. But this hiatus only allows
the novelist to marshal his stylistic forces for a new
rhythmic movement of far greater solemnity that,
with old motifs, will carry the narrative through
the death of the fugitive. Nevertheless, the focus
remains on Carker's consciousness as the register of
both inner and outer scene. In so doing, Dickens
simply repeats across the entire chapter the same
rhythmic rise and fall, acceleration and deceleration,
that has already served him so well.

Less obviously "rhetorical" and rhythmic though
this interlude may be, the ground is being prepared
for the grandest orchestration of the "rush of Death"
motif when it is finally identified as a speeding locomotive, the instrument of Carker's destruction. During the night, the manager "started up and listened,
in a sudden terror" as the "ground shook, the house
rattled, the fierce impetuous rush was in the air."
The "rush of Death" is no "fancy," but the reality
of a passing train; and Carker feels as if "he had
been plucked out of its path, and saved from being
torn asunder" (XIX, 387). All the terms of the
"fancy" first noticed outside Dijon are now translated

into a literal description of a rushing locomotive, to which is added the daemonic suggestions clustered around the carriage ride through France. Strangely fascinated and yet horrified, Carker ventures out along the tracks as another train goes by: "A trembling of the ground, and quick vibration in his ears; a distant shriek; a dull light advancing, quickly changed to two red eyes, and a fierce fire, dropping glowing coals; an irresistible bearing on of a great roaring and dilating mass; a high wind, and a rattle —another come and gone, and he holding to a gate, as if to save himself!" (XIX, 388). In making this essential connection between the "rush of Death" motif and an actual locomotive, between a psychological phenomenon and its counterpart in the object-world, Dickens employs all the usual features of the melodramatic voice to announce the manager's doom.

There follows another pause, during which the rhythms relax and lengthen into the more deliberate and solemn tempo of the novelist's death scenes. Arising at dawn to await the coming of the train that is to carry him to safety, Carker sees the rising sun:

So awful, so transcendent in its beauty, so divinely solemn. As he cast his faded eyes upon it, where it rose, tranquil and serene, unmoved by all the wrong and wickedness on which its beams had shone since the beginning of the world, who shall say that some weak sense of virtue upon earth, and its reward in heaven, did not manifest itself, even to him? If ever he remembered brother or sister with a touch of tenderness and remorse, who shall say it was not then?

He needed some such touch then. Death was on him. He was marked off from the living world, and going down into his grave.

. . . He saw the man from whom he had fled, emerging from the door by which he himself had entered there. And their eyes met.

In the quick unsteadiness of the surprise, he staggered, and slipped onto the road below him. But recovering his feet immediately, he stepped back a pace or two upon that road, to interpose some wider space between them, and looked at his pursuer, breathing short and quick.

He heard a shout—another—saw the face change from its vindictive passion to a faint sickness and terror—felt the earth tremble—knew in a moment that the rush was come—uttered a shriek—looked round—saw the red eyes, bleared and dim, in the daylight, close upon him—was beaten down, caught up, and whirled away upon a jagged mill, that spun him round and round and struck him limb from limb, and licked his life up with its fiery heat, and cast his mutilated fragments in the air.

When the traveller, who had been recognized, recovered from a swoon, he saw them bringing from a distance something covered, that lay heavy and still, upon a board, between four men, and saw that others drove some dogs away that sniffed upon the road, and soaked his blood up, with a train of ashes. (XIX, 390-391)

Dickens prepares the reader for the death of the fugitive by his slow-paced description of the rising sun, by the rhetorical questions calculated to arouse sympathy for the man, and by his oracular announcement of Carker's approaching death; for death in Dickens' hands is always a dignified and solemn occasion, to which a certain religious fatality adheres. The pace slows, the sentence elements lengthen into a periodic construction that builds toward the two questions, and diction and imagery take on Biblical overtones. The outright annunciation of the manager's death surrounds Dickens with a priest-like authority and omniscience, as he stands before the reader dressed in all the trappings of Old Testament prophecy. The statement constitutes an almost ritualistic confirmation of a surmise the reader has long held and the fugitive long dreaded; and by intruding at this point in the narrative, when an "accident" brings poetic justice, Dickens invites the reader to join him in the contemplation of a just fatality.

After this affirmation of the presence of an omniscient narrator, Dickens quickly appropriates Carker's point of view for the narration of the actual moment of his death; and the onrushing locomotive is described as if the fugitive were seeing it bearing down upon him. This final realization of the "rush of Death" motif—the trembling ground, the rush, the red eyes, and all the rest—carries one stunning innovation: the shriek of the whistle becomes the shriek of the terrified victim. Fragmented sentence structure, abrupt punctuation, concrete images, and brief syntactical elements communicate the effect of an hysterically heightened consciousness at the moment of death. The shift to the passive voice marks the precise time of death, and a corresponding alteration in tempo from the jagged, hammering measure of the first few lines to the sweeping rhythms of the concluding lines, with their looping "and" connectives, suggests the spinning forward motion of the locomotive that is the instrument of Carker's death. Dickens then abruptly shifts his narrative perspective once more, to the horrified gaze of Dombey, the witness of this terrible scene, who is allowed to see the grisly evidence of the man's death in terms all the more telling for being indirect—the "something on a board," the sniffing dogs, and the ashes. A falling measure, meanwhile, together with a lengthened period, allows this sensational episode to terminate in an appropriate stillness.

The elaborate manipulation of almost every rhythmic resource of syntax, rhetoric, and repeated motif operates upon this episode with the same emotional force as their musical counterparts in an old fashioned melodrama or a modern motion picture soundtrack. However much Dickens was intent on collapsing narrative in upon psychological projection, on condensing event in a recording consciousness, in order to thrust the reader all the more dramatically into the center of the episode, he was not behindhand in augmenting the emotional impact of this melodramatic set-piece with every "musical," "poetic," or rhythmic device at his disposal. A full scale of tempos is exploited as accompaniment to the narrative, ranging from frantic hurry, through foreboding measures, to the solemn ritual beat that announces Carker's fate. This chapter is a complexly orchestrated climacteric of prose rhythms that, like a well wrought piece of symphonic music, brings together a host of lesser themes and variations with which prose style has been playing a deliberate game of development since the introduction of the railroad motif and its associated measures early in the novel. Now they come together and are resolved in this chapter, to reappear only in muted form a few chapters later when Dombey, ruined, alone, and remorseful, is saved from suicide by the timely intervention of his daughter Florence. Nor is this episode "musical" merely in the way that Dickens handles local prose rhythms and sentence structure; in a deeper sense style appropriates the musical method of development by theme, refrain, and motif—not only in texture, nor yet simply in some single passage or chapter, as above, but across the whole fabric of the novel. Formal plot structure and setting integrate *Dombey and Son* around a unified action played out beside the sea; but this exoteric unity is augmented by an esoteric integrity of image and motif—an atmospheric unity —handled in the manner of a musical score which has the same relationship to plot, setting, character, and theme as a score has to its scenario.

We may see this better by turning to examine a pathetic and sentimental passage, in which the same principles govern the deployment of rhythmic language as in sensational episodes. In such passages, however, the pace is slower, syntax is somewhat simpler, although parallelism and periodicity continue, and repeated refrains in image and motif often are the means of effecting a pathetic indirection. In *Dombey and Son,* the determining rhythms for such scenes are not derived from the terrific beat of rushing trains but rather from the more languid measures of ocean waves, in token of the fact that the protagonists of these episodes are allied with those eternal values associated with the sea, as opposed to the time-bound materialists such as Dombey and Carker who are linked to rhythms of the railroad. Thus the management of style offers a musical counter-theme in narrative on which to base a kind of rhythmic counterpoint in prose. A case in point is the death scene of little Paul Dombey, the merchant's son and heir.

In accord with Dickens' practice of projecting the reader into his scenes, the style of narrative in this episode simulates the point of view of the dying child himself as he dimly perceives his approaching death. The claims of decorum are met by simplifying diction and syntax to suggest a child's consciousness, and rhythm is based on a succession of relatively simple clauses linked by the most elementary of seriatim connectives: the aim is to evoke a sense of life slowly and painlessly ebbing away. A motif—the light glimmering on the sickroom wall like water—is introduced and repeated across the entire passage to imply the presence of the river of life that is passing and of the eternal ocean of death that lies beyond. The poetic organization of these measures imparts to this episode its melodramatic qualities.

Typically, Dickens prepares the reader for this final scene in the boy's life by careful earlier development of the motif of ocean waves, first at Mrs. Pipchin's establishment in Brighton and at Dr. Blimber's school, where Paul's preoccupation with the mysterious message embodied in the murmuring sea is designed to suggest not only his approaching death but as well to ally him with those eternal values of the human spirit which his father so conspicuously lacks. Paul's death scene in Chapter XVI, then, comes as the culmination of a long-anticipated process or pattern with broad ramifications throughout the symbolic system of the novel. For our present purposes, however, the episode itself is of major interest. It begins in the following manner:

When the sunbeams struck into his room through the rustling blinds, and quivered on the opposite wall like golden water, he knew that evening was coming on, and that the sky was red and beautiful. As the reflection died away, and a gloom went creeping up the wall, he watched it deepen, deepen, deepen, into night. Then he thought how the long streets were dotted with lamps, and how the peaceful stars were shining overhead. His fancy had a strange tendency to wander to the river, which he knew was flowing through the great city; and now he thought how black it was, and how deep it would look, reflecting the hosts of stars—and more than all, how steadily it rolled away to meet the sea.

As it grew later in the night, and footsteps in the street became so rare that he could hear them coming, count them as they passed, and lose them in the hollow distance, he would lie and watch the many-coloured ring about the candle, and wait patiently for day. His only trouble was, the swift and rapid river. He felt forced, sometimes, to try to stop it—to stem it with his childish hands—or choke its way with sand—and when he saw it coming on, resistless, he cried out! But a word from Florence, who was always at his side, restored him to himself; and leaning his poor head upon her breast, he told Floy of his dream, and smiled.

When day began to dawn again, he watched for the sun; and when its cheerful light began to sparkle in the room, he pictured to himself—pictured! he saw—the high church towers rising up into the morning sky, the town reviving, waking, starting into life once more, the river glistening as it rolled (but rolling fast as ever), and the country bright with dew. Familiar sounds and cries came by degrees into the street below; the servants in the house were roused and busy; faces looked in at the door, and voices asked his attendants softly how he was. Paul always answered for himself, "I am better. I am a great deal better, thank you! Tell papa so!"

By little and little, he got tired of the bustle of the day, the noise of carriages and carts, and people passing and repassing; and would fall sleep, or would be troubled with a restless and uneasy sense again—the child could hardly tell whether this were in his sleeping or his waking moments—of that rushing river. (XVIII, 255-256)

Although these lines form only a small portion of the chapter devoted to Paul's death, they are sufficiently representative of the whole. In them a strong sense of rhythm is apparent, but the tempo is modeled on the languid, long-drawn cadences of ocean waves rather than on the furious forward motion of the locomotive that governs the passage that narrates Carker's flight. Connectives assist in creating the oceanic rhythms by maintaining only a rudimentary relationship between sentence elements, a step appropriate to the intention of stressing the sense of stasis and stability in the scene. Thus a certain equilibrium or equivalence is indicated by such conjunctions as "and," "but," "then," "and now," "and then," and "that . . . and that," an essentially static addition and opposition which seem to level part to part. There is even a wave-like structure in the periods of the mainly compound-complex sentences that distinguish this episode. Ordinarily, they open with some introductory element, usually a subordinate clause, which prefaces a centrally located main clause; and this in turn is modified by another subordinate element that trails away to end the sentence. The opening of the second paragraph is a case in point: "As it grew later . . . and footsteps became so rare that he could hear them, count them as they passed, and lose them . . . he would lie and watch . . . and wait. . . ." Rise, peak, fall, a rocking motion like the action of waves, is the basic pattern of sentence structure throughout this passage. Brief excitations occur infrequently, as in the third paragraph, but the overall development of the episode is languid in tempo and at heart static, in sharp contrast to the staccato reaching after climax of the flight from Dijon. Rather, the topography of Paul's death is level, a compound of back-and-forth, to-and-fro relationships that are as unprogressive as Carker's escape is progressive. The rhetorical organization of the account of Paul's death is designed to project the feeling of an eternal, immutable, finally immortal quality that is associated throughout the novel with the values for which the boy stands, just as Carker, Dombey, and their circle are uniformly depicted in rhythms that indicate the essential transience of the way of life they represent.

As in the episode of Carker's flight, a rhythmic repetition of the dominant motif of the "golden ripple," itself a theme that participates in the novel's wider system of oceanic imagery, often joins with other motifs whose place of origin and development lies outside a particular chapter such as that devoted to Paul Dombey's death. In this case, the theme of Paul's "old fashioned" qualities, which has been a constant motif betokening the boy's commitment to the eternal verities of the human heart in contrast to his father's transient materialism, now reappears at the moment of his death in combination with the "golden ripple" to define the meaning of the novel's water symbolism:

The golden ripple on the wall came back again, and nothing else stirred in the room. The old, old fashion! The fashion that came in with our first garments, and will last unchanged until our race has run its course, and the wide firmament is rolled up like a scroll. The old, old fashion—Death!

Oh thank GOD, all who see it, for that older fashion yet, of Immortality! And look upon us, angels of young children, with regards not quite estranged, when the swift river bears us to the ocean! (XVIII, 261)

The dual values of the novel's water imagery, which alternatively typify mortal transience and the eternal immortality of the spirit, are now established. In the meantime, this chapter has very fully exploited the motif of the golden ripple's appearance and disappearance in connection with yet another rhythmically repeated theme, the journey down the river of life in time of the boat of the boy's spirit to the ocean of death—which is also the sea of immortal life to those whose values are founded on the human spirit.

Like the railroad theme, then, which reappears across the whole scope of the novel in a kind of extended process of repetition, and which carries in its dynamic rhythms suggestions of time and, alternatively, retribution or progress, so too the motif of the ocean and its waves invokes in its extensive repetitions overtones of permanence, alternatively of the inescapable conditions of mortality and of those eternal values which transcend death, destruction, and suffering. To Dombey, for example, the frustration of his vain effort to establish an imperishable earthly mercantile dynasty is uniformly described in terms of maritime disaster. The death of his first wife in childbirth, the death of his son and heir, Paul, the quite literal shipwreck of his vessel, the "Son and Heir," which begins the process that culminates in the bankruptcy of his firm, the bankruptcy itself, and the break-up of his home following the flight of the second Mrs. Dombey, Edith Granger, and the casting-out of Florence—all these episodes are described as disasters at sea, as they must be to a man such as Dombey, whose life is committed to the things of this world that must and do pass away. To the other characters in the novel—Florence and those located around the Wooden Midshipman—on the contrary, maritime adversity of a literal or figurative nature results in happiness primarily because they possess spiritual resources which ally them with what is eternal. The Wooden Midshipman itself, for example, is consistently likened to a tight ship capable of riding out the storm of life's mortal sea because its "crew" of inhabitants have taken the necessary spiritual measures to protect themselves from the temporal disasters inseparable from life in time.[3]

Time and eternity, transience and permanence, temporal process and timelessness, are thus the presiding themes of *Dombey and Son;* and in this fact lies the ultimate use of the devices of rhythm and repetition that Dickens exploited so fully in the texture of his novel. For the entire extent of *Dombey and Son* is dominated by two narrative rhythms, one suggesting temporal change and progress derived from the dynamic, onrushing rhythms of the railroad, and the other, evoking the permanent facts of mortality and immortality, based on the languid, tranquil rhythms of ocean waves, which alternate in correspondence with the novel's contrasting groupings of the characters, their values and attitudes. Thus the personages located around Dombey's business house and mansion tend to be associated with the narrative rhythms of the railroad, because in those cadences are embodied the transitoriness of the values to which they ascribe. Against this measure, with its suggestions of the swift passing of time, lies the quieter prose tempo of sea waves, which is employed to narrate events in the lives of those whose allegiance is pledged to eternal things. Florence Dombey in her father's deserted mansion, Captain Cuttle in lone command of the shop—"vessel," the Wooden Midshipman, when Walter Gay and Sol Gills appear lost at sea, and as we have seen, Paul Dombey's brief life in the novel—these are instances in which the narrative pace approximates the enduring cadences of the sea. In contrast, even the episode in which Dombey contemplates suicide following the wreck of both his business house and his home is carried on in the hurrying rhythms of the scenes devoted to the rail journey and to Carker's flight from Dijon.

It is not too much to say that narrative tempo in *Dombey and Son* is deployed to reinforce theme and plot structure with a congruent atmospheric system derived from and consonant with a figurative scheme that is based on the naturalistic materials of setting and action. It is this remarkable integration of symbol and setting, action and atmosphere, narrative and style, and literal and figurative dimensions of meaning that gives to *Dombey and Son,* and to Dickens' novels generally, that unique coherence necessary for the creation of a compact poetic universe under the inimical conditions of serial publication.

At first blush it must surely seem that poetic universes bear little direct and demonstrable relationship to early Victorian theatrical idioms. In one sense this is true, for having developed my approach at the outset, I have felt that I might expect a generous reader to grant me a certain freedom to exploit it to the utmost, without recalling at every point the first principles upon which a particular reading is based, provided that I do no violence to the initial premise, and that I give him something in the way of a better understanding of Dickens' stylistic methods in exchange for his forbearance. At the same time, it is well to remember the kinship to melodramatic idioms, however primitive those originals may have been, of Dickens' exploitation of musical procedures in narrative style, however subtle they may have become in their mediation in prose fiction. For in theatrical melodrama rhythm and music were used as Dickens employed them: to define the emotional quality of a scene, to identify and heighten an expectation or an atmosphere, and to discriminate between moral identities of different characters or groups of characters.

Where Dickens departs from his theatrical prototypes—aside from the transmutations required by the very different language of prose—is in the broader structural uses to which he puts his management of the composer's methods, a task to which melodrama playwrights and arrangers do not seem to have addressed themselves. In this latter technique Dickens stands closer to that unique modern form, the motion picture with soundtrack, which was born out of the unholy union of melodrama and twentieth-century technology. Nowadays we are accustomed to listening to the musical score of a motion picture transcribed from its soundtrack, knowing that the music was augmenting the form and feeling of the cinema from which it was taken and that its effects on the audience went largely unnoticed during projection. A musical theme linked to a character, setting, or situation is introduced and developed during the course of the movie in ways that reflect and reinforce the movements in plot and characterization through the special idioms of music—counterpoint, fugue, development, and the like. On a record such a score has a more or less completely realized form of its own, thus lending to the visual and spoken portions of the film a supplemental musical structure. An exactly comparable transmutation of the potentialities of early Victorian theatrical melodrama is to be found in Dickens' mature narrative prose style. There the exploitation of the rhythmic resources of rhetoric, syntax, and motif lend to local texture the same kind of augmentation of mood and tone as that to be gained from an orchestra in a pit or in a recording studio. And in *Dombey and Son* and *Bleak House,* at least, we have seen how Dickens assumed the composer's mantle to score his novels around a counterpoint of prose rhythms and rhythmically repeated and varied images and motifs to achieve a consummately orchestrated symphonic development of theme and counter-theme. If this thesis be correct, Dickens' melodramatic prose style stands in the same kind and degree of relationship to its theatrical prototype as the modern motion picture stands to its nineteenth-century progenitor.

APPENDIX A
An Evening at a
Victorian Playhouse

From Francis Wey, *Les Anglais Chez Eux,* trans. Valerie Pirie (New Haven, Conn., 1936). This volume originally appeared in 1856, but it appears on good authority to have been the result of visits to England spread over the period of at least a decade. The text below follows that of Jacob Korg, ed., *London in Dickens' Day* (Englewood Cliffs, N. J., 1960), pp. 144-147.

I remember once being present at a revue where each character stood for one of the chief events of the year. France was represented by a milliner, for before Malakoff the only field of glory we were allowed was the one of fashion. Britannia as Minerva was equipped with helmet and lance. John Bull, the citizen-king, with a baggy check coat, a congested, drunken countenance, wore a tinsel crown and held a sceptre. He had a large lion's tail fastened to the seat of his trousers, which being set in motion by some mechanism, stood straight up as a sign of anger or pride, or whenever he turned his back on the public. This trivial buffoonery never failed to let loose a perfect storm of hilarity. When this grotesque creature approached the actress impersonating France with jokes which we guessed from their success to be obscene, my friends gave signs of unequivocal discontent, but fortunately the action was so disconnected and impossible to follow that their attention soon wandered. Our nation was so abused in this play that the public kept turning round to see what effect it was having on the "Frenchies." Happily, most

of the allusions were entirely lost on us, but when John
Bull started to thrash Marianne we got up and left with
quiet dignity. Jeered at on the stage, derided in the
audience, the French tourist in those days expiated the
weakness of his Government.

That evening had left such a disagreeable impression
on my mind that I was anxious to obliterate it by
witnessing a Christmas pantomime under more auspicious circumstances.

During the last week of the year all the smaller
theatres get up one of those extravaganzas which constitute Londoners' only amusement during those fes-
tive days. Society goes to them on the sly, and it is the
general subject of conversation for a month at least.
A good pantomime epitomises the events and ideas of
the moment. It must be up to date, scourge the people's
bugbear and flatter its idol. It has full license to be
coarse and would be disappointing if it were not. The
Princess' and the Surrey Theatres have had the greatest
successes for this Christmas season of 1856. The first
with *Harlequin,* the second with *The Prince of Pearls.*
Although in the first-mentioned the meeting on the stage
of Henry VIII and Cardinal Wolsey with the characters
of the *Gaaza Ladra* rather tickled me, and, although
the scenery was charming and the ballet dancers a treat
to behold, yet I will confine myself to a description of
The Prince of Pearls, which was perhaps the greater
success of the two.

The managers, Messrs. Shepherd and Creswick, are
evidently quite aware of their supremacy as proved by
the self-sufficiency of their posters. Their announcement
contains the following gems:

"The Pantomime at the Surrey Theatre is the best
in London, it has been got up regardless of cost. . . .
Specialists of every category have been consulted, arch-
aeologists, zoologists, phrenologists, and physiologists.
The supernatural parts have been treated with circum-
spection—our witches are really *old.* Our fairies just
sufficiently so to exhibit limbs, eyes, wings, and smiles
fit to turn the heads of all young mortals who behold
them. . . . The comic parts will keep the public in such

roars of laughter that if their buttons do not fly off their seams will surely burst, etc."

I must admit that the case was barely overstated.

The play opens in the den of three witches, *by a remarkably savage scene.* But the various incidents of the drama are less *savage* than one might have feared from such an ominous beginning. From the cavern we are wafted to the Prince's Palace, where twenty-four oysters disgorge twenty-four pearls in the guise of twenty-four alluring dancers. And so all along graceful fantasy will be interwoven with the ugliness of brutal parody which is the main subject of the entertainment. This parody is composed of a medley of various dramas, *Jane Shore,* Shakespeare's *Richard III* and Delavigne's *Enfants d'Edouard.* Enormous cardboard heads conceal the actors', who wear historical costumes cleverly exaggerated. No words can give a correct idea of the cunning hideosity of these masks, scientifically moulded, as the management proclaims, with the aid of a phrenologist. The melancholy of Hastings, the brutality of Tyrrel, the sufferings of Jane Shore, the sensuality of the Archbishop of Canterbury, are wonderfully imprinted on those pasteboard countenances. But the palm must go to Richard III for the ease with which he carries his hump and his buffoon-like ferocity. Gloucester is a hybrid figure, half ogre, half mountebank, seasoning his cruelty with mock gallantry. To emphasize this trait he never appears on the stage without a quizzing glass. Richard III, Henry VIII, and Charles I are the three kings most familiar to the London cockneys. In this country blood keeps the memory green.

When Gloucester visits the little princes in the tower they are dressed in nightshirts and velvet caps, and are wearing the ribbon and star of St. George. He makes them eat boiling pap with a large wooden spoon with which he raps them on the nose—to the public's huge delight. Now and then there is a break in the farce and the spectator is transported to the ethereal regions of unreality—where fairies and genii float in landscapes of gold, crystal and diamonds. And so one moves alternately from dreams of bliss to the horror of nightmares.

But that is not all. Each of these historical impersonations plays a dual role; so that at a given moment the
most unexpected transformations take place. Conquer-
ors and conquered, executioners and victims cast off
their dramatic garb and take part in a dishevelled
Bacchanalia. The plaintive Jane Shore is now Columbine, Richard III a clown, Hastings Harlequin, and the
murdered princes pantaloons. All the characters join
in a rough-and-tumble, and the pantomime commences
in real earnest. Blows are freely exchanged with any
available instruments, the actors kick, laugh, yell, jest,
roar and rollick in an indescribable pandemonium.
Thereupon mock policemen intervene and are roughly
handled by the actors. Meanwhile the background representing the various London districts moves slowly
past. Then comes a scene of political satire. The General
Staff of the British Army drag themselves in on crutches;
Cobden and his adherents are flogged like schoolboys;
food adulterers are belaboured by the people.

Suddenly the scene changes to a market-place and is
swarming with live chickens, turkeys, pigeons, ducks.
They squawk with fright and many of them jump or
fly among the audience; a general uproar ensues, while
on the stage sheep and calves have made their appearance and a pig is having its tail twisted and squealing
the house down. How would it be possible to describe
such a hurly-burly of an entertainment which lasts
three hours without a break; which is acted with such
rapidity that notices have to be posted up to explain
the acts, and which brings into contact Cobden, Richard III, Columbine, Hastings, Lord Raglan, the Prince
of Pearls, Admiral Napier, the Queen of Grapes, the
Emperor of the French and Queen Victoria.

England's ally has not been forgotten. Four men
stagger in with a bale of goods on which is written
French divertissement. With a touch of his wand Harlequin has wrought a miracle. The bale opens and dis-
gorges a tower bearing the name of Malakoff printed
across a tricolour flag, and out of this tower steps a
memeluke of three years old representing Turkey lib-
erated. The orchestra play *Partant pour la Syrie* and

the audience yells *hurrah!* I must be even more sensitively patriotic than I realised, for my heart was thumping and I had an overwhelming impulse, which fortunately I was able to repress, to kiss every pretty English girl in the theatre. Meanwhile Admiral Napier had appeared in full-dress uniform, ordered a few Cossacks to be put in irons, shaken the editor of the *Times* by the hand, been chaired, then discarding his uniform danced a frantic jig with Harlequin. It all ended by a scene in an enchanted island lit by multi-coloured Roman candles. From the centre rose an enormous spray of flowers, supporting the figures of Queen Victoria and Napoleon III standing hand-in-hand. These parts were taken by small children in consideration of the demands of perspective. The Prince of Pearls and the Queen of Grapes crowned them with laurel wreathes, the young ladies of the ballet grouped themselves around with their legs in the air, Columbine and the clown fell on their knees, Richard III's soldiers presented arms and the curtain fell to the majestic strains of *God Save the Queen.*

No words can express the animation, the gaiety, the boldness, the madness, the incoherence, the coarseness, the splendour, the whimsical poetry, and the brutality of these Christmas pantomimes. Their greatest charm is their unexpectedness and diversity. At the Princess's Theatre I saw a whole militia composed of ostriches ten feet high. At the Surrey, Gloucester's soldiers, most beautifully and correctly dressed, wore leopard's heads. It would be impossible to imagine entertainments better calculated to cheer the spirits and divert the eyes. . . .

APPENDIX B
The News of Nemo's Death
Reaches Cook's Court

BY THIS TIME the news has got into the court. Groups of its inhabitants assemble to discuss the thing; and the outposts of the army of observation (principally boys) are pushed forward to Mr. Krook's window, which they closely invest. A policeman has already walked up to the room, and walked down again to the door, where he stands like a tower, only condescending to see the boys at his base occasionally; but whenever he does see them, they quail and fall back. Mrs. Perkins, who has not been for some weeks on speaking terms with Mrs. Piper, in consequence of an unpleasantness originating in young Perkins [*sic*] having "fetched" young Piper "a crack," renews her friendly intercourse on this auspicious occasion. The potboy at the corner, who is a privileged amateur, as possessing official knowledge of life, and having to deal with drunken men occasionally, exchanges confidential communications with the policeman, and has the appearance of an impregnable youth, unassailable by truncheons and unconfinable in station-houses. People talk across the court out of window, and bare-headed scouts come hurrying in from Chancery Lane to know what's the matter. The general feeling seems to be that it's a blessing Mr. Krook warn't made away with first, mingled with a little natural disappointment that he was not. In the midst of this sensation, the beadle arrives.

The beadle, though generally understood in the neighbourhood to be a ridiculous institution, is not without a certain popularity for the moment, if it were only as a man who is going to see the body. The police-man considers him an imbecile civilian, a remnant of the barbarous watchmen-times; but gives him admission, as something that must be borne with until Government shall abolish him. The sensation is heightened, as the tidings spread from mouth to mouth that the beadle is on the ground, and has gone in.

By and by the beadle comes out, once more intensify-ing the sensation, which has rather languished in the interval. He is understood to be in want of witnesses, for the Inquest to-morrow, who can tell the Coroner and Jury anything whatever respecting the deceased. Is immediately referred to innumerable people who can tell nothing whatever. Is made more imbecile by being constantly informed that Mrs. Green's son "was a law-writer his-self, and knowed him better than anybody"— which son of Mrs. Green's appears, on inquiry, to be at the present time aboard a vessel bound for China, three months out, but considered accessible by telegraph, on application to the Lords of the Admiralty. Beadle goes into various shops and parlours, examining the inhabi-tants; always shutting the door first, and by exclusion, delay, and general idiotcy, exasperating the public. Policeman seen to smile to potboy. Public loses inter-est, and undergoes reaction. Taunts the beadle, in shrill youthful voices, with having boiled a boy; choruses fragments of a popular song to that effect, and import-ing that the boy was made into soup for the workhouse. Policeman at last finds it necessary to support the law, and seize the vocalist; who is released upon the flight of the rest, on condition of his getting out of this then, come! and cutting it—a condition he immediately ob-serves. So the sensation dies off for the time; and the unmoved policeman (to whom a little opium, more or less, is nothing), with his shining hat, stiff stock, inflex-ible great-coat, stout belt and bracelet, and all things fitting, pursues his lounging way with a heavy tread: beating the palms of his white gloves one against the other, and stopping now and then, at a street-corner, to look casually about for anything between a lost child and a murder.

Under cover of the night, the feeble-minded beadle comes flitting about Chancery Lane with his summonses, in which every Juror's name is wrongly spelt, and nothing rightly spelt but the beadle's own name, which nobody can read or wants to know. The summonses served, and his witnesses forewarned, the beadle goes to Mr. Krook's, to keep a small appointment he has made with certain paupers; who, presently arriving, are conducted upstairs; where they leave the great eyes in the shutter something new to stare at, in that last shape which earthly lodgings take for No one—and for Every one.

And all that night, the coffin stands ready by the old portmanteau; and the lonely figure on the bed, whose path in life has lain through five-and-forty years, with no more track behind him, that any one can trace, than a deserted infant.

Next day the court is all alive—is like a fair, as Mrs. Perkins, more than reconciled to Mrs. Piper, says, in amicable conversation with that excellent woman. The Coroner is to sit in the first-floor room at the Sol's Arms, where the Harmonic Meetings take place twice a-week, and where the chair is filled by a gentleman of professional celebrity, faced by Little Swills, the comic vocalist, who hopes (according to the bill in the window) that his friends will rally round him, and support first-rate talent. The Sol's Arms does a brisk stroke of business all the morning. Even children so require sustaining, under the general excitement, that a pieman who has established himself for the occasion at the corner of the court, says his brandy-balls go off like smoke. What time the beadle, hovering between the door of Mr. Krook's establishment and the door of the Sol's Arms, shows the curiosity in his keeping to a few discreet spirits, and accepts the compliment of a glass of ale or so in return.

At the appointed hour arrives the Coroner, for whom the Jurymen are waiting, and who is received with a salute of skittles from the good dry skittle-ground attached to the Sol's Arms. The Coroner frequents more public-houses than any man alive. The smell of sawdust, beer, tobacco-smoke, and spirits, is inseparable in his vocation from death in its most awful shapes. He is conducted by the beadle and the landlord to the Harmonic Meeting Room, where he puts his hat on the piano, and takes a Windsor-chair at the head of a long table, formed of several short tables put together, and ornamented with glutinous rings in endless involutions, made by pots and glasses. As many of the Jury as can crowd together at the table sit there. The rest get among the spittoons and pipes, or lean against the piano. Over the Coroner's head is a small iron garland, the pendant handle of a bell, which rather gives the Majesty of the Court the appearance of going to be hanged presently.

Call over and swear the Jury! While the ceremony is in progress, sensation is created by the entrance of a chubby little man in a large shirt-collar, with a moist eye, and an inflamed nose, who modestly takes a position near the door as one of the general public, but seems familiar with the room too. A whisper circulates that this is Little Swills. It is considered not unlikely that he will get up an imitation of the Coroner, and make it the principal feature of the Harmonic Meeting in the evening.

"Well, gentlemen—" the Coroner begins.

"Silence there, will you!" says the beadle. Not to the Coroner, though it might appear so.

"Well, gentlemen," resumes the Coroner. "You are impanelled here, to inquire into the death of a certain man. Evidence will be given before you, as to the circumstances attending that death, and you will give your verdict according to the—skittles; they must be stopped, you know, beadle!—evidence, and not according to anything else. The first thing to be done, is to view the body."

"Make way there!" cries the beadle.

So they go out in a loose procession, something after the manner of a straggling funeral, and make their inspection in Mr. Krook's back second floor, from which a few of the Jurymen retire pale and precipitately. The beadle is very careful that two gentlemen not very

neat about the cuffs and buttons (for whose accommodation he has provided a special little table near the Coroner in the Harmonic Meeting Room) should see all
there is to be seen. For they are the public chroniclers
of such inquiries, by the line; and he is not superior
to the universal human infirmity, but hopes to read
in print what "Mooney, the active and intelligent beadle
of the district," said and did; and even aspires to see
the name of Mooney as familiarly and patronisingly
mentioned as the name of the Hangman is, according to
the latest examples.

Little Swills is waiting for the Coroner and Jury
on their return. Mr. Tulkinghorn, also. Mr. Tulkinghorn is received with distinction, and seated near the
Coroner; between that high judicial officer, a bagatelle-
board, and the coal-box. The inquiry proceeds. The
Jury learn how the subject of their inquiry died, and
learn no more about him. "A very eminent solicitor
is in attendance, gentlemen," says Coroner, "who, I am
informed, was accidentally present, when discovery of
the death was made; but he could only repeat the evidence you have already heard from the surgeon, the
landlord, the lodger, and the law-stationer; and it is
not nesessary to trouble him. Is anybody in attendance
who knows anything more?"

Mrs. Piper pushed forward by Mrs. Perkins. Mrs.
Piper sworn.

Anastasia Piper, gentlemen. Married woman. Now,
Mrs. Piper—what have you got to say about this?

Why, Mrs. Piper has a good deal to say, chiefly in
parentheses and without punctuation, but not much to
tell. Mrs. Piper lives in the court (which her husband
is a cabinet-maker), and it has long been well beknown
among the neighbours (counting from the day next but
one before the half-baptising of Alexander James Piper
aged eighteen months and four days old on accounts
of not being expected to live such was the sufferings
gentlemen of that child in his gums) as the Plaintive—
so Mrs. Piper insists on calling the deceased—was reported to have sold himself. Thinks it was the Plaintive's air in which that report originated in. See the

Plaintive often and considered as his air was feariocious and not to be allowed to go about some children being timid (and if doubted hoping Mrs. Perkins may be brought forard for she is here and will do credit to her husband and herself and family). Has seen the Plaintive wexed and worrited by the children (for children they will ever be and you cannot expect them specially if of playful dispositions to be Methoozellers which you was not yourself). On accounts of this and his dark looks has often dreamed as she see him take a pick-axe from his pocket and split Johnny's head (which the child knows not fear and has repeatually called after him close at his eels). Never however see the Plaintive take a pick-axe or any other wepping far from it. Has seen him hurry away when run and called after as if not partial to children and never see him speak to neither child nor grown person at any time (excepting the boy that sweeps the crossing down the lane over the way round the corner which if he was here would tell you that he has been seen a-speaking to him frequent).

Says the Coroner, is that boy here? Says the beadle, no, sir, he is not here. Says the Coroner, go and fetch him then. In the absence of the active and intelligent, the Coroner converses with Mr. Tulkinghorn.

O! Here's the boy, gentlemen!

Here he is, very muddy, very hoarse, very ragged. Now, boy!—But stop a minute. Caution. This boy must be put through a few preliminary paces.

Name, Jo. Nothing else that he knows on. Don't know that everybody has two names. Never heerd of sich a think. Don't know that Jo is short for a longer name. Thinks it long enough for *him*. *He* don't find no fault with it. Spell it? No. *He* can't spell it. No father, no mother, no friends. Never been to school. What's home? Knows a broom's a broom, and knows it's wicked to tell a lie. Don't recollect who told him about the broom, or about the lie, but knows both. Can't exactly say what'll be done to him arter he's dead if he tells a lie to the gentlemen here, but believes it'll be something wery bad to punish him, and serve him right—and so he'll tell the truth.

"This won't do, gentlemen!" says the Coroner, with a melancholy shake of the head.

"Don't you think you can receive his evidence, sir?" asks an attentive Juryman.

"Out of the question," says the Coroner. "You have heard the boy. 'Can't exactly say' won't do, you know. We can't take *that,* in a Court of Justice, gentlemen. It's terrible depravity. Put the boy aside."

Boy put aside; to the great edification of the audience; especially of Little Swills, the Comic Vocalist.

Now. Is there any other witness? No other witness.

Very well, gentlemen! Here's a man unknown, proved to have been in the habit of taking opium in large quantities for a year and a half, found dead of too much opium. If you think you have any evidence to lead you to the conclusion that he committed suicide, you will come to that conclusion. If you think it is a case of accidental death, you will find a Verdict accordingly.

Verdict accordingly. Accidental death. No doubt. Gentlemen, you are discharged. Good afternoon.

While the Coroner buttons his great-coat, Mr. Tulkinghorn and he give private audience to the rejected witness in a corner. . . .

For some little time the Jurymen hang about the Sol's Arms colloquially. In the sequel, half a dozen are caught up in a cloud of pipe-smoke that pervades the parlour of the Sol's Arms; two stroll to Hampstead; and four engage to go half-price to the play at night, and top up with oysters. Little Swills is treated on several hands. Being asked what he thinks of the proceedings, characterises them (his strength lying in a slangular direction) as a "rummy start." The landlord of the Sol's Arms, finding Little Swills so popular, commends him highly to the Jurymen and public; observing that, for a song in character, he don't know his equal, and that that man's character wardrobe would fill a cart.

Thus, gradually the Sol's Arms melts into the shadowy night, and then flares out of it strong in gas. The Harmonic Meeting hour arriving, the gentleman of professional celebrity takes the chair; is faced (red-faced) by Little Swills; their friends rally round them, and support first-rate talent. In the zenith of the evening, Little Swills says, Gentlemen, if you'll permit me, I'll attempt a short description of a scene of real life that came off here to-day. Is much applauded and encouraged; goes out of the room as Swills; comes in as the Coroner (not the least in the world like him); describes the Inquest, with recreative intervals of pianoforte accompaniment to the refrain—With his (the Coroner's) tippy tol li doll, tippy tol lo doll, tippy tol li doll, Dee!

The jingling piano at last is silent, and the Harmonic friends rally round their pillows. Then there is rest around the lonely figure, now laid in its last earthly habitation; and it is watched by the gaunt eyes in the shutters through some quiet hours of the night. If this forlorn man could have been prophetically seen lying here, by the mother at whose breast he nestled, a little child, with eyes upraised to her loving face, and soft hand scarcely knowing how to close upon the neck to which it crept, what an impossibility the vision would have seemed! O, if, in brighter days, the now extinguished fire within him ever burned for one woman who held him in her heart, where is she, while these ashes are above the ground!

. . . Then the active and intelligent, who has got into the morning papers as such, comes with his pauper company to Mr. Krook's, and bears off the body of our dear brother here departed, to a hemmed-in churchyard, pestiferous and obscene, whence malignant diseases are communicated to the bodies of our dear brothers and sisters who have not departed; while our dear brothers and sisters who hang about official back-stairs—would to Heaven they *had* departed!—are very complacent and agreeable. Into a beastly scrap of ground which a Turk would reject as a savage abomination, and a Caffre would shudder at, they bring our dear brother here departed, to receive Christian burial.

With houses looking on, on every side, save where a reeking little tunnel of a court gives access to the iron gate—with every villainy of life in action close on death, and every poisonous element of death in action close on life—here, they lower our dear brother down a foot or two: here, sow him in corruption, to be raised in corruption; an avenging ghost at many a sick-bed-side: a shameful testimony to future ages, how civilization and barbarism walked this boastful island together.

Come night, come darkness, for you cannot come too soon, or stay too long, by such a place as this! Come, straggling lights into the windows of the ugly houses; and you who do iniquity therein, do it at least with this dread scene shut out! Come, flame of gas, burning so sullenly above the iron gate, on which the poisoned air deposits its witch-ointment slimy to the touch! It is well that you should call to every passer-by, "Look here!"

With the night, comes a slouching figure through the tunnel-court, to the outside of the iron gate. It holds the gate with its hands, and looks in between the bars; stands looking in, for a little while.

It then, with an old broom it carries, softly sweeps the step, and makes the archway clean. It does so, very busily and trimly; looks in again, a little while, and so departs.

Jo, is it thou? Well, well! Though a rejected witness, who "can't exactly say" what will be done to him in greater hands than men's, thou art not quite in outer darkness. There is something like a distant ray of light in thy muttered reason for this:

"He wos wery good to me, he wos!" (XXII, 162-172)

NOTES

CHAPTER ONE

1 See *Unto This Last* (1862) in *Works*, ed. E. T. Cook and Alexander Wedderburn (39 vols.; 1903-1912), XXXVII, 31n.

2 "Dickens: The Two Scrooges," in *Eight Essays* (New York, 1954), p. 3. Reprinted from *The Wound and the Bow* (Boston, 1941).

3 See, for example, J. B. van Amerongen, *The Actor in Dickens* (New York, 1927); F. Dubrez Fawcett, *Dickens the Dramatist* (London, 1952); S. J. A. Fitz-Gerald, *Dickens and the Drama* (London, 1910); and Thomas E. Pemberton, *Charles Dickens and the Stage* (London, 1888).

4 Two short studies are valuable: R. C. Churchill, "Dickens, Drama, and Tradition," *Scrutiny*, X (1942), 358-375, and reprinted in *The Importance of Scrutiny*, ed. Eric Bentley (New York, 1948), pp. 182-202; and Sergei Eisenstein, "Dickens, Griffith, and the Film Today," *Film Form and The Film Sense* (New York, 1957), pp. 195-255, and published originally in *Film Form* (New York, 1948). Dickens' relations with the theater of his own day are fully chronicled by Edgar Johnson, *Charles Dickens: His Tragedy and Triumph* (2 vols.; New York, 1952). One further study, Robert Garis, *The Dickens Theatre* (Oxford, 1965), which appeared in print during the writing of these pages, is valuable but general in its remarks.

5 See Dickens' "Dullborough Town," from *The Uncommercial Traveller*, in *Works*, National Edition, ed. B. W. Matz (40 vols.; London, 1906-1908), XXX, 152-153 (hereafter cited as *Works;* all citations to Dickens' works in the text, unless specified otherwise, are to this edition); and "Introductory Chapter" to *Memoirs of Joseph Grimaldi, Works*, XXXIV, 340-343. Also Johnson, I, 22-24, *passim.*

6 Johnson, I, 49.

7 John Forster, *The Life of Charles Dickens*, ed. J. W. T. Ley (London, 1928), pp. 59-60 (hereafter cited as *Life*). Earle Davis' *The Flint and the Flame* (Columbia, Mo., 1963) contains an interesting discussion of Mathews' influence on Dickens' characterization.

8 Among others, Dickens wrote *The Village Coquettes*, a burletta, and *The Strange Gentleman*, a farce based on his sketch, "The Great Winglebury Duel"; both were performed successfully in 1836; *Is She his Wife?*, another farce, was performed in 1837, and *The Lamplighter*, a comedy, in 1838. He dramatized his Christmas story, *The Battle of Life*, with the Keeleys in 1846; and with Wilkie Collins' help he wrote *No Thoroughfare*, a drama, in 1867: see *Works*, XXXVI, 253-463.

Dickens' journalism includes many reviews of important theatrical productions, like those of Macready's *Lear* and Benedick, Talfourd's *Virginie*, and a revival of Jerrold's *Black-Ey'd Susan*, all in the *Examiner* (Feb. 4, 1838; March 3, 1843; May 12, 1848), in *Works*, XXXV, 3-7, 25-28, 89-90. An important defense of the popular theater is to be found in "The Amusements of the People," *Household Words* (March 30 and April 30, 1850), in *Works*, XXXV, 112-125. See also, *ibid.*, XXXVI, 10-16, 96-102; and XXXIV, 479-485.

9 Johnson, I, 424, 570-571; II, 623, 645-646, 734-735, 828, 843, 868. Among other rôles, Dickens played Sir Epicure Mammon in *The Alchemist*, Bobadil in *Every Man in his Humour*, Shallow in *The Merry Wives of Windsor*, and Richard Wardour in *The Frozen Deep*.

10 Among his theatrical friends, Dickens could number William Macready, one of the great nineteenth-century tragedians and an important innovator in Shakespearean production; Douglas Jerrold, author of some of the earliest domestic melodramas to have any worth, such as *Black-Eyed Susan* and *The Rent Day;* Sheridan Knowles, a prolific writer of classically inspired tragedies and of broad comedies and farces; Thomas Noon Talfourd, jurist and author of *Ion* (1835), a celebrated tragedy of the day; Clarkson Stanfield, a distinguished scenic designer; Tom Taylor, a leader in the realistic movement of the middle years of the century; Charles Fechter, a French tragedian of considerable talent; the two Charles Mathews, father and son, who variously encouraged better standards of acting and production; and a host of lesser lights.

11 Johnson, I, 537, II, 611-612, 1099, 1150-1151, and *passim*.

12 *The Speeches of Charles Dickens*, ed. K. J. Fielding (Oxford, 1960), pp. 73-80, 92-97, 110-127, 138-142, 162, 184-188, and *passim*.

13 Johnson, II, 1057-1058.

14 *Ibid.*, I, 523-532.

15 *Ibid.*, II, 1142ff.

16 "*Hard Times:* An Analytical Note," in *The Great Tradition* (London, 1950), pp. 227-248.

17 J. W. T. Ley, *The Dickens Circle* (London, 1919), p. 75.

18 *The Letters of Charles Dickens*, Nonesuch Edition, ed. Walter Dexter (3 vols.; 1938-1939), III, 461. Hereafter cited as *Letters*.

19 *Ibid.*, II, 624.

20 *Ibid.*, III, 138.

21 Richard Stang, *The Theory of the Novel in England, 1850-1870* (New York and London, 1959), p. 100.

22 *Ibid.*, pp. 101-103. See also Fred W. Boege, "Point of View in Dickens," *PMLA*, LXV (1950), 90-105.

23 *Letters*, III, 125. See also Harland S. Nelson, "Dickens' Plots: 'The Ways of Providence' or the Influence of Collins?", *Victorian Newsletter*, 19 (1961), 11-14.

24 *Life*, p. 76. Dickens often voiced similar sentiments both in and about his works. In *Bleak House* he underscored the unitary tendency in things: "What connexion can there have been between many people in the innumerable histories of this world, who, from opposite sides of great gulfs, have, nevertheless, been very curiously brought together!" (*Works*, XXII, 248). Of *Little Dorrit* he wrote, "It struck me that it would be a new thing to show people coming together, in a chance way, as fellow-travellers . . . as happens in life; and to connect them afterwards, and to make the waiting for that connection a part of the interest" (*Life*, p. 624). See also *Works*, III, xvii, xx; and John Henry Raleigh, "Dickens and the Sense of Time," *NCF*, XIII (1958), 127-137.

25 "The Amusements of the People," *Household Words* (March 30 and April 30, 1850), in *Works*, XXXV, 112-125.

26 This quotation is taken from the preface to *Bleak House* (*Works*, XXII, xv) because of its succinctness. But see the statement of editorial policy for *Household Words*, in which Dickens held that one of his aims was "to show to all, that in all familiar things . . . there is Romance enough, if we will find it out" (XXXV, 107). He carried out this policy in his journalism to the hilt, as Monroe Engel demonstrates in "Dickens on Art," *MP*, LII(1955), 25-38.

27 *Life*, p. 728. Dickens was often struck by what he called the "fantastic fidelity" of his characters to their originals (*ibid.*, p. 726), by which he meant something more specific, I believe, than a mere superlative: he was getting at the notion of imaginative projection of character. To Bulwer-Lytton he once wrote that "I think it is my infirmity to fancy or perceive relations in things which are not apparent generally" (*ibid.*, p. 721).

28 "The Spirit of Fiction," *All the Year Round*, XVIII (July 27, 1867), 120. George Santayana agreed with Dickens. Those who think Dickens exaggerated "have no eyes and no ears" but "only notions of what things and people are": "Dickens," in *Soliloquies in England* (London, 1922), pp. 65-66.

29 "Spirit of Fiction," p. 120.

30 For example, see "Address on Completion of the First Volume of *Bentley's Miscellany*," *Works*, XXXIV, 337-338, in which he likens his editorial position to that of a stage manager.

31 According to J. W. T. Ley in a footnote to Forster's *Life*, p. 728, n. 474a.

32 As quoted by Forster, *Life*, p. 720. Lewes' remarks are contained in his essay, "Dickens in Relation to Criticism," *Fortnightly Review*, Feb., 1872, pp. 141-154, and reprinted in *The Dickens Critics*, ed. George H. Ford and Lauriat Lane, Jr. (Ithaca, N. Y., 1961), pp. 54-74. There are many shrewd comments on Dickens' strategy in the novel in George H. Ford's *Dickens and*

his Readers (Princeton, 1955) and in Miriam Allott's *Novelists on the Novel* (New York and London, 1959).

33 This is confirmed by Forster *(Life*, p. 481), who arrived in Paris the day after Dickens had written the death of Paul, and who found the novelist desolated. The death of Little Nell affected Dickens similarly *(Life*, p. 150).

34 *Ibid.*, p. 146.

35 *Ibid.*, p. 378.

36 *Letters,* II, 825.

37 *Life*, p. 646.

38 *Ibid.*, p. 689.

39 Johnson, II, 1004. Johnson's account of Dickens' response to his readings is the most complete: II, 531-532, 790-791, 853-854, 874, 904, 916, 936-937, 940, 999-1000, 1004-1005, 1009, 1080, 1082-1083, 1102-1104, 1106, 1144-1145.

40 *Ibid.*, II, p. 1144.

CHAPTER TWO

1 While marred by inaccuracies and omissions, Allardyce Nicoll's *A History of the English Drama, 1660-1900* (5 vols.; Cambridge, 1955), III and IV, remains the best source on the general features of the Georgian and Victorian theater. An excellent overall review is to be found in George Rowell, *The Victorian Theatre, A Survey* (Oxford, 1956), and in the introductory chapters of Winton Tolles, *Tom Taylor and the Victorian Drama* (New York, 1940). On theatrical conditions especially, see E. B. Watson, *Sheridan to Robertson: A Study of the Nineteenth-Century London Stage* (Cambridge, Mass., 1926). Two studies with some relevance to Dickens' knowledge of theatrical conventions and traditions are F. J. H. Darton, *Vincent Crummles: His Theatre and his Times* (London, 1926), and V. C. Clinton-Baddeley, *All Right on the Night* (London, 1954), of which the latter is the more valuable. Also useful is Ernest Reynolds, *Early Victorian Drama (1830-1870)* (Cambridge, 1936). Among the hosts of memoirs by theatrical personages in the nineteenth century, the following are especially valuable: Westland Marston, *Our Recent Actors* (2 vols.; London, 1881); J. R. Planché, *Recollections and Reflections* (2 vols.; London, 1872); W. B. Jerrold, "Introductory Memoir," *The Works of Douglas Jerrold* (4 vols.; London, 1863-1864). See also G. H. Lewes' acute appraisals of Victorian actors and forms in *On Actors and the Art of Acting* (New York, 1957), originally published in 1875. *The Oxford Companion to the Theatre* (Oxford, 1951), is a mine of general information.

2 Nicoll, III, 194 and 230; IV, 4-6 and 137-140; Rowell, pp. 8-13. See also Allarydyce Nicoll, "The Theatre," in *Early Victorian England,* ed. G. M. Young (2 vols.; London, 1934), II, 265-282, esp. p. 267. Two of Dickens' closest friends, Bulwer-Lytton and Macready, lead the fight to repeal the Licensing Act of 1737: Nicoll, IV, 5 and Reynolds, pp. 149-150.

3 Rowell, pp. 10-12.

4 Nicoll, IV, 137ff.; Rowell, pp. 66-70; Tolles, pp. 35-44; and V. C. Clinton-Baddeley, *The Burlesque Tradition in the English Theatre after 1660* (London, 1952), pp. 8ff., and pp. 88-120.

5 The following description of pantomime is a collation of a number of primary and secondary sources. Perhaps the best short account of the form is "Traditions of the Pantomime," in Clinton-Baddeley's *All Right on the Night*, pp. 201-234. See also the same author's *Burlesque*, pp. 88-120, *passim*. The best general history of pantomime is Maurice Willson Disher, *Clowns and Pantomimes* (London, 1925), with many contemporary illustrations. Other sources, in the order of their relative importance, are: Rex Pogson, "The Pantomime Tradition," *Manchester Review* (Winter, 1955), 3-14; Albert Edward Wilson, *King Panto: The Story of Pantomime* (New York, 1935); Andrew Halliday, *Comical Fellows; or, The History and Mystery of the Pantomime* (London, 1863); R. J. Broadbent, *A History of the Pantomime* (London, n.d.). Halliday and Broadbent are valuable chiefly for their descriptions of later pantomime productions. See also Cyril W. Beaumont, *The History of Harlequin* (London, 1926), and Allardyce Nicoll's *The World of Harlequin* (Cambridge, 1963). Certainly the most fully and carefully documented of recent studies of English pantomime is that of Thelma Niklaus, *Harlequin Phoenix; Or, The Rise and Fall of a Bergamask Rogue* (London, 1956). Her account of later eighteenth-century and early nineteenth-century pantomime, while unsympathetic, is informative: see pp. 137-174.

6 The text is preserved in *Fairburn's Description of the Popular and Comic New Pantomime Called Harlequin and Mother Goose, or The Golden Egg . . .* (3rd ed.; London, [n.d.]), in the Theatre Collection of the Princeton University Library. Clinton-Baddeley, *All Right on the Night*, p. 226, indicates the pioneering nature of this pantomime.

7 See the Pope-Arbuthnot *Memoirs of Martinus Scriblerus*, as quoted by Clinton-Baddeley, *All Right on the Night*, p. 227.

8 *Ibid.*

9 *Ibid.*, p. 226.

10 *Ibid.*, pp. 213-214; Clinton-Baddeley, *Burlesque*, pp. 108-111; Nicoll, IV, 136.

11 Clinton-Baddeley, *All Right on the Night*, p. 214.

12 Clinton-Baddeley, *Burlesque*, pp. 109-111.

13 This pantomime, which does not appear in Nicoll's hand-list of plays in his *History of the English Drama, 1660-1900*, is preserved in a printed playbook (London, [n.d.]) in the Theatre Collection of the Princeton University Library.

14 *Victorian Theatre*, p. 66.

15 Leo Hughes, *A Century of Farce* (Princeton, 1956), p. 19.

16 Hughes, pp. 19-49, *passim;* Nicoll, IV, 138-142.

17 Tolles, pp. 35-37.

18 *Ibid.*

19 Nicoll, IV, 136-137.

20 Tolles, p. 35; Nicoll, IV, 135-136.

21 Tolles, pp. 37-38; Rowell, pp. 66-70; Hughes, pp. 124-126; Nicoll, IV, 147-154.

22 Tolles, p. 21.

23 As quoted by Tolles, p. 36.

24 Clinton-Baddeley, *Burlesque,* pp. 111ff. See also: H. Granville-Barker, "Exit Planché, Enter Gilbert," in *The Eighteen-Sixties: Essays by Fellows of the Royal Society of Literature,* ed. John Drinkwater (London, 1932); Dugald MacMillan, "Planché's Early Classical Burlesques," *SP,* XXV (1928), 340-345; and "Some Burlesques with a Purpose," *PQ,* VIII (1929), 255-263; T. F. D. Croker and S. Tucker, eds., *Extravaganzas of J. R. Planché* (5 vols.; London, 1879).

25 Tolles, p. 21. Clinton-Baddeley, *Burlesque,* p. 88, agrees with Tolles that melodrama had become all but a recognizable form in England by the 1790's through its independent development out of such native materials as the dumb-show dramas of the Royal Circus and Georgian blank-verse tragedy. However, Clinton-Baddeley also variously ascribes its origin to French *melodrame,* German translations, and a native theater "already deeply involved in sensationalism." Nicoll, IV, 212-213, cites George Lillo's *The London Merchant* (1730) as evidence of an early taste for the sort of thing melodrama later provided; and Maurice Willson Disher, *Blood and Thunder: Mid-Victorian Melodrama and its Origins* (London, 1949), pp. 19ff., traces the beginnings of the form back to the literary influence of Madame de Maintenon. Rowell, pp. 39ff., substantially concurs in Clinton-Baddeley's opinion of the inclusive origins of the form.

26 Rowell, pp. 46-51; Disher, *Blood and Thunder,* pp. 142-147; Nicoll, IV, 332.

27 Hughes, pp. 99-100; Disher, *Blood and Thunder,* p. 60.

28 Jerrold's melodrama is reprinted in *Nineteenth-Century Plays,* ed. George Rowell (London, 1953). Gay's ballad is reprinted in *A Collection of English Poems: 1660-1800,* ed. Ronald S. Crane (New York, 1932), pp. 373-375. The vital role played by nautical song in the development of melodrama is indicated by Maurice Willson Disher, *Victorian Song: From Dive to Drawing Room* (London, 1955), pp. 48-49. Rowell agrees, pp. 47-50.

29 Tolles, pp. 66-67, 96-97; Nicoll, IV, 100ff.

30 See Rowell's excellent first chapter, pp. 1-30, *passim.*

31 See Alan S. Downer, "Plays and Painted Stage: Nineteenth-Century Acting," *PMLA,* LXI (1946), 522-576.

32 Instead of cluttering this text with an extended account of nineteenth-century theatrical forms, I have placed in Appendix A a very full description of a typical Christmas pantomime by a foreign visitor to England during the middle years of the century.

33 The following discussion of the grotesque style is largely drawn from Wolfgang Kayser, *The Grotesque in Art and Literature,* trans. Ulrich Weisstein (Bloomington, Ind., 1963), who traces its emergence in *commedia dell' arte.* There is, of course,

a very large literature on the grotesque, principally in German, which is very fully discussed by Kayser. Nearer to home are two recent studies which appeared in print during the period when the present study was being written: Mark Spilka, *Dickens and Kafka* (Bloomington, Ind., 1963) and Taylor W. Stohr, *Dickens: The Dreamer's Stance* (Ithaca, N. Y., 1965). Both of these studies, while valuable and sometimes pertinent to our concerns here, take a view of the grotesque which is essentially post-Freudian and psychoanalytic, more concerned with theme and motif than with style and technique, and hence explore another territory altogether than that examined in these pages.

34 Kayser, pp. 95-96.

CHAPTER THREE

1 This line of argument does not propose to denigrate the many other sources of inspiration that played upon the novelist's imagination: his immersion in children's literature, nursery rhymes, fairy tales, *The Thousand and One Nights, Gulliver's Travels,* Hogarth's engravings, the novels of Smollett and Sterne, the Gothic novel, Defoe and *Pilgrim's Progress,* not to mention the Bible and the Anglican prayer book, all of which possess in different degrees and kinds elements of the grotesque like that in Dickens' work. Indeed, much of this material was a staple of early Victorian pantomime, burlesque, and extravaganza.

2 As quoted by Kayser, p. 158.

3 So powerful must have been the hold of this theatrical metaphor on Dickens' imagination that he sometimes accidentally transposes the two realms. Here Dickens reverses the settled order of comparison and has the supernumeraries' roles taken by tradesmen, rather than the other way around.

CHAPTER FOUR

1 Students of Dickens will recognize the indebtedness of this chapter to earlier commentators, of whom the chief is J. Hillis Miller, *Charles Dickens: The World of His Novels* (Cambridge, Mass., 1958). A fuller acknowledgment will be found in my article, "Unity and Coherence in *The Pickwick Papers," SEL,* V (Fall, 1965), 663-676, which approaches this novel from a somewhat different angle than that developed in these pages.

CHAPTER SIX

1 William Axton, *"Dombey and Son:* From Stereotype to Archetype," *ELH,* XXXI (Sept., 1964), 301-317.

2 As this volume was being readied for the press, an admirable essay on this very subject came to my attention: Martin Meisel, "Miss Havisham Brought to Book," *PMLA,* LXXXI (June, 1966), 278-285. Professor Meisel's wholly convincing thesis is that a con-

siderable portion of Dickens' conception of the character of Miss Havisham and of the "expectations" theme may have had its inception in one of Charles Mathews' "At Home's" for the year 1831, when the novelist-to-be was still contemplating an acting career. The inseminating image seems to have been the "White Woman of Berners' Street," who reappears not only in Wilkie Collins' novel but in a sketch of Dickens, "Where We Stopped Growing" (*Household Words*, VI [Jan. 1, 1853], 361-363). In *Great Expectations*, of course, she is Miss Havisham.

3 The size of the secondary literature that has grown up around *Great Expectations* lately constitutes virtually a canon of its own. The reading of the structure and themes of the novel proposed in these pages accords with the generally accepted view that it is a *bildungsroman* in which Pip learns to acknowledge the human condition and his participation in evil. My differences from the prevailing criticsm lie in the nature and place of the patricular evil that Pip shares. See Johnson, II, 972-994; G. Robert Stange, "Expectations Well Lost: Dickens' Fable for his Time," *College English*, XVI (Oct., 1954), 9-17; Julian Moynahan, "The Hero's Guilt: The Case of *Great Expectations*," *Essays in Criticism*, X (Jan., 1960), 60-79; and Dorothy Van Ghent, "On *Great Expectations*," *The English Novel: Form and Function* (New York, 1953), pp. 125-138.

4 Dickens appears to have been fully conscious of the grotesque quality of *Great Expectations*. In a letter to Forster sometime in September, 1860, marking what his biographer calls the "germ of Pip and Magwitch," (*Life*, p. 733) Dickens wrote, "For a little piece I have been writing—or am writing; for I hope to finish it to-day—such a fine, new, and grotesque idea has opened upon me, that I begin to doubt whether I had not better cancel the little paper, and reserve the notion for a new book. . . . But it so opens out before *me* that I can see the whole of a serial revolving on it, in a most singular and comic manner . . ." (*Letters*, III, 182). Again, sometime in October, he wrote about "the grotesque tragicomic conception that first encouraged me" as though it were the pivot of the story (*ibid.*, p. 186).

CHAPTER SEVEN

1 A much fuller discussion of this entire episode will be found in Chapter Ten of this study.

2 So pervasive are Dickens' borrowings of this sort from the theater that another full-length study could be made of this technique solely in the light of nineteenth-century actors' manuals and the conventional methods of staging, massing, blocking, and lighting employed in the playhouses of his day, as well as the typical "business" of pantomime and burlesque. Such a project is beyond the scope of this study, aside from this brief mention. Some other aspects of Dickens' debt to the popular theater are discussed by Earle Davis in *The Flint and the Flame*.

CHAPTER EIGHT

[1] There are a host of other instances: the macabre description of the slum, Tom-all-Alone's, in *Bleak House;* the survey of Coketown in *Hard Times,* with its memorable image of great steam pistons moving up and down like the nodding heads of melancholy elephants; the haunting vision of Marshalsea Prison that broods over *Little Dorrit,* or Mrs. Clennam's disintegrating house in the same novel; Boffin's dust heaps in *Our Mutual Friend;* or the Peggotys' ship-home in *David Copperfield.* The list could be extended indefinitely.

[2] "The Undivided Imagination: *Bleak House,*" in *Craft and Character . . . In Modern Fiction* (New York, 1957), p. 28.

[3] However, such a position has been advocated by Dorothy Van Ghent among others in her influential "On *Great Expectations,*" in *The English Novel: Form and Function* (New York, 1953), pp. 125-138. The same point is made in her essay, "The Dickens World: The View from Todgers's," *Sewanee Review,* LVIII (1950), 419-438.

Many of Mrs. Van Ghent's observations on this passage—as well as on a passage in *Martin Chuzzlewit* depicting the roof-top view from Mrs. Todgers' boarding-house—coincide with those stylistic features already isolated and discussed in this chapter, leaving aside their similarity to devices of the popular theater which was not part of her purpose. As she says of the "view from Todgers's":

"Much of the description is turned upon the conservative 'seemed to be' and 'as if,' and the pathetic fallacy provides a familiar bourgeois security, but the technique changes in the middle, betrayed by a discomfort which the 'as if's' are no longer able to conceal. The prospect from Todgers's is one in which categorical determinations of the relative significance of objects . . . have broken down, and the observer of Todger's roof is seized with suicidal nausea at the momentary vision of a world in which significance has been replaced by naked and aggressive existence. . . . The point of view is hallucinated and often fearful, as the insecure and ill-fed child's might be. It is not childish. The grotesque transpositions are a coherent imagination of a reality that has lost coherence, comic because they form a pattern integrating the disintegrated and lying athwart the reality that has not got iteslf imagined. Everything has to be mentioned . . . for, assuming that there is coherence in a world visibly disintegrated into things, one way to find it is to mention everything. Hence the indefatigable attention to detail. No thing must be lost, as it is doubtless essential to the mysterious organization of the system. The system itself is assumed to be a nervous one, and for this reason Dickens's language has its almost inexhaustible vitality and vivacity. . . ."

These are by now familiar formulations, although the terminology is different in important and, I think, crucial ways; of this, more later. Meanwhile, Mrs. Van Ghent generalizes about Dickens' characterization and scenic description: "The animation of inanimate objects suggests both the quaint gaiety of a forbidden life and an aggressiveness that has got out of control—an aggressiveness they have borrowed from the human economy. . . . His description of people [shows] a reciprocal metaphor: people are described by nonhuman attributes, or by such an exaggeration of or emphasis on one part of their appearance that they seem to be reduced wholly to that part, with an effect of having become "thinged" into one of their own bodily members or into an article of their clothing or into some inanimate object of which they have made a fetish. . . . People were becoming things, and things . . . were becoming more important than people. People were being de-animated, robbed of their souls, and things were usurping the prerogatives of animate creatures. . . . This picture, in which the qualities of things and people were reversed, was a picture of a daemonically motivated world, a world in which "dark" or occult forces or energies operate not only in people . . . but also in things. . . ."

Valuable as Mrs. Van Ghent's services have been to our better understanding of Dickens' vision and technique, and they are considerable, her generalizations are, I believe, open to demurrer. One may, for example, accept the view that Dickens' descriptions are marked by the use of the simile and pathetic fallacy without dismissing these devices as "conservative" or as conducive to "bourgeois security"; for as we have seen, Dickens' grotesquerie consists precisely in the ambivalence created by the simile between the reality-status of the object world and the imaginative reordering of that world. Nor can the use of pathetic fallacy be a security device if it is later construed as evidence of the way in which things are "usurping the prerogatives of animate creatures." One may concur with Mrs. Van Ghent that the novelist's grotesque transpositions demonstrate a coherent imagination dealing with incoherence and disintegration; but one need not conclude therefrom that it is reality itself which is incoherent. The thesis advanced in these pages is, rather, that Dickens wished to employ incoherence in order to dislodge his readers' conventional view of things. Similarly, there are no surprises to be found in the idea of the "inexhaustible vitality and vivacity" of Dickens' language, his "indefatigable attention to detail," and his belief in the "mysterious organization of the system"—indeed, even the conception that the system is a "nervous" one—but it need not follow that these stylistic features suppose a world in which humanity has leaked out into things and things are possessed by some daemonic energy, even though one is willing to grant the fact of characterization-by-thing.

In short, the same data may lead to quite different conclusions, and one need not posit a narrative perspective of an "insecure, ill-fed child" to account for the fact that Dickens characterizes by leitmotif and employs pathetic fallacy. It is true that the novelist depicts a world in which he carefully omits "the categorical determinations of the relative significance of objects," but this may be more a tactic than a conviction. In a fact-minded age, when the tendency is to be "frightfully literal and catalogue-like," a writer gifted with the ability to see "relations in things not apparent generally" and dedicated to a "fanciful" treatment of reality might— and I believe did—attempt to subvert the conventional "categorical determinations" of his readers in order to open their eyes to the vitality and vivacity of the familiar world. An object-world embodied in similes drawn from incongruous realms of familiar life, riddled with pathetic fallacy, and proliferate with realistic details may emanate from a healthy if manic vision which perceives in the commonplace scene a quick and exuberant liveliness and fresh curiosity. To such a perspective the conventional man's dullness of vision seemed a tragic imprisoning of the imagination; and the process of releasing the common reader's sight from its blinders might well have taken the form of removing from description those "categorical determinations of the relative significance of things."

Moreover, the familiar scene that Dickens regarded was alive for him in two important respects that are quite irrelevant to twentieth-century existential presuppositions. First, as John Holloway has so well demonstrated in *The Victorian Sage,* the physical world to the Victorian gave vivid if tacit evidence of a lively and comprehensible order. To contradict Coleridge, things as things were not fixed and dead but doubly suggestive of controlling life and motive, both as an extension of the men and society which made them and as obscure testimony of a divine hand working in and through them. All that was required to see this "open secret" was an eye educated to perceive the self-evident fact of the living fabric of the human and physical realms, their interpenetration in a significant moral unity. Second, to Dickens as to Disraeli the world through which unseeing men moved was a vital and dramatic entity. The popular theater disoriented and reorganized this mode of nonsight into an enjoyable and comprehensible vision by grotesquely mixing animate and inanimate realms, heightening, stylizing, and vivifying the commonplace, and setting all in antic motion. It remained only for a serious, realistic novelist such as Dickens to exploit these techniques in fiction for the purpose of demonstrating how the familiar scene engages dimensions of meaning far beyond its existence in a physical sense.

CHAPTER NINE

[1] E. M. Forster, *Aspects of the Novel* (New York, 1927), pp. 107-109.

[2] See William Axton, "The Trouble with Esther," *MLQ*, XXVI (Dec., 1865), 545-558.

[3] In Chapter XXV, installment eight, for October, 1852, and in Chapter LIV, installment seventeen, for July, 1853, two and eleven months, respectively, after his introduction in Chapter XIX, installment six, for August, 1852.

4 In Chapter XI, installment four, for June, 1852. It is the first chapter of that installment. Since the episode is far too long to quote here in its entirety, I have lodged it in Appendix B.

5 A reader has pointed out very aptly that the mock coroner's inquest in the Harmonic Meeting Room of the Sol's Arms owes much to a form of dramatic entertainment in vogue during the middle years of the century, "Lord Chief Baron" Renton Nicholson's satirical "Judge and Jury" improvisations. See John L. Bradley, ed., *Rogue's Progress* (Boston, 1965).

6 See Chapter XXXIII, in XXIII, 17-18: "Now do those two gentlemen not very neat about the cuffs and buttons who attended the last Coroner's Inquest at the Sol's Arms, reappear in the precincts with surprising swiftness (being, in fact, breathlessly fetched by the active and intelligent beadle), and institute perquisitions through the court, and dive into the Sol's parlour, and write with ravenous little pens on tissue-paper. Now do they note down, in the watches of the night, how the neighbourhood of Chancery Lane was yesterday, at about midnight, thrown into a state of the most intense agitation and excitement by the following alarming and horrible discovery. Now do they set forth how it will doubtless be remembered, that some time back a painful sensation was created in the public mind, by a case of mysterious death from opium occurring in the first floor of the house occupied as a rag, bottle, and general marine store shop, by an eccentric individual of intemperate habits, far advanced in life, named Krook; and how, by a remarkable coincidence, Krook was examined at the Inquest, which it may be recollected was held on that occasion at the Sol's Arms, a well-conducted tavern, immediately adjoining the premises in question, on the west side, and licensed to a highly respectable landlord, Mr. James George Bogsby. Now do they show (in as many words as possible). . . ." And so on.

7 This system of imagery is far more pervasive in *Bleak House* than might appear at first glance. Put briefly, one of the novel's schemes of imagery contrasts the "brilliant circle" of the "Fashionable World" with the mighty planetary universe. But further, this fits into an elaborate system of cosmological and theological imagery which suggests that obsolescent institutions such as Chancery and the aristocracy are not only threatened with natural extinction but also with a congruent divine judgment. The latter is engaged by images of the Deluge which dominate the early chapters of the novel and by later images of Armageddon, chiefly located in Krook's death by spontaneous combustion. The Dedlocks and Chancery are made to appear to be hanging poised between the flood and the last trump.

CHAPTER TEN

1 The flight of Sikes in *Oliver Twist* and the attack on Jacob's Island in the same novel are typical instances. Others include the mob scenes in *Barnaby Rudge,* Jonas Chuzzlewit's return from the

murder of Montague Tigg, the "oak tree" passages in *A Tale of Two Cities,* the meeting between Esther and her natural mother in *Bleak House,* and Mr. Dombey's suicidal despair near the end of *Dombey and Son.*

2 One calls to mind the death of little Paul Dombey, of Jo and Gridley in *Bleak House,* of Magwitch in *Great Expectations,* of Little Nell in *The Old Curiosity Shop,* and many more. Florence Dombey's lonely vigil in her father's deserted mansion or Captain Cuttle's long watch over the Wooden Midshipman are characteristic.

3 This matter has been dealt with at some length in a recent article: William Axton, "Tonal Unity in *Dombey and Son,*" *PMLA,* LXXVIII (Sept., 1963), 341-348.

INDEX

WILLIAM F. AXTON, the author of this book, is a native of Louisville, Kentucky. A graduate of Yale University, he holds the M.A. degree of the University of Louisville and the Ph.D. degree of Princeton University. He has taught at Miami University, Brown University, and, since 1961, the University of Kentucky, where he is an associate professor of English.

Circle of Fire was composed and printed at the University of Kentucky. It is set in Linotype Baskerville, with ATF Bulmer used for the large display and ATF Garamond initials for the chapter openings. The book is printed on Warren Olde Style Antique Wove paper and bound by the C. J. Krehbiel Company in Interlaken Arco Linen cloth. The book and the jacket were designed by Robert James Foose.